ANIMALS

EMOTION & MORALITY

D1509098

B. A. Dixon

ANIMALS
EMOTION & MORALITY

Marking
the Boundary

Prometheus Books
59 John Glenn Drive
Amherst, New York 14228-2119

Published 2008 by Prometheus Books

Animals, Emotion, and Morality: Marking the Boundary. Copyright © 2008 by B. A. Dixon. All rights reserved. No part of this publication may be reproduced, stored in a retrieval system, or transmitted in any form or by any means, digital, electronic, mechanical, photocopying, recording, or otherwise, or conveyed via the Internet or a Web site without prior written permission of the publisher, except in the case of brief quotations embodied in critical articles and reviews.

Inquiries should be addressed to
Prometheus Books
59 John Glenn Drive
Amherst, New York 14228–2119
VOICE: 716–691–0133, ext. 210
FAX: 716–691–0137
WWW.PROMETHEUSBOOKS.COM

12 11 10 09 08   5 4 3 2 1

Library of Congress Cataloging-in-Publication Data

Dixon, B. A. (Beth A.), 1957–
    Animals, emotions, and morality : marking the boundary / B. A. Dixon
        p. cm.
    Includes bibliographical references and index.
    ISBN: 978–1–59102–629–7 (pbk.)
    1. Emotions in animals. 2. Psychology, Comparative. 3. Ethics. I. Title.

QL785.27.D59 2008
591.5—dc22

2008016532

Printed in the United States of America on acid-free paper

CONTENTS

Chapter One

INTRODUCTION

U sually when I tell my friends and colleagues that I am writing about the topic of animal emotion, they immediately want to know whether I think animals *do* have emotions. My answer is a little complicated. "Well, it depends on what you mean." This sounds like a way of avoiding the question, but as I will describe, the settings in which we attribute emotions to animals are various. Some of these, I believe, are not philosophically innocent. Throughout this book I explain why it is incorrect to attribute *some* kinds of emotions to animals, what I call "morally laden emotions." So if we are inclined to attribute these kinds of emotions to our pets or to wild animals, then we are more than likely unwarranted in doing so. But my critical remarks are not aimed at our ordinary ways of talking about animals. I am not interested in trying to correct our common-sense views about what animals are like psychologically. Rather,

I direct my criticisms to the philosophical conclusions about the moral status of animals that we may be tempted to infer from attributing to animals morally laden emotional states. Sometimes these philosophical contexts are easy to identify because they are articulated by professional philosophers who are writing specifically for other professional philosophers—but not always. Many scholars write for popular audiences, and, alternatively, what popular writers have to say is often relevant in academic settings. So what counts as a philosophical context is sometimes difficult to discern. Animal stories and anecdotes are also used as evidence of emotions in animals. This contributes to blurring what counts as a scholarly or a philosophical conclusion. The animal narrative may function as a methodology in cognitive ethology, as a way of educating nonspecialists about how animals and humans are alike and how they are different, and also as a form of literary entertainment for both children and adults. Here there is no neat and tidy distinction about which animal stories are "off limits" and which are "legitimate" in the inquiry about whether or not real animals have emotions and other psychological states. This is why my discussion of texts includes popular writing about animal emotion, philosophical arguments about the emotional and moral capacities of animals, and research data about animal emotion in cognitive ethology.

It is probably wise to lay out a few assumptions right at the start in order to anticipate possible misunderstandings. First, I believe that the study of animal minds that is called "cognitive ethology" is an important research program. I share with most cognitive ethologists the general view that it is correct to use intentional language to describe how animals think. It is my opinion that some animals have certain kinds of beliefs and desires even though they do not have what we would call a human language. Moreover, I agree with most of my friends and colleagues that it would be counterintuitive to say that animals do not have emotions at all, even though I will qualify this claim in the philosophical analysis that follows.

What kind of contribution can a philosopher make to the study of the animal mind? Allen and Bekoff distinguish between empirical and theoretical approaches to this interdisciplinary topic. "The task of . . . understanding the bases for mental-state attributions is at the same time a philosophical project and a scientific project. It is a philosophical project because it requires philosophical investigation of mentalistic concepts and of the aims and methods of cognitive ethology; it is a scientific project because impoverished knowledge of animal behavior results in impoverished arguments and faulty conclusions."[1] I agree with this way of characterizing the division of labor between philosophers and scientists and the need to collaborate about the conclusions we are warranted in drawing about the psychological states of animals. I see my work as a contribution to this effort since my focus is to investigate the *particular* mentalistic concept of animal emotion. But I would add to this the need to engage in a conceptual analysis of moral concepts as well when these are used to infer something about what animals are like. When conceptual analysis is paired with empirical research about the capacities of animals, then we are better situated to explain precisely how humans and animals are the same and how they are different.

SOME QUESTIONS

One aim I have in writing this book is to invite the reader to engage in philosophical inquiry. Stories about animals are a wonderful occasion for doing so. If the story is good, we develop a concern for the main actors and the circumstances of their lives. The best kind of philosophical analysis of an animal story includes an appreciation of the main characters in that story, but it also raises questions about the concepts used and the conclusions that may be drawn from the story itself. By way of illustration consider this story I came across in *National Geographic World,* a magazine for young people interested in nature and science. The article is titled "Do Animals Have Feelings?"

> A scientist sat observing wild chimpanzees in Tanzania, in Africa. The chimp she called Flint had always been unusually attached to his mother. Even as an adolescent, he shared her nest at night. When his mother died, Flint withdrew from other chimps. He hardly ate. He climbed a tree to the nest he and his mother had shared. For a long time he stood there, staring into space. "It was as though he were remembering," says Jane Goodall, the world famous National Geographic explorer-in-residence who witnessed the scene.[2]

As Goodall reports elsewhere, Flint stayed by his mother's body for ten days. Finally, Flint himself lay down and died. Goodall concluded that Flint must have died from grief.[3] The author of "Do Animals Have Feelings?" goes on to say, "Stories like this suggest that animals have emotional feelings. Add up all such stories (there are many) and they suggest something more: *evidence.* It is evidence that researchers like Goodall hope will convince skeptics of something most people with pets already believe: that animals *do* have feelings."[4] Besides the endearing pictures of chimps and giraffes gently nuzzling one another and a polar bear playing with a sled dog, there are other examples to suggest that animals have emotions. "There are many people who believe that animals can feel compassion, too. An adult elephant was once seen trying to rescue a baby rhinoceros that was stuck in the mud in Kenya. Over and over, the elephant used its tusks to try to push or lift the rhino despite charges by the rhino baby's mother, who did not appreciate the elephant's efforts. Was the elephant showing compassion, while the rhino mother was expressing fear or anger?"[5]

The author goes on to note that not everyone accepts the conclusion that animals have feelings. Joseph LeDoux, a professor of neuroscience at New York University, comments that there is no "experiment" we can do to confirm this conclusion: "an animal can't tell you how it feels; there is no way you can prove it." But this kind of skeptical response did not prevent Goodall from continuing her research. "Look into a chimp's eyes," she says, "and you know you're looking into the mind of a thinking, feeling being." The conclusion leaves the reader a little bit up in the air but optimistic. An answer to the question "Do animals have feelings?" will be forthcoming once more observations of animals are undertaken and more data is collected. In the meantime we are urged by Goodall to "give all creatures the benefit of doubt."

This narrative setting contains all the ingredients of the topic I want to examine; it includes a story about animal emotion that immediately engages the reader and an interpretation of the story that points to a conclusion about how similar animals are in relation to humans. But it also raises more questions than it answers. For example, did Flint really die of grief? We do use the expression "dying of grief," but what does this literally mean when we speak about human beings? A grieving person may be brought low by the death of a loved one. So maybe to die of grief is to be so psychologically incapacitated that nothing about living interests one. Under what circumstances are we so affected? And what does this possibility imply about our relations with those about whom we grieve and our attempts to lead a fulfilling life? The very nature of grief and its role in a particular life is the territory into which we have stumbled. How are such questions settled—by research into brain physiology and function? By observing animal behavior?

By gazing into the eyes of animals? It seems unlikely that the nature of grief and the role it plays in living a meaningful life will be *entirely* explained in any of these ways. These questions about grief are conceptual. I do not mean by this that the issue of animal emotion is *only* a conceptual one, but it is at least partly so because emotions can be characterized in various ways depending on the goals of the speaker and how she chooses to use these concepts. This means that the conclusions we might be tempted to draw from animal stories and anecdotes are not always clearly defined or obviously true. A philosopher's guide to reading animal stories should begin by demonstrating to the reader that there are conceptual puzzles worth thinking about lurking just below the surface of these stories. By way of introduction to what follows in this book, I focus on three philosophical questions we might ask that are inspired by the *National Geographic* article: In what sense are humans and animals emotional kin? What is the connection between animal emotion and morality? Are human beings unique with respect to morality?

EMOTIONAL KINSHIP

"Look into a chimp's eyes," Goodall says, "and you know you're looking into the mind of a thinking, feeling being." What Goodall surely means by this is that by looking into a chimp's eyes we will recognize a kindred soul, a being just like us in some respects though not in all respects. Having emotions and being capable of feeling matters to us; otherwise, it would not be worth mentioning with such alacrity by Goodall or anyone else. Imagine instead if Goodall remarked that chimps and humans shared the property of having teeth and because of this we were kin. While true, it misses the mark for capturing what many believe is distinctive of humans. Why is emotionality a distinctive and noteworthy feature of a person or an animal? By way of an answer consider a bit of science fiction.

Fans of the original *Star Trek* series as well as *Star Trek: The Next Generation* are familiar with the characters Spock and Data. Even though Spock is a Vulcan hailing from another planet and Data is an android made up entirely of machine parts, Spock and Data are alike in several fundamental ways. Neither has the capacity for emotions, but both have the ability to engage in highly complex rational thinking. Because Data is, in fact, a rather sophisticated computer, he is actually better at certain kinds of thinking tasks than humans. He apparently has a larger database than humans and he can process information more quickly than we can. But when it comes to situations that require feeling and emotionality, Data falls short of human expertise. As the story goes, this is because Data fails to have the emotion chip in his central processing unit.

Data aspires to be human, but the one recurring obstacle is his inability to feel emotions. This capability is understood to be what is distinctive about human beings; not our rationality, not our language ability, and not our ability to walk on two legs. In my opinion, the very best episodes of this series are about Data's attempt to negotiate what it means to be human where emotionality is a prominent feature of human life. One comic episode involves Data attempting to play poker, which, as we all know, requires a certain amount of deception in facial expression and attitude. He fails miserably. In another heartrending episode, Data builds an android offspring, Lal, who surprises everyone by doing things that Data cannot. One difference in her abilities is that she can feel emotions. Tragically, Lal has a malfunction and does not survive. Is it because her emotionality compromises her wiring and software? The story hints that emotions are destructive in this way. What is fascinating about Data, in particular, is the ambiguity that surrounds his character. We know that he doesn't have the emotion chip but we are always left with the idea that he is very much like us even with respect to his emotionality. His loyalty, friendships, and camaraderie with his shipmates are never in question. Moreover, his efforts to save his "daughter" Lal are the kind of heroics that bring tears to our eyes. What else to call it but love?

The important idea that emerges from these episodes is that emotions are defining of humanness—not merely in our capacity to have experiences, per se, but as a way of negotiating what has meaning in our lives. Data's attitude toward raising his daughter can be understood only by attributing to him a sense of parental love. His friendships with crewmates are not merely simulations of human friendships; they are genuinely marked by respect, loyalty, and reciprocity. So it is not raw feelings that Data aspires to have but the display and realization of emotionality that emerges in rather complex ways in the context of living a life. What the writers of this series manage to demonstrate is that emotionality is connected in various ways with the activities of living that have value for most of us: parenting, friendships, or losing a child. Sometimes my students wonder why we should be spending so much time trying to answer the question "Do animals have emotion?" My answer is that the concept of emotion is intimately connected with what has value in our lives. And when emotions are connected to value, they are morally significant.

If animals are like humans because we share emotionality, we must ask further what concept of emotion we have in common that explains our "emotional kinship." The concept of emotion we settle on should do justice to those animal stories and narratives that attribute emotions to animals and that compare humans and animals in just this respect. For example, the story Jane Goodall tells about Flint seeks to explain why Flint acted despondently, even neglecting his own welfare, by referring to the grief he felt when his mother died. So the operative concept of grief that makes sense of Flint's story is one that should explain how the conceptual content of grief is tied to the loss of a loved one. Not just any theory of the emotions will do the explanatory work required of it in the narrative settings that I examine throughout this book.

In chapter 2 I consider what kind of theory of emotion is appropriate to the job of explaining our emotional kinship with animals. I suggest that our alleged emotional kinship with animals depends on a conception of the emotions that is value-laden. As animal emotion is described in narratives, stories, and anecdotes, it occupies a strikingly similar role as it does in human lives. In this way our emotional kinship with animals comes to stand for our moral kinship with animals.

THE MORAL KINSHIP HYPOTHESIS

Was the elephant in Kenya being compassionate by trying to rescue the baby rhino from the mud? If so, we might say that the elephant was virtuous in the same way that human beings who act compassionately, generously, bravely, or loyally have a virtuous moral character. At the very least, we are tempted to morally praise people who are motivated to perform right actions. Is the same true for animals?

In some narrative settings emotional kinship is taken to imply a deeper commonality between humans and animals, and that is the capacity for morality. What it means to say that animals are moral beings in this particular sense needs to be carefully distinguished from other philosophical positions about the moral status of animals. I borrow (or perhaps *appropriate*) the expression "moral kinship" from Jamieson and Bekoff, who say, "While there is no purely logical connection between views about mental continuity and views about moral continuity, there are important psychological connections. A culture that recognizes its behavioral and emotional kinship with nonhuman animals is one that is likely to recognize its moral kinship as well."[6] In this passage the authors may be saying only that if animals share with humans psychological states like emotions, then we may be more likely to think that animals are *morally considerable*. In this sense an animal (or a human) is morally considerable if we believe that it has some moral claim on us. This might mean that I take into account how to treat an animal in my moral deliberations about what it is right to do.[7] Alternatively, we might understand the concept of moral kinship as one way of alleging that animals share with humans the more robust property of *being moral*. If humans and animals are moral kin in this sense, then animals have the capacity for morality in ways that resemble human morality. I wish to use the designation "Moral Kinship Hypothesis" to stand for this stronger position about the moral status of animals and to refer to a cluster of views that either argue for moral kinship in this sense or assume that it is true. Before we go on to identify particular versions of the Moral Kinship Hypothesis, we should say something more about how this sense of moral kinship differs from standard ways of talking about the moral status of animals.

It is by now traditional in the literature about ethics and animals to classify some animals as *moral patients* while denying them the status of being *moral agents*.[8] This distinction is owed to Tom Regan, who characterizes moral agency in the following way:

Moral agents are individuals who have a variety of sophisticated abilities, including in particular the ability to bring impartial moral principles to bear on the determination of what, all considered, morally ought to be done and, having made this determination, to freely choose or fail to choose to act as morality, as they conceive it, requires. Because moral agents have these abilities, it is fair to hold them morally accountable for what they do. . . . Normal adult human beings are the paradigm individuals believed to be moral agents.[9]

There is no general consensus about what "sophisticated abilities" are required to qualify as a moral agent in this sense, though by some accounts this may involve being able to evaluate reasons for acting and being able to conceptualize rights and duties. For example, when Marc Hauser argues that animals are not moral agents, he lists six conditions that he believes must be satisfied, including having a sufficient amount of control over one's passions; being able to "consider the beliefs, desires, and needs of others when planning an action"; and being able to "understand the norms of action and emotion in society."[10] The details of the conditions for moral agency in this sense are not crucial to characterizing the idea of moral kinship since those who seek to establish that humans and animals are moral kin typically do not believe that animals are moral agents by virtue of satisfying highly rationalistic conditions of the sort listed above.

Regan also maintains that some animals and some human beings should be classified as moral patients, a category that he characterizes in the following way:

Moral patients lack the prerequisites that would enable them to control their own behavior in ways that would make them morally accountable for what they do. A moral patient lacks the ability to formulate, let alone bring to bear, moral principles in deliberating about which one among a number of possible acts it would be right or proper to perform. Moral patients, in a word, cannot do what is right, nor can they do what is wrong. Granted, what they do may be detrimental to the welfare of others. . . . But even when a moral patient causes significant harm to another, the moral patient has not done what is wrong. Only moral agents can do what is wrong. Human infants, young children, and the mentally deranged or enfeebled of all ages are paradigm cases of human moral patients.[11]

The Moral Kinship Hypothesis is the view that humans and animals share the capacity for morality but in a way that is not reducible to saying either that animals are moral agents (in the sense identified above) or that they are moral patients. This is so because animals undoubtedly fail to be highly rational in the way Regan requires for moral agency. But *arguably* they exceed the conditions Regan articulates for being merely moral patients since many believe that they are capable of performing right or wrong actions for which they may be morally commended or blamed. This is not because animals "deliberate about moral principles," but because they have emotions in the morally relevant sense.[12] In addition, it is thought that some animals have the relevant freedom or autonomy to choose right actions over wrong actions. The Moral Kinship Hypothesis does not presume that animals are exactly like adult human beings in the realization of our moral capacities. But those who endorse this hypothesis maintain that what animals share with humans still deserves to be called "morality."

Who endorses the Moral Kinship Hypothesis and what are their reasons? In chapters 3 through 7 I explain and evaluate some of these views more carefully, but for now we can get a sense of what the following writers have in common. Marc Bekoff says, for example,

If one is a good Darwinian and believes in evolutionary continuity, it seems premature to claim that *only* humans can be empathic and moral beings. As we increasingly come to recognize that animals share their emotions with us it becomes increasingly difficult to deny their existence.[13]

. . . It is self-serving anthropocentric speciesism to claim that we are the *only* moral beings in the animal kingdom.[14]

Both Steve Sapontzis and David DeGrazia argue that animals are moral *agents*, though they do not mean by this that animals satisfy the highly rationalistic conditions that we have identified with moral agency as Regan and Hauser use this term.[15] DeGrazia says, "These examples support the attribution of moral agency—specifically, actions manifesting virtues—in cases in which the actions are not plausibly interpreted as instinctive or conditioned. On any reasonable understanding of moral agency, some animals are moral agents. This conclusion, again, contradicts the assumption, common even among contributors to animal ethics, that nonhuman animals may be 'moral patients' (bearers of moral status) but not moral agents."[16] Evelyn Pluhar reserves the term "full persons" to designate the kind of moral agency characteristic of human beings, requiring "intelligence, rationality, creativity, and communication skills," but she is also prepared to classify some animals as moral agents in a slightly different sense.[17]

Is it really so clear, however, that the capacity for moral agency has no precedent in any other species? Certain other capacities are required for moral agency, including the capacities for emotion, memory, and goal-directed behavior. As we have seen, there is ample evidence for the presence of these capacities, if to a limited degree, in some nonhumans (again, just as evolution would lead us to expect). Not surprisingly, then, evidence has been gathered that indicates that nonhumans are capable of what we would call "moral" or "virtuous" behavior.[18]

Frans de Waal argues that apes occupy the "ground floor of the tower of morality" by sharing moral sentiments with humans.[19] And Gary Francione cites de Waal's conclusion approvingly by claiming that "[t]he similarities between humans and animals are not limited to cognitive or emotional attributes alone. Some argue that animals exhibit what is clearly moral behavior as well. . . . There are numerous instances in which animals have acted in altruistic ways toward unrelated members of their own species and toward other species, including humans."[20] Aristotle is arguably committed to the Moral Kinship Hypothesis because he appears to formulate conditions for being morally responsible that animals can satisfy.[21] Richard Sorabji supplies reasons for supporting this interpretation of Aristotle, and in chapter 7, "Bad Wolves," we investigate the plausibility of holding some animals morally appraisable for their actions.[22] A number of popular writers about animals express a commitment to the Moral Kinship Hypothesis as well. In this respect the most notable is Kristin Von Kreisler, who wrote a book titled *Beauty in the Beasts: True Stories about Animals Who Choose to Do Good.*[23]

By referring to these writers' views collectively as a "hypothesis," I mean to call attention to the fact that despite differences in the individual articulation of the position and why each writer endorses this position, claims about our moral kinship with animals require philosophical justification. In the remaining chapters we will evaluate the reasons and arguments that philosophers, ethologists, and laypeople have given for believing that moral kinship holds between humans and animals.

The Moral Kinship Hypothesis gets its initial plausibility by attributing to animals emotional states that are conceptually connected to morality in ways that I will describe in the next section. I call these "morally laden" emotions. If it is correct to attribute to some animals "morally laden emotions," then the Moral Kinship Hypothesis is true.

MORALLY LADEN EMOTIONS

Imagine a human being who is described as ashamed, jealous, caring, sympathetic, or compassionate. Crediting a person with these emotions implies much more than that she is in a particular neurophysiological state or that she has a feeling or sensation of the body. Being called a compassionate person or a jealous person refers to the disposition or moral character of that person. We imply something about how she typically acts as well as her motivations to act on particular occasions. We may extend to her our moral praise or blame depending on what she knows and the circumstances surrounding her action. Moreover, when emotions are *appropriate* feelings, they cluster around other qualities of a person, such as integrity and strength of purpose, being trustworthy, being a loyal and caring friend, and having self-worth and a sense of pride as well as humility about one's accomplishments.[24] When we credit human beings with having integrity, being committed, being trustworthy, or being a loyal friend, there is no denying that we are *morally* commending that person. Likewise, when animals are credited with these kinds of states, we will think the same. An animal who is motivated to act from compassion is morally praiseworthy. And an animal that is described as having friendships characterized by commitment and trust is morally meritorious. In many narrative settings about our emotional kinship with animals, emotions are construed as valued contributions to living a morally good life. When emotions are understood in this way they are morally laden. Specifically, *morally laden emotions are those emotional states that imply by the context of use that the subject who has these emotions is a moral being.* To be moral in this sense is consistent with what the Moral Kinship Hypothesis implies about some animals. Animals may not have the full range of moral capacities included in highly rationalistic definitions of moral agency, but their moral status is more robust than that of moral patients since they may perform actions that are good or evil. Further, they may be morally appraisable for these actions because they are motivated to act from emotional states that are appropriate to the circumstances.

Some emotions more directly implicate the moral capacities of a subject because of the *kind* of emotion experienced. Shame, guilt, or jealousy, for example, may be the kinds of emotions that we associate with moral failure. Some emotions, like compassion, are prime candidates for being moral virtues. But even anger can be morally laden if it is about a state of affairs in the world that we judge to be unfair or inequitable. Our guide in this matter is the context of use.

Who believes that some animals have morally laden emotions? It is not hard to find examples of this view, though it is not always recognized as a position that requires justification. Some attribute morally laden emotions to animals by way of arguing explicitly for what I am calling the Moral Kinship Hypothesis. Steve Sapontzis, David DeGrazia, and Kristin Von Kreisler employ the argumentative strategy of attributing to animals motivational states like compassion or kindness and then inferring from this that animals are morally virtuous. Frans de Waal argues that some chimpanzees have the rudiments of morality because it is correct to attribute to them moral sentiments such as sympathy. But in most other settings where animals are credited with morally laden emotions, writers do not explicitly present an argument for moral kinship. I am referring here to how animal emotions are characterized in the work of Darwin, Pluhar, Masson, Masson and McCarthy, Wise, Francione, Bekoff, and Goodall, to name a few who have written about animal emotion.[25]

EVALUATING THE MORAL KINSHIP HYPOTHESIS

Throughout chapters 3 through 7, I evaluate the plausibility of the Moral Kinship Hypothesis. I proceed by explaining and evaluating one particular route that some philosophers, ethologists, and popular writers have used to establish this hypothesis, and that is by attributing to some animals morally laden emotions.

In order to evaluate the claim that some animals have morally laden emotions, we will need to specify what account of morality is either explicitly or implicitly relied on and how emotions contribute to this account of morality. The philosophical lens that I focus on narratives about animal emotion in the remaining chapters is designed to clarify exactly how emotions are connected to these moral background conditions. Sometimes, for example, it is argued that animals have moral virtue because they are motivated to perform right actions by emotional states like compassion. What it means to have a virtue and what counts as the right motivational state is the topic examined in chapter 3. Philosophers as well as cognitive ethologists appeal to Darwin's principle about evolutionary continuity to conclude that some animals have morally laden emotions *in some lesser degree* than human beings. So in chapter 4 we look more carefully at what Darwin meant by evolutionary continuity and how this idea might be used to conclude that animals have merely a little bit of those morally laden emotions that adult human beings employ as mature moral reasoners. Frans de Waal argues that the origins of morality can be found in apes, our closest anthropoid relatives. De Waal's argument depends on attributing to some chimpanzees "moral sentiments" such as cognitive empathy. In chapter 5 we specifically focus on how empathy must be characterized in order to make this emotional state morally significant. In the course of discussing primate moral sentiments, we discover that de Waal occasionally likens the emotional capacities of chimpanzees to children's emotional responsiveness at an early stage of their moral development. The idea that children and animals are alike in their emotional and cognitive capacities is a popular view that has cultural and historical antecedents. In chapter 6 we investigate how the practice of moral appraisal applies to children and whether or not it appropriately extends to nonhuman subjects. Our emotional responses and practical attitudes toward some wild and domestic animals might be interpreted to imply that some animals are the proper subjects of moral responsibility ascriptions according to certain philosophical theories of moral responsibility. The topic of chapter 7 concerns how to interpret what it means to be a proper target of the reactive attitudes and to be *fairly* morally appraisable.

All of these positions that I survey have something in common, and that is the attempt to mark our close moral affinity with animals—our moral kinship—because animals share with us morally laden emotions. What is typically missing from the positions I explain and evaluate is how the concept of a morally laden emotion depends critically on other related moral concepts such as virtue, moral motivation, ethical perception, or those moral practices that surround the moral appraisal of children. If emotions *are* conceptually connected to morality, then we are owed a precise account of the nature of morality and how emotions contribute to this moral domain.

METHODOLOGY

Ideally, what kind of methodology should we use to establish that animals have morally laden emotions? Martha Nussbaum's commentary on the differences between animal and human emotions is instructive.[26] She remarks, "In short, in an ethical and social/political creature, emotions themselves are ethical and social/political, parts of an answer to the questions, 'What is worth caring about?' 'How should I live?'"[27] Nussbaum makes it clear that to conclude that an animal is ethical and social/political, one must argue for this claim. This kind of argument will proceed by stating and examining the ethical theory endorsed, identifying the emotion state concepts employed, as well as taking into consideration the empirical data about the cognitive capacities of animals that are relevant to a particular theory of ethics and the emotional concepts attributed to the animal. The argumentation about this issue is complex because it combines conceptual issues about the nature of morality and empirical data about cognition in animals and humans, as this is relevant to a particular conception of morality.

But notice also that in the passage above Nussbaum says that once it has been established that an animal is ethical then we can conclude that the emotions attributed to that animal are ethical. In other words, the direction of argumentation goes from first establishing that a particular kind of animal is ethical (by using the argumentative strategies described in the previous paragraph) to saying something about the kinds of emotions that animal has.

By contrast the narratives examined in chapters 3 through 7 begin by attributing to an animal an emotion of a certain kind, like compassion or shame. If we also believe that emotional states like compassion or shame have moral connotations, then we may be tempted to infer that some animals are moral beings. If so, this would be a startling conclusion since we will have moved from the claim that animals and humans are *emotional* kin to the claim that animals and humans are *moral* kin, but without bothering to formulate the philosophical and empirical argument that supports such an inference.

Using narratives about animal emotion to conclude that animals are moral beings is not necessarily an illegitimate way of arguing, but it does demand that the reader exercise close scrutiny of the narrative context to ensure that the attribution of certain kinds of emotional states to an animal is warranted in the narrative setting in which it occurs. This is exactly the rationale for examining stories and anecdotes about animal emotion in the chapters that follow.

TELLING TALES

My love of animal stories is one reason why I have structured this book around the stories themselves. But there is also an important philosophical issue here that deserves our attention. Recall the story of Flint, the chimp who is reported to have died of grief. The author writing for *National Geographic World* says, "Stories like this suggest that animals have emotional feelings. Add up all such stories (there are many) and they suggest something more: *evidence.* It is evidence that researchers like Goodall hope will convince skeptics of something most people with pets already believe: animals *do* have feelings."[28] This passage raises questions about what we can reliably conclude about the real qualities of animals from the stories we read about animals and how these are interpreted and explained. In particular, what role should stories and anecdotes about animals play as evidence for the conclusion that animals have morally laden emotions?

Chapter 8 is devoted to answering these questions by examining the animal narrative itself and the role it plays in our efforts to establish that animals do or do not have emotions. Animal stories are used variously both to entertain children and adults as well as to educate us about the similarities and differences between humans and animals. Because this is so, it is worthwhile to carefully consider how we decide whether an animal story is true and literal, and what standards we should invoke for determining this. In this chapter I recommend some guidelines for how to read an animal story so as to locate the limits of "fancy." Readers are urged to consider the cultural context of the story, the conceptual analysis of emotion state terms and descriptions within the story, and the normative values that some animal stories encourage us to embrace. By paying attention to these particular features of the story itself, we can begin to see how that story contributes to our understanding of what animals are like, both figuratively and literally.

MARKING THE BOUNDARY

In all the animal narratives discussed throughout this book, the attribution of morally laden emotions to animals implies that we do share with animals something more than emotionality, and that is *moral kinship*. If animals and humans are moral kin in this sense, then human beings are not unique with respect to the capacity for morality. Our moral kinship implies that we are located alongside animals in the natural world rather than distinct from animals and nature.

 While there are undoubtedly many commonalities between animals and humans, I believe that moral kinship is not one of them. By suggesting that humans may be unique with respect to morality, I leave myself open to the charge that I am arguing for human superiority over animals. But this is decidedly not my position. Identifying differences between humans and animals need not imply human superiority even though there are historical antecedents for just such a misplaced view.

Can one maintain that humans are unique in some respect

without maintaining that humans are superior? I believe so. Marking the boundary between humans and animals involves noting biological differences. But it is also a conceptual issue about the nature of the emotions as well an ethical issue about what we value in a human life and our normative judgments about where we ought to locate human beings with respect to the natural world. As I explain in chapter 9, marking the boundary between humans and animals may not be merely a matter of identifying one single feature or characteristic that humans have and that some animals lack, such as language, self-awareness, or rationality.[29] A more complex (and less tidy) picture of how animals and humans are different emerges from our attention to the variety of ways in which the concept of emotion is used in narratives about animals and humans, as well as how emotions are embedded in the practice of morality.

NOTES

1. Colin Allen and Marc Bekoff, *Species of Mind: The Philosophy and Biology of Cognitive Ethology* (Cambridge, MA: MIT Press, 1997), p. 2.

2. Aline Alexander Newman, "Do Animals Have Feelings?" *National Geographic World,* June 2001, 28.

3. Jane Goodall, *Through a Window* (Boston: Houghton Mifflin, 1990), p. 165.

4. Newman, "Do Animals Have Feelings?" p. 28.

5. Ibid., p. 30.

6. Dale Jamieson and Marc Bekoff, "Afterword: Ethics and the Study of Animal Cognition," in *Readings in Animal Cognition,* ed. Marc Bekoff and Dale Jamieson (Cambridge, MA: MIT Press, 1996), p. 360.

7. The two main kinds of philosophical arguments in the traditional literature about ethics and animals are advanced by Peter Singer (equality of interests) and Tom Regan (rights). Each con-

cludes that animals are morally considerable. For Singer, who uses the ethical theory of utilitarianism to make his case, animals are morally considerable because they are capable of pleasures and pains. For Regan, some animals have certain rights, including the right to respectful treatment, because they are subjects-of-a-life, where this is sufficient for attributing to some animals inherent value. Being a subject-of-a-life, for Regan, *does* involve the capacity for emotion as one of a cluster of psychological properties that Regan believes it is correct to attribute to some animals. See Tom Regan, *The Case for Animal Rights* (Berkeley: University of California Press, 1983); Peter Singer, *Animal Liberation* (New York: Avon Books, 1975).

8. Regan, *The Case for Animal Rights.* See chapter 5.2 especially.

9. Ibid., pp. 151–52.

10. Marc D. Hauser, *Wild Minds: What Animals Really Think* (New York: Henry Holt and Company, 2000), pp. 249–53.

11. Regan, *The Case for Animal Rights*, pp. 152–53.

12. Regan himself does not interpret animal emotion in this particular way. Emotions are one of several psychological states that Regan argues some animals have in order to qualify as being subjects-of-a-life. Even though this status is sufficient for attributing rights to animals, they are still classified as moral patients on Regan's view. See ibid., pp. 243–48.

13. Marc Bekoff, "Wild Justice and Fair Play: Cooperation, Forgiveness, and Morality in Animals," *Biology and Philosophy* 19 (2004): 492.

14. Ibid., p. 515. Bekoff concludes this article by saying, "It is still far too early to draw the uncompromising conclusion that human morality is different in kind from animal morality and walk away in victory." Ibid., p. 516.

15. See chapter 3 in S. F. Sapontzis, *Morals, Reason, and Animals* (Philadelphia: Temple University Press, 1987).

16. David DeGrazia, *Taking Animals Seriously: Mental Life and Moral Status* (Cambridge: Cambridge University Press, 1996), p. 203.

17. Evelyn B. Pluhar, *Beyond Prejudice: The Moral Significance of Human and Nonhuman Animals* (Durham, NC: Duke University Press, 1995), p. 2.

18. Ibid., p. 55.

19. See Frans B. M. de Waal, *Good Natured: The Origins of Right and Wrong in Humans and Other Animals* (Cambridge, MA: Harvard University Press, 1996); Frans B. M. de Waal, "Morally Evolved: Primate Social Instincts, Human Morality, and the Rise and Fall of 'Veneer Theory,'" in *Primates and Philosophers: How Morality Evolved*, ed. Steven Macedo and Josiah Ober, *University Center for Human Values* series (Princeton, NJ: Princeton University Press, 2006).

20. Gary L. Francione, "Animals—Property or Persons?" in *Animal Rights: Current Debates and New Directions*, ed. Cass R. Sunstein and Martha C. Nussbaum (Oxford: Oxford University Press, 2004), pp. 128–29.

21. Aristotle, *Nicomachean Ethics*, 2nd ed., trans. Terence Irwin (Indianapolis: Hackett, 1999). See Book 3.1.

22. Richard Sorabji, *Animal Minds and Human Morals: The Origins of the Western Debate* (Ithaca, NY: Cornell University Press, 1993). See especially chapter 9.

23. Kristin Von Kreisler, *Beauty in the Beasts: True Stories of Animals Who Choose to Do Good* (New York: Jeremy P. Tarcher/Putnam, 2001).

24. Justin Oakley, *Morality and the Emotions* (London: Routledge, 1992), ch. 2.

25. Some of these positions will be discussed in later chapters. See Charles Darwin, *The Descent of Man; and Selection in Relation to Sex* (Amherst, NY: Prometheus Books, 1998); J. M. Masson and S. McCarthy, *When Elephants Weep: The Emotional Lives of Animals* (New York: Delacorte, 1995); Jeffrey Moussaieff Masson, *Dogs Never Lie about Love: Reflections on the Emotional World of Dogs* (New York: Three Rivers Press, 1997); Pluhar, *Beyond Prejudice*; Steven M. Wise, *Rattling the Cage: Toward Legal Rights for Animals* (Cambridge, MA: Perseus Books, 2000); Steven M. Wise, *Drawing the Line: Science and the Case for Animal Rights* (Cambridge, MA: Perseus Books, 2002); Marc Bekoff, *Minding Animals: Awareness, Emotions, and Heart* (Oxford: Oxford University Press, 2002); Marc Bekoff, ed., *The Smile of a Dolphin: Remarkable Accounts of Animal Emotions* (New York: Discovery Books, 2000); Francione, "Animals—Property or Persons?"; Goodall, *Through a Window*.

26. Martha C. Nussbaum, *Upheavals of Thought: The Intelligence of Emotions* (Cambridge: Cambridge University Press, 2001).

27. Ibid., p. 149.

28. Newman, "Do Animals Have Feelings?" p. 28.

29. See, for example, Hauser, *Wild Minds*; Richard Joyce, *The Evolution of Morality* (Cambridge, MA: MIT Press, 2006); Christine M. Korsgaard, "Morality and the Distinctiveness of Human Action," in *Primates and Philosophers: How Morality Evolved.*

Chapter Two

EMOTIONAL KINSHIP

My main objective in this chapter is to clarify the concept of emotion used in narratives about our emotional kinship with animals. This is not an exhaustive survey of all such stories and anecdotes but a sampling of the kind of story that will be the focus of our philosophical analysis. What is distinctive about some declarations of our emotional kinship with animals is that they require a certain kind of theory about what the emotions are. I explain how Martha Nussbaum's eudaimonistic theory of the emotions captures this sense of emotional kinship by characterizing emotions in a way that connects them to what has value in both human and animal lives.

By the end of the chapter I hope to have positioned the reader to see how some narratives about emotional kinship rely on or presuppose a particular account of the emotions;

how such narratives invite us to endorse a stronger thesis about moral kinship; and finally, what kind of philosophical analysis is required to evaluate the plausibility that some animals have morally laden emotional states.

ANIMALS ARE LIKE US

When Theophrastus, a student of Aristotle's, claimed that humans and animals are kin, he meant by this that animals are like humans in certain respects, including their bodily composition, such as fluids and tissues, but also appetites, emotions, perceptions, and even reasoning. This sense of kinship does not depend on ancestry but on *likeness* and "the sharing of food, habits and race."

> In this way, too, we class all humans as related both to each other and to all animals. For their bodily origins (*arkhai*) are by nature the same. By this I do not mean to refer to the primary elements, since plants also are made of these, but for example skin, flesh and the type of fluids that are natural to animals. And much more are they related through their souls being no different in nature, I mean in their appetites (*epithumiai*), anger (*orgai*), and again in their reasonings (*logismoi*) and above all in their senses (*aisthêseis*). But as with their bodies, some animals have souls more finely tuned, others less so, but they still all by nature have the same origins. And this is shown by their passions (*pathê*) being akin (*oikeiotês*).[1]

Writing in 1903, John Burroughs declares that animals can be "kin" with humans because they share emotions even when there is doubt about "how far our psychology applies to the lower animals," and even if one doubts that the intellectual and reasoning processes of animals are like our own. Here

Burroughs comments about Charles Roberts's collection of nature stories, *Kindred of the Wild.*[2]

> True it is that all the animals whose lives are portrayed—the bear, the panther, the lynx, the hare, the moose, and others—are simply human beings disguised as animals; they think, feel, plan, suffer, as we do; in fact, exhibit almost the entire human psychology. But in other respects they follow closely the facts of natural history, and the reader is not deceived; he knows where he stands. Of course it is mainly guesswork how far our psychology applies to the lower animals. That they experience many of our emotions there can be no doubt, but that they have intellectual and reasoning processes like our own, except in a very rudimentary form, admits of grave doubt. But I need not go into that vexed subject here. They are certainly in any broad generalization our kin, and Mr. Roberts's book is well named and well done.[3]

[handwritten marginal note: all examples are mammals]

These passages allow us to see that very different assumptions about what animals are like and what they are capable of may underlie claims about our emotional kinship with animals. For example, when Burroughs attributes emotions to some animals he does not apparently believe that this commits him to the idea that animals can *reason* like us, except in "very rudimentary form." When we turn to more contemporary writers who declare our emotional kinship with animals, we should seek clarity about what it means to share this capacity. The best approach, I believe, is to tease out of the narrative context itself how the nature of emotion is characterized. Or, if this is not sufficiently clear, we should ask what kinds of emotional states are credited to animals in the narrative and how these are connected to other capabilities it is believed animals have.

The particular kinds of narratives that interest me throughout this book are those in which the attribution of emotions to animals points to a fundamental likeness between humans and animals. Sue Savage-Rumbaugh writes, for example, "With bonobos, I experience a similar two-way understanding. I know how they feel and they know how I feel. This is possible because of the expressions that emanate from their faces, the way they interpret the feelings of others, the depth of their commitment to one another, and the understanding of one another that they share. Their sharing of emotional perspective is of a peculiarly human sort."[4] Savage-Rumbaugh is searching for a way to identify the very respect in which animals are like humans, singling out emotion as a way of marking that commonality. But here emotions are conceptually connected to "interpreting the feelings of others," "being committed to one another," and "understanding one another." It is in these ways that bonobos are like human beings.

Sometimes narratives about our emotional kinship with animals do not merely declare our emotional commonality but suggest also that animals are exemplars for human beings. Michael Tobias has had the experience of swimming with a dozen whale sharks. He writes,

> These sharks came up to us in the water, swam around us and with us, and truly wanted to make some sort of metaphysical, primal exchange. We swam side by side, entered into trust and fellowship, extended every mutual admiration, displayed all the forces of poetry and passion and delight that can be interpreted according to any free range of the senses.
>
> . . . What feelings did they have? I'm certain that between them, at the heart of their ancient relationship, was the very essence of bliss as the poets and saints have always thought of it. A joy that we spend our lives aspiring to. An integrity that has no conflict. They aren't sabotaging themselves, or acting out conflicts between their conscious and subconscious selves. Nor are they solitary. They move fre-

quently together, inches apart, and it's clear to the observer that they deeply love and are committed to one another.[5]

In this passage, whale sharks are credited with trust, fellowship, mutual admiration, integrity, commitment, love for one another, and bliss, as well as a freedom from what is emotionally problematic in humans; namely, conflict and sabotage. In this way Tobias suggests that whale sharks are living better than human beings because they experience those particular emotions that we hold in high esteem such as joy and love while avoiding the entanglements of human emotional life.

In an article titled "Our Emotional Kin," primatologists Deborah Fouts and Roger Fouts say, "In our more than thirty years of living with and studying chimpanzees, we've come to believe that we share all our emotions with them. Such differences that exist are merely of degree—differences that probably have a greater range within our own species than between ours and theirs."[6] The authors go on to describe this short anecdote titled "Compassion for Fellow Chimpanzees."

Moja and Dar, chimpanzees who are social siblings, have been a part of Washoe's family for many years. Moja, the oldest sister, was known to bully and tease her younger brother, Dar, when he was young. It took a number of years for Dar to fully trust her and to allow their friendship to flourish. One cool fall day, Dar and Moja sat side by side and Dar began touching a sore on his arm. Moja looked over at Dar, then looked at his sore and kissed him on the ear. Dar again touched his sore, and Moja leaned over and kissed it and they began to groom. Sometimes a kiss will make it better.[7]

The emotional states of chimpanzees that the authors identify here are caring and compassion toward a younger sibling who is injured. But these emotions are also connected to being capable of trusting and developing lasting friendships.

These passages illustrate a few main ideas about the concept of emotional kinship that I wish to examine more carefully. First, of course, is the idea that some animals have emotions and that they are like us in this respect. Comparisons of emotional similarity between humans and animals capture one sense in which we are "kin" to animals. But when it is claimed that we share emotions with animals, what does this mean exactly? We can complete the inquiry by examining the narrative context itself for clues about how animals and humans are alike.

Importantly, these passages do not suggest that because animals have emotions they are lustful, moved by beastly impulses, bodily appetites, or passions. The pejorative characterization of the emotions as irrational and bodily is not remotely implicit in these claims about our emotional kinship with animals. Instead writers point to various ways in which the emotions are valued, construing emotions in ways that are commendable and connecting these with other characteristics that we might even aspire to develop in our own lives. Bonobos "interpret the feelings of others," express a "depth of commitment to one another"; sharks have "integrity" and engage in relationships of "trust, fellowship," and deep love and commitment to each other; chimpanzees feel compassion for their siblings who are injured. When used in these ways emotions are valued contributions to living a life rather than what is undesirable, irrational, and out of our control.

If we are interested in animal emotion as a way of explaining how animals might be capable of trust, loyalty, integrity, long-term friendship, or compassion, then we should choose a characterization of the nature of emotion that does justice to the way in which emotional experience makes possible relationships of trust, lives lived with integrity, deep and lasting friendships, and motivating states like compassion. In other words, the concept of emotional kinship as it is articulated in some narrative settings about animals demands a certain kind of account of what the emotions are. At the very least, whatever definition of emotion we employ should be sensitive to an agent's psychology since it is these kinds of intentional states that make sense of what it means to have lasting friendships, to trust, and to be motivated to action by compassion, for example. As I will suggest later in this chapter, a eudaimonistic theory of the emotions does exactly this kind of explanatory work by making reference to a subject's beliefs, desires, and appraisals of the world and connecting these to valuing people, projects, or states of affairs. To get a clearer idea about the concept of emotion we are trying to capture in these narrative settings, consider a different context where emotions are also attributed to nonhumans.

Contemporary emotion researchers Paul Ekman, Carroll Izard, and Robert Plutchik claim that emotional expression has an adaptive role in helping organisms deal with survival issues in the environment.[8] This leads Plutchik to say that "[t]he concept of emotion is applicable to all evolutionary levels and applies to all animals as well as humans."[9] Indeed, the logical extension of this idea that the concept of emotion is applicable to animals in virtue of the adaptive role that these states play across species can be found in Terry McGuire's article "Emotion and Behavior Genetics in Vertebrates and Invertebrates."[10] McGuire says, "I define 'emotion' in an invertebrate as a change in the internal systems of the invertebrate so that it is more likely to perform a particular behavior."[11] By this definition, according to McGuire, fruit flies and other insects have emotions. And McGuire also suggests that the relevant plasticity of behavior singled out by this definition implies that emotions can be found in mollusks and crustaceans, as well as in reptiles, amphibians, birds, and mammals.[12]

There is nothing wrong with adopting a definition of emotion that has the consequence that fruit flies have emotions.

But notice what is missing from this claim about insect emotion. The context of attribution does not include reference to, for example, compassion as a motivating intentional state, loyalty to friends, or integrity—the kinds of emotions and contextual detail that are salient to the narratives about emotional kinship we have already discussed. Since McGuire is clearly not attempting to persuade us that fruit flies and humans are emotional kin in the sense we are describing, the context of emotional attribution does not demand a theory of emotion that is sensitive to the *value* of integrity, friendships, and caring about a sibling.

I do not maintain that the theory of emotions I will use can be applied with equal success to every declaration that we share emotions with animals. However, the few examples used above are intended to be illustrative of the way in which emotions are characterized in the stories and narratives I discuss throughout this book. In other words, the focus of my philosophical inquiry is delineated roughly by those writers who claim that animals are like humans in sharing emotions, where emotions are characterized as valued contributions to living a good life. I plan to expand on this in the following section. But it is perfectly reasonable to insist that not all contexts where emotions are attributed to animals characterize emotions in this way. McGuire's research program, for example, relies on a definition of emotion that specifies "changes in the internal system of an animal making it more likely to perform a particular behavior." This is one such context that eludes any mention of the psychology or the intentional state of the animal. For this reason it is not a candidate for the analysis of emotional states that I use throughout this work. However, it sometimes happens that writers will claim that humans and animals share emotions, but they do not define what emotions are nor do they supply contextual details that help us to understand what intentional states, if any, are attributed to both animals and humans. In these cases the reader has every right to be puzzled about what concept of emotion is being used and to demand clarity about this concept.

EUDAIMONISTIC EMOTIONS

What explains the concept of emotion used to characterize our emotional kinship with animals is a theory about how emotions are connected to what has value in a life, such as friendship, integrity, caring for a sibling, or trust. One theory of the emotions that captures how emotions are value-laden in this way is a eudaimonistic theory, explained by Martha Nussbaum in her book *Upheavals of Thought*.[13] Nussbaum articulates a view about emotions as essentially constituted by cognitions (beliefs, judgments, or appraisals) that are imbued with value and that reflect the importance of people, events, and projects in our lives. The theory is called *eudaimonistic* by connection to Aristotle's conception of human flourishing; an answer to the question "How should a human being live?" On Nussbaum's account, emotions are about a person's flourishing, since they reflect "the person's own commitment to the object as a part of her scheme of ends."[14] To understand how this is so, consider the following three stories about grief as it is felt or experienced by an animal whether fictional or real.[15] From these stories we can learn something about the nature of grief and about what we share with animals.

Wild with Grief

In the story "Lobo: The King of the Currumpaw," Ernest Thompson Seton describes the old, gray wolf Lobo as "a giant among wolves."[16] Not only is Lobo larger and stronger than any ordinary wolf, he is more cunning and wily than any wolf that has roamed the cattle range of northern New Mexico. This allows Lobo and his small pack to rule his territory with a "despotic power," killing livestock at will. Seton writes that Lobo and his pack "often amused themselves by killing sheep" and on one night in November 1893, they killed two hundred and fifty sheep "apparently for the fun of it." Lobo "scorned his enemies," the hunters, and successfully eluded capture by all the best wolf hunters hired to capture him with poisons, traps, or dogs. When Joe Calone is hired to destroy Lobo and fails repeatedly, Lobo moves his family of wolf pups to the cliffs near Joe's home. "'There's where he lived all last summer,' said Joe, pointing to the face of the cliff, 'and I couldn't do a thing with him. I was like a fool to him.'"[17]

Lobo's eventual downfall is precipitated by Seton himself, who takes on the challenge of capturing and killing the dreaded wolf to collect the rich bounty of $1,000. With great care he places a combination of large traps around poisoned meat and around a heifer's head. This does not fool Lobo, but the head attracts his mate, the white wolf Blanca, who is caught in the trap and killed later by Seton.

The ruin of Lobo is brought about by his feelings for his lost mate, Blanca. Seton describes Lobo as one among many heroes who have "fallen through the indiscretion of a trusted ally."[18] Seton drags Blanca's carcass over five or six traps he has laid. Lobo follows the trail "recklessly," without his ordinary caution and care and apparently beside himself with sorrow. Eventually he stumbles into a trap. Seton takes him back to the ranch, alive but weakened. The story ends with Lobo's death. Seton writes, "A lion shorn of his strength, an eagle robbed of his freedom, or a dove bereft of his mate, all die, it is said, of a broken heart; and who will aver that this grim bandit could bear the threefold brunt, heart-whole?"[19]

What can we learn about the nature of emotion from this story? We know that it is to Lobo's credit that he avoids capture, year after year, by his cautiousness, experience, and his cunning ability to discern poisons and traps. Lobo is wise in the ways of being hunted, and the evidence of this is his success in remaining free to live his independent life. But when Blanca is killed, Lobo is what we might call "grief stricken." He mourns out loud in sorrow, and his ordinary caution is forgotten. Seton uses the word "reckless" several times to describe Lobo's unthinking racing about; as if avoiding traps is the least of his concerns when compared to the loss of his mate.

Lobo's sorrow is appropriate to the loss of an object of love. It is what any of us might feel in reaction to the tragic demise of someone we adore. And it is also within our range of experience to see that sorrow and grief can temporarily, or, for some, pathologically, blind us to reason and deliberation and impede us in the pursuit of what we ordinarily believe is appropriate action. In other words, what Seton describes about Lobo's experiences and behavior resonates with our own experiences and actions, and to some extent, makes more perspicuous both the value of love and our emotional vulnerability incurred by such relationships.

A Barnyard Tale of Friendship and Loss

E. B. White's story *Charlotte's Web* has at least one thing in common with Seton's story about Lobo.[20] We can learn from the animals in *Charlotte's Web* something about the nature of grief and loss as it figures into the living of a good life. Wilbur is a lonely pig who has many barnyard acquaintances but no real friends until he meets Charlotte, a spider who lives in a web in the corner of the barn. When a goose inadvertently lets slip that Wilbur is headed for slaughter and destined to be bacon on the table, Wilbur is horrified and desperate. Charlotte devotes herself to saving Wilbur. Her plan involves weaving words into her web to draw the farmer's attention to

Wilbur and his extraordinary qualities. She writes, "Some Pig," "Terrific," and "Radiant." As one might expect, Wilbur becomes a local legend. If he wins a prize at the fair, Charlotte guarantees that the farmer will never sacrifice Wilbur for food. Wilbur does become a prize-winning pig through Charlotte's efforts. But the spider's life cycle draws to a close. She dies, leaving an egg sack containing 514 of her offspring.

Wilbur's immediate reaction to Charlotte's death is to cry and carry on. But this is only temporary. He designs and implements a plan to move the egg sack from the fair back to his own barn. Wilbur is not made crazy with grief nor is he debilitated in his sorrow like the wolf Lobo. Instead his sorrow moves him to action. The installation of the egg sack is a kind of memorial to Charlotte. Even though she dies alone, she is remembered and, in a sense, lives on in the family of spiders that she produces. Wilbur declares, "She was brilliant, beautiful, and loyal to the end. I shall always treasure her memory. To you, her daughters, I pledge my friendship, forever and ever."[21] How Wilbur feels about the death of Charlotte cannot be understood without the background details that include the mutual friendship he shares with the spider. Her warmth, concern, and efforts to save him from slaughter and her continuous loyalty to him make up this friendship. It is in this context that his sorrow is understood.

In this setting, emotion is not an obstacle to clear thinking, as it apparently was for Lobo. The experience of sadness does not interfere with the continuation of a rewarding life. Wilbur is certainly not indifferent to Charlotte's death, but his feelings are transformed into fond memories that override his sadness. The narrative has a hopeful quality about it that Charlotte is not entirely and irrevocably lost. Her death is not the final act, in part, because her children come to supply a continuation of the intimacy and friendship that Wilbur desires without actually replacing her as an individual with her own personality and talents. This is not unlike what *we* might feel toward the relations of those we have lost. A certain physical resemblance or shared mannerism can sometimes be a reminiscent and comforting reminder of that person who has died.

Dying of Grief

Jane Goodall writes about the chimpanzees of Gombe from the vantage point of a lifetime of observing them and living with them.[22] She is witness to countless details about the lives of individual chimpanzees; activities that range over births, deaths, changes of social status, aggression, leadership, food foraging, and mating. So when Goodall writes about the experiences of eight-year-old Flint, we understand her remarks as informing us about a culture that is alien to most of us. She is an anthropologist telling us about an unfamiliar tribe of people whom she has come to know over the course of many years, explaining and interpreting for us what their behaviors really mean. Her writing has a kind of authority that derives from the quantity and variety of her experiences.

Flint was eight and a half years old when his mother, Flo, died. At this time he no longer needed her for milk, but Goodall suggests that he was *psychologically* dependent on her, so much so that her death created in him a depression from which he could not recover. As the story is told, Flint died from grief: "But, dependent as he was on his mother, it seemed that he had no will to survive without her. His whole world had revolved around Flo, and with her gone life was hollow and meaningless."[23] Flint did not follow his brother and the other chimpanzees in the group but returned to the place his mother died. There he sat, lethargic and despondent. "The last time I saw him alive, he was hollow-eyed, gaunt and utterly depressed, huddled in the vegetation close to where Flo had died."[24] Within days he became weaker, and he eventually died after making his way slowly to the exact spot Flo's body had lain.

As before, I want to ask what we can learn about the particular emotion of grief from this narrative. Despite the fact that most of us know very little about chimpanzees, this story about one individual chimpanzee is powerfully clear. We not only understand Flint's behavior when it is described in this way, we empathize with him. This is so because the experience of loss when it manifests itself as depression is an all-too-familiar human experience. Who among us has not had an experience that approximates this kind of hopelessness about life, where nothing motivates and nothing interests? The death of a parent has this very real potential for each of us. Even if we have not had exactly this reaction to exactly this set of circumstances, we can imagine how losing the person who has cared for and nurtured us can create a hopelessness and loneliness from which we may not feel capable of extricating ourselves.

I think we do learn something about the concept of grief from seeing how Lobo grieves for his lost mate, Blanca, Wilbur for the loss of his spider friend, Charlotte, and Flint for the death of his mother. The animals described in these stories—both fictional and real—grieve for objects dearly valued. In this sense they are like human beings who suffer these kinds of losses. This is most noticeable in Goodall's descriptions of Flint and other chimpanzees. If we begin reading Goodall's story wondering what chimpanzees are really like psychologically and behaviorally, the answer is quite plain. They are like us. And so an explanation about the role of grief and loss as it figures into human lives is equally suitable to explain how Flint experiences the loss of his mother. The source of our empathy for Flint is the recognition of grief and loss in our own case.

The eudaimonistic theory of the emotions can help us to articulate the concept of emotion that underlies our emotional kinship with animals. This theory can be briefly sketched by reference to four main ideas.[25]

First, emotions are about the world insofar as they point to or are directed at objects, persons, or states of affairs. All three animal narratives I discuss here illustrate that grief is an intentional state. Lobo's misery is directed at the loss of his mate, Blanca. The sadness Wilbur feels is about the loss of his intimate friendship with Charlotte when she dies. And Flint's depression and despondency are about the death of his mother.

Second, the object of emotion is interpreted by or seen through the eyes of the agent. In particular, grief is shaped by an interpretation of events by the subject who experiences the grief. Blanca's death is acknowledged by the ranchers, but it is cause for jubilation and not mournfulness as Lobo experiences the loss of his mate. The barnyard animals recognize that Charlotte has died. This fact is not in dispute. But no one other than Wilbur is motivated to memorialize her life by moving her egg sack back to the barn. It is only Wilbur who seeks to preserve the memory of his intimate friendship with Charlotte. So it is with the chimpanzee Flint. While Goodall herself is sad about the death of Flint's mother, only Flint is incapacitated by the loss—or so the narrative implies. In each of these cases, the experience of grief is informed by the particular relationship that each subject bears to the object of grief, the loss of a mate, friend, or mother. We cannot explain the emotion without reference to the particular way in which each subject regards or understands the loss. As Nussbaum puts it, in grief we see the object "through one's own window."[26]

Third, as these descriptions imply, emotions essentially involve beliefs, judgments, or appraisals about the object (of grief). Seton describes Lobo's emotion when Blanca is killed by attributing to him certain beliefs and knowledge states, including the knowledge of how she died. "As evening fell he seemed to be coming toward the home cañon, for his voice sounded continually nearer. There was an unmistakable note of sorrow in it now. It was no longer the loud, defiant howl, but a long, plaintive wail; 'Blanca! Blanca!' he seemed to call. . . . It was sadder than I could possibly have believed. . . . He seemed to know exactly what had taken place, for her blood had stained the place of her death."[27] Goodall explains Flint's experience of grief by conjuring up for us a scene. Flint gazes motionlessly at an empty nest. Then he walks slowly away "with the movements of an old man." Goodall suggests that he must have thought something when he gazed with wide eyes at the empty nest. She suggests the following, "Memories of happy days gone by to add to his bewildered sense of loss? We shall never know."[28] The beliefs that Goodall tentatively attributes to Flint reinforce her description of the experience of grief from Flint's point of view that the loss of his mother rendered his life "hollow and meaningless."

Finally, and perhaps most important to the account of emotions we are exploring, is the way in which the concept of grief captures a kind of valuing, both of the object of grief and also as a measure of the various ways in which things external to the agent figure into the goals and projects of a good life. We can see plainly how this point is realized in all three narratives. In *Charlotte's Web* it is friendship that plays a central role in Wilbur's life. Preserving Charlotte's offspring is a memorial to the importance of intimate and trusting relationships. Lobo's actions are testimony to the importance that companionship plays in the living of a good life. Goodall explains Flint's despondency and eventual death as the result of grief. Again, we see that according to this interpretation of how and why Flint dies, there is contained an appreciation for the value of Flo and her nurturing relationship with her son. But we also see how she figures into Flint's life and his well-being. Flint's death may well represent a choice that a life without the presence of a nurturing parent is not a life worth living.

Using a eudaimonistic theory of the emotions captures the concept of grief that is salient in these stories because it best explains the intentional states of those who grieve. As such, it is a plausible candidate for what animals and humans share in those contexts where it is claimed that animals and humans are emotional kin. Jane Goodall remarks, for example, "It is hard to empathize with emotions we have not experienced. . . . It was not until I knew the numbing grief that gripped me after the death of my second husband that I could even begin to appreciate the despair and sense of loss that cause young chimps to pine away and die when they lose their mothers."[29] In this passage Goodall makes it clear that grief plays the same role in both human lives and chimpanzee lives. And, if we somehow fail to understand what we share with Lobo after reading the story "Lobo: The King of the Currumpaw," Ernest Thompson Seton addresses the reader directly by saying, "[W]e and the beasts are kin. Man has nothing that the animals have not at least a vestige of, the animals have nothing that man does not in some degree share."[30]

However, even if we use a eudaimonistic theory of the emotions to explain grieving animals in these particular stories, it might be thought that we have captured only the concept of *human* grief and what this experience is like for us. Perhaps we cannot assume from this that real animals have emotions in just this way, or that animals themselves engage in the kind of valuing that is characteristic of the intentionality associated with grief and other emotional states as *we* experience them.

Marc Bekoff suggests, for example, that we may not necessarily assume that animal emotion is exactly like human emotion because, "even among humans joy, for example, feels different to different people, and humans also display fear, bereavement and grief, and anger in a wide variety of ways."[31] Elsewhere Bekoff suggests that there may be species-specific emotions. "Species differences in the expression of emotions and what they feel like also need to be taken into account. Even if joy and grief in dogs are not the same as joy and grief in chimpanzees, elephants, or humans, this does not mean that there is no such thing as dog-joy, dog-grief, chimpanzee-joy, or elephant-grief. Even wild animals (for example, wolves), and their domesticated relatives (dogs), may differ in the nature of their emotional lives."[32]

In response, despite the obvious fact that individuals may experience emotions in rather different ways, this does not preclude an attempt to supply a theory of the emotions—one that seeks to specify underlying commonalities that are true for most people. A general theory of the emotions may satisfy this demand while still allowing that there are individuals who experience particular emotions in various ways. In fact, the advantage of trying to formulate such a general theory is that it aims for a specification of the essential or defining features of grief, for example, that are characteristic of all or most individual experiences. The mere fact that there is variability in the emotional experiences of human beings does not preclude us from attempting to say what is central to certain kinds of emotions or to emotions more generally.[33]

But even so, Bekoff is right that there are bound to be differences in how we explain human emotions and animal emotions. Nussbaum takes account of these differences by building into her theory several qualifications. First, although a eudaimonistic theory characterizes the emotions of a creature as "evaluative appraisals" of the world, these appraisals do not necessarily take the form of "objects of reflexive self-consciousness." Even though it may be accurate to ascribe intentional states to animals, this need not be taken to imply that animals who have emotions reflect on their own intentional states.[34]

A second modification of her theory Nussbaum notes is that the cognitive appraisals of the world attributed to those animals that have emotions need not entail attributing to the animal linguistic symbolism in order to accurately capture the cognitive content of the animal's emotional state.[35] While Nussbaum does not argue for a sharp discontinuity in cognitive capacities between humans and animals, she does identify several capacities as being more highly developed in human beings, such as temporal thinking, the capacity for generalizing, the degree of self-understanding, and the capacity for language or other forms of symbolic representation. The degree of development of these cognitive capacities in humans and animals shapes the kinds of emotions capable of being experienced. She remarks,

> Some emotions will prove altogether unavailable to many animals, to the extent that the sort of thinking underlying them proves unavailable: hope, for example, with its robust sense of future possibility; guilt with its keen identification of a past wrongdoer with the agent's own present self; romantic love, to the extent that it involves a temporal sense of aim and aspiration, and a fine sense of particularity; compassion, to the extent that it calls upon a sense of general possibility and fellow feeling; types of shame that involve thought of a norm against which one has measured oneself and found oneself wanting; and even some forms of anger, fear, and grief, to the extent to which they require causal and temporal judgments.[36]

Even without ascribing language to an animal we can refer to the evaluative content of eudaimonistic emotional states by making use of approximate translations in our language, though Nussbaum admits there is always room for distortion in such cross-species translations. In fact, she insists that in "*good* animal narratives" (my italics) there is always a cautious use of linguistic content in specifying an animal's emotional states. I will have more to say about what these constraints are in chapter 8, where I discuss stories about animal emotion and morality.

There may not be unanimity about which "emotions will prove altogether unavailable to many animals." In particular, the narratives and anecdotes about animal emotion discussed in forthcoming chapters ascribe to animals morally laden emotions—emotions such as compassion, empathy, or sympathy. Nonetheless, the approach Nussbaum seems to employ is a good model for how we should proceed to investigate whether or not some animals have morally laden emotions. Nussbaum identifies both a theoretical part of the project, which is to examine what intentional content is implied by emotion state concepts such as compassion, and an empirical investigation that looks to see what cognitive capacities it is appropriate to ascribe to certain kinds of animals. In this way we can make the best possible judgment about whether it is warranted to attribute to an animal a particular kind of emotion. In the remainder of this work we focus exclusively on the theoretical part of this methodology in order to supply an analysis of those emotion state terms and moral concepts that some writers use to attribute morally laden emotions to animals.

CONCLUSION

In this chapter I have suggested that in order to capture how some writers characterize our emotional kinship with animals, we should use a eudaimonistic theory of the emotions that explains how emotions are intentional and directed upon those things that have value in a life. This way of characterizing emotions is forward looking as well. The stories and anecdotes about animal emotion that we examine in later chapters also describe our emotional kinship in this way; suggesting by the kinds of emotions we share with animals and how these are construed that emotions are connected to what has importance and value in the living of a life for both humans and animals.

But the narratives examined in later chapters also make a stronger claim about what we share with real animals, since they argue in one way or another that the Moral Kinship Hypothesis is true *because* some animals have morally laden emotional states. Our investigation of this possibility will focus on a number of attempts to establish that some animals have these kinds of emotions. We can now go on to examine how emotions can be morally laden against some particular set of background assumptions about morality. We begin with a story that ascribes to a dog named "Heart" the moral virtue of compassion.

NOTES

1. Iamblichus, "Lives of Pythagoras," in *The Pythagorean Source-book and Library*, ed. K. S. Guthrie (Grand Rapids, MI: Phanes Press, 1987), p. 3.25. This passage is quoted in Richard Sorabji, *Animal Minds and Human Morals: The Origins of the Western Debate* (Ithaca, NY: Cornell University Press, 1993), pp. 177–78.

2. Charles G. D. Roberts, *The Kindred of the Wild: A Book of Animal Life* (Boston: L. C. Page, 1902).

3. John Burroughs, "Real and Sham Natural History," in *The Wild Animal Story*, ed. Ralph Lutts (Philadelphia: Temple University Press, 1998), p. 131.

4. Sue Savage-Rumbaugh, Stuart G. Shanker, and Talbot J. Taylor, *Apes, Language, and the Human Mind* (Oxford: Oxford University Press, 1998), p. 238.

5. Michael Tobias, "A Gentle Heart," in *The Smile of a Dolphin: Remarkable Accounts of Animal Emotions*, ed. Marc Bekoff (New York: Discovery Books, 2000), p. 172.

6. Deborah Fouts and Roger Fouts, "Our Emotional Kin," in *The Smile of a Dolphin*, Bekoff, p. 205.

7. Ibid.

8. See Paul Ekman, "Expression and the Nature of Emotion," in *Approaches to Emotion*, ed. K. Scherer and P. Ekman (Hillsdale, NJ:

Erlbaum, 1984); Carroll Izard, *Human Emotions* (New York: Plenum, 1977); Robert Plutchik, *Emotion: A Psychoevolutionary Synthesis* (New York: Harper and Row, 1980).

9. Plutchik, *Emotion*, p. 129.

10. Terry R. McGuire, "Emotion and Behavior Genetics in Vertebrates and Invertebrates," in *Handbook of Emotions*, ed. Michael Lewis and Jeannette Haviland (New York: Guilford Press, 1993).

11. Ibid., p. 158.

12. Ibid.

13. Martha C. Nussbaum, *Upheavals of Thought: The Intelligence of Emotions* (Cambridge: Cambridge University Press, 2001).

14. Ibid., pp. 31–33.

15. The reader might object that we will learn nothing about the emotional states of real animals by reading fictional characterizations of animals that are depicted as grief-stricken. Perhaps. I will suggest a way of analyzing how to read animal stories for their literal versus "fanciful" content in chapter 8. But for now I will say that these stories about animal grief and narratives about emotional kinship have something in common, and that is a particular concept of emotion. The narratives about grieving animals help us to fix the kind of theory that best explains what it is that animals and humans share. But additionally there is some value in grouping these stories together without regard for their literal truthfulness. The reader may notice how the concept of grief is constant across these different narratives, applying equally well to stories about fictional animals who act like human beings, as well as to real animals that are described in ways that are familiar and characteristic of human beings. This is perhaps how it should be if the concept of emotion that underlies claims about our emotional kinship with animals actually captures those particular respects in which we are alike.

16. Ernest Thompson Seton, *Wild Animals I Have Known* (New York: Charles Scribner's Sons, 1911), pp. 17–54.

17. Ibid., p. 51.

18. Ibid., p. 54.

19. Ibid., pp. 53–54.

20. E. B. White, *Charlotte's Web* (New York: HarperCollins, 1952).

21. Ibid., p. 182.

22. Jane Goodall, *Through a Window* (Boston: Houghton Mifflin, 1990).

23. Ibid., p. 196.

24. Ibid.

25. See Nussbaum, *Upheavals of Thought*, pp. 27–30.

26. Ibid., p. 28.

27. Seton, *Wild Animals I Have Known*, pp. 46–47.

28. Goodall, *Through a Window*, p. 196.

29. Ibid., p. 17.

30. "Note to the reader" in Seton, *Wild Animals I Have Known*.

31. Marc Bekoff, *Minding Animals: Awareness, Emotions, and Heart* (Oxford: Oxford University Press, 2002), p. 103.

32. Ibid., p. 119. See also Marc Bekoff, "Wild Justice and Fair Play: Cooperation, Forgiveness, and Morality in Animals," *Biology and Philosophy* 19 (2004): 495.

33. Nussbaum describes her methodology in proposing a general theory of the emotions in the following way,

What, then, is the starting point of the investigation? It is plain that it must be experience. . . . I will start from instances of emotion as people identify them in daily life, but I will ultimately argue that we should admit other instances that are not always correctly identified. . . . In such cases, I do believe that we need to return, at the end, to people and their judgments: we need to be able to show people that positing a fear of death is a good way of unifying diverse experiences in the given case, and explaining actions that otherwise would not be so well explained. If we do not come back to the phenomena with a sense of new illumination, then our own explanatory account is in trouble. Nonetheless, we should insist that philosophy may, indeed should, be responsive to human experience and yet critical of the defective thinking it sometimes contains.

Nussbaum, *Upheavals of Thought*, pp. 9–11.

34. Ibid., p. 126.
35. Nussbaum writes,

There are many kinds of cognitive activity or seeing-as in which ideas of salience and importance figure: there are pictorial imaginings, musical imaginings, the kinetic forms of imagining involved in the dance, and others. These are not all reducible to or straightforwardly translatable into linguistic symbolism, nor should we suppose that linguistic representing has pride of place as either the most sophisticated or the most basic mode. (Ibid., pp. 127–28)

36. Ibid., pp. 146–47.

Chapter Three

EMOTIONS AND
MORAL VIRTUE

In the last chapter we explored the concepts of emotional and moral kinship as these ideas figure into stories and anecdotes about animal emotion. Here we examine one particular way in which the emotions can be morally laden, and that is when they are connected to moral virtue.

According to Ernest Thompson Seton, the story of Lobo illustrates that animals and humans share the emotion of grief as well as love. This is at least one feature of our commonality that makes us kin. These emotions figure into the living of animal lives in much the same way that emotions figure into our human lives as motivations to act and sometimes as impediments to successful living. But most importantly the emotions Lobo is credited with are value-laden. Lobo deserves our respect because he dies with dignity and because he dies as a result of his unwavering love for his mate, Blanca. These qualities of Lobo are *moral virtues*. We praise human beings who exemplify such characteristics and dispositions to act. One way in which emotions are conceptually linked to morality is when certain emotional states function as motivations to act in ways that are morally commendable. In these cases we may come to believe that a person has a good moral character and that she is morally virtuous. Seton reminds us that being constant in love and being motivated by that emotional state is a virtue that we recognize in people. But he also urges us to see this virtue in Lobo as he displays his love and fidelity to Blanca, even to his own detriment.[1]

When descriptions of emotional states are characterized as virtues they are morally laden in the following way. If an animal is depicted as loving, sympathetic, or compassionate, we may come to believe that the animal displays an admirable quality of character. Seton's description of Lobo's grief plays exactly this role because the emotion of grief is connected to the moral virtue of love-constancy. Lobo is not simply an object of pity. He is deserving of our moral praise for the qualities of character that his grief-stricken actions reveal. In such cases where the emotion attributed to an animal is morally laden, our kinship with animals goes beyond our shared capacity for emotion. If animals are virtuous, then they are also moral. And it is this more important and fundamental characteristic that it is alleged animals share with human beings. I say *fundamental* because while most of us believe that there are many similarities between humans and animals, for example, having skin or teeth, some properties we believe are more important than others. Some features of human beings are closer to capturing what we think is essential to our nature. Being moral is that kind of feature. It is a capacity that we exercise when we are at our best. So if it should turn out that animals and humans are alike in being moral, then we must acknowledge that we, as a species, are not exceptional in this respect. This startling and intriguing possibility is why it is worth devoting our attention to the idea that animals have emotions, like compassion, that are morally laden. To judge whether or not animals are moral in just this sense by displaying virtue of character, we need to be quite precise about what virtues are and what kind of agency is required for virtue.

In this chapter I look closely at the emotion of compassion and at the stories we tell about animals that seem to display this emotion. I use these stories to ask what it means for compassion to be a moral virtue or a trait of moral character. It might seem excessively pedantic to focus on definitions of compassion and how these various definitions are used. But I will try to show that important philosophical conclusions about animals depend on just what we do mean by compassion, especially when it is connected to moral virtue. As before, telling the stories is the first order of business. The philosophical work follows.

COMPASSIONATE ANIMALS

"Heart" was an abandoned dog found curled under a log near a pond in California. He was barely breathing and suffering from wounds and loss of blood. Heart was rescued along with his daughter, "Soul," a five-month-old puppy found nearby. Their rescuer, Leo Grillo, reconstructed the story of what happened.

> Heart and Soul had been dumped in the wilderness, Grillo figured. They'd walked for miles to find a warm, dry hiding place and food. As they searched, they'd met a coyote pack, just eager for a meal. . . . Reading the paw prints like the words in a book, Grillo concluded that the hungry coyotes circled the father and daughter and got ready to kill.

But Heart probably lured the coyotes away to give Soul the chance to run and hide. As the coyotes cut off Heart's escape, the fight began in earnest; and he defended his daughter with every bit of strength he had. The dog won, and the coyotes ran away. Heart dragged himself to the ditch behind the log, where Soul came and curled up beside him.[2]

Jeffrey Masson writes that compassion is the essence of a dog's inner life. In his book *Dogs Never Lie about Love*, he reports a story as told to him by Rich McIntyre about an injured alpha male wolf that fell behind his pack because he was limping. "The wolf would rush forward on three legs and momentarily catch up. Then he would drop back several hundred yards, and the other pack members would halt and patiently wait for him to reach them."[3] What is central to our interest is what these authors say about the animals described and why they act. This will tell us what the authors believe is morally relevant about an animal's behavior as well as the motivational state attributed to that animal. Jeffrey Masson says about the wolves that wait for their limping leader, "This act seems to illustrate the complex state we refer to as compassion. I would suggest that waiting for the animal is the same order of compassion as we witness among humans."[4]

Von Kreisler describes Heart's defense of his daughter in the following way: "Animals understand another's situation, and often they try to offer comfort or support, both of which, of course, have kindness in them. But so often animals choose to do more than just be sensitive. They dive in and act in sometimes amazing and dramatic ways to solve whatever problem another may be having. The action, which is often absolutely selfless, turns the empathy into kindness. Compassion, in fact, is empathy, in action."[5]

References to emotions and animal virtue also appear in philosophical texts. David DeGrazia and Steven F. Sapontzis credit some animals, both domestic and wild, with moral virtue in order to argue that some animals are moral agents.[6] Both argue that some animals are moral agents because they perform actions that manifest virtues.[7] DeGrazia's evidence for this are cases where animals appear to behave altruistically and in ways that we would describe as compassionate. For example, DeGrazia reports that the chimpanzee Washoe acted "compassionately" and with "considerable altruism" when she risked drowning herself to save a young chimp.[8] In case we are skeptical about whether or not these animals really display virtues, DeGrazia reminds us that when human beings act from the right motivational state they need not provide elaborate reasons for acting. A human mother who rushes into a burning building to save a child may act virtuously by displaying courage or compassion even though she may only explain her act by saying, "The child was still in there!"[9] DeGrazia insists that this is a case where she acts for moral reasons and in such a way as to override her instincts or conditioning. According to DeGrazia, if animals or humans sometimes do act to override instincts or conditioning, then they sometimes do qualify as moral agents.

There are two philosophical questions we should ask about these descriptions of what animals do and why they act. First, what is the nature of a compassionate state? And second, how is the emotion of compassion conceptually linked to morality, in particular, moral virtue? Von Kreisler comments on what is morally salient about these kinds of examples.

> Whatever their reason, they made a choice to act differently than they had before. On their own, without being asked or forced, they were showing goodness; you could even call it virtue. To me, goodness, or virtue, means right action and impeccable behavior. It means displaying commendable qualities—such as cooperation, courage, and loyalty—which

are all abstract nouns that need active, freely chosen verbs to bring them to life. Goodness also implies a moral sense of right and wrong, an expectation of how one should be treated or should treat others with fairness, helpfulness, and sympathy. I believe that all animals, and not just mine, can have this moral sense and, more important, that they can act on it to show benevolence.[10]

In this passage Von Kreisler suggests that compassion, for example, is morally significant because it is a virtue. More specifically,

- Compassion leads to right action;
- Compassion is a commendable quality or trait of a person or an animal;
- If a person or an animal has compassion, then she has a sense of right and wrong and an understanding of how one should be treated.

Anyone interested in ethical issues will see this as an opportunity to investigate a number of ideas that underlie the claim that some animals have moral virtue. For example, I can't help wondering about the following additional questions: Does the emotional state of compassion always lead to right action? If not, in what circumstances do we morally commend those for feeling compassionate? Do we have to learn how to develop a compassionate disposition or trait of character? If not, why do we morally praise human beings who act compassionately? What does a person or an animal understand when she has compassion? And, more generally, what is a moral virtue? I believe any adequate account of the relation between the emotions and moral virtue should answer these questions. Since we are looking closely at stories and anecdotes about animal compassion in particular, we should begin by characterizing what kind of emotional state this is and how it is specific to moral virtue.

WHAT IS COMPASSION?

Seton tells us that humans and animals are kin because we share emotions as well as moral virtues. If we are trying to explain how animals and humans are alike in sharing emotions and moral virtue, then we should use a conception of emotion that captures exactly the sense in which emotions are morally significant. What we should demand is a conception of compassion that specifies why it is a praiseworthy motivational state and why this should count as displaying a virtue. In this way we may be able to formulate what it means for an animal to have a "moral sense of right and wrong," as Von Kreisler puts it.

To see why we must pay attention to the concepts and definitions we use, suppose that we tried to characterize compassion as a "simple-feeling state" that is more like a sensation of the body rather than a complex set of beliefs and judgments about the world. If compassion is defined merely as a sensation, then we will be unable to explain why we classify acts performed out of compassion as morally virtuous. Bodily sensations are not voluntary acts, let alone praiseworthy ones, so it is not appropriate to commend a person or an animal for having such a sensation. In other words, when compassion is defined as a bodily state it is not morally laden.

What account of compassion should we use in order to explain its moral significance?[11] In chapter 2 we saw the basic outlines of Martha Nussbaum's eudaimonistic theory of emotions. This cognitive-evaluative theory of the emotions we judged to be suitable for capturing the concept of emotional kinship used in some narratives about animal emotion. Additionally, Nussbaum devotes several chapters of her book *Upheavals of Thought* to explaining the emotional state of compassion. Her definition and explication of this concept illustrates how this particular emotion can be morally significant. Nussbaum defines compassion as "a painful emotion occasioned by the awareness of another person's undeserved misfortune."[12] The cognitive structure of compassion has three necessary conditions.

First is the idea that the state of being compassionate implies the belief or judgment that the misfortune or suffering is serious, or has "size." The intuition here is that feeling compassion toward another is not automatically extended to anyone regardless of their misfortune. Some losses are genuinely trivial compared to others. For example, we do not believe that Imelda Marcos, former first lady of the Philippines, deserves our compassion because she cannot find exactly the right shade of green in her search for yet another pair of shoes. But what constitutes a *serious* loss? Nussbaum suggests that there is considerable unanimity across time and place. Consider, for example, what Aristotle says about tragic plots and those that are worthy of pity on the part of the audience. They concern, "death, bodily assault or ill-treatment, old age, illness, lack of food, lack of friends, separation from friends, physical weakness, disfigurement, immobility, reversals of expectations, absence of good prospects."[13] The determination of seriousness or size of misfortune is not made from the point of view of the object of our compassion—the person to whom we direct our emotion. Even if Ms. Marcos were overcome with grief about her frustrated search for chartreuse shoes, this is not likely to affect our disposition to feel compassionate toward her. But, additionally, even if a person has adjusted her expectations or is even stoic under extremely adverse circumstances (poverty or loss of loved ones), this attitude normally will not interfere with our assessment that her plight is worthy of compassion. In other words, the point of view of the onlooker is central to the determination that the misfortune is serious.[14] This is not to say that the judgment of the sufferer is always irrelevant. Adopting just this point of view and seeing things through the eyes of the sufferer is sometimes revealing about what can count as a serious loss or misfortune.[15]

The second necessary condition required in Nussbaum's specification of the cognitive structure of compassion is the belief or judgment that the misfortune is undeserved, the sufferer is not at fault, or the degree of suffering is out of proportion to the blameworthiness of the object of our compassion. Here also there is a rather finely tuned assessment required of the circumstances surrounding *how* a person fares in the world and *why*. We can see how assessing fault is central to this emotion by considering examples where we are inclined to withhold our compassion. Imagine a drunk driver who totals his car in an accident. Though he must suffer in paying damages for the car, his plight is brought about by the poor decision to drink and drive. We see the sufferer here as blameworthy for his circumstances, and, for most of us, this judgment interferes with our feeling of compassion. But suppose, alternatively, that he has killed a member of his own family in a drunken-driving accident. While he is still at fault, we might believe that the kind of suffering he experiences is out of proportion to his fault. In this kind of case, we are likely to extend our compassion to him though perhaps in a qualified way. The assessment of fault depends, in part, on a determination of responsibility and blame. Sometimes a person may fall into misfortune through no fault of her own. But the extent to which she contributes to her misfortune in ways that are blameworthy, either by carelessness, negligence, or risk taking, determines the degree of compassion we extend to a person who suffers or interferes with our ability to feel compassion altogether.

As Nussbaum describes it, a third condition necessary for compassion is the "judgment of similar possibilities." We feel compassion toward those who undeservedly experience misfortune in those cases where we imagine ourselves suffering in similar circumstances. The object of our pity and compassion is relevantly like us in her susceptibility and vulnerability. Aristotle says that pity or compassion is about those circumstances "which the person himself might expect to suffer, either himself or one of his loved ones." And this feeling is contingent on having some "experience and understanding of the suffering."[16]

The cognitive-evaluative account of emotions allows us to see exactly why a person should be praised for having the right emotional state. If the onlooker goes wrong about directing her compassion to those who suffer only trivial annoyances or to those who bring misfortune upon themselves through their own fault, we say that compassion is not praiseworthy or, perhaps, we say that the emotion is not compassion. If the emotion is misdirected, inappropriate, or if the agent has undeveloped moral sensibilities, then we do not morally commend that person for having compassion.

Let me summarize what we have learned about the emotion of compassion and how it is morally significant. For ease of exposition I distinguish between *thin* and *thick* accounts of what compassion is. A thin account is one that characterizes this emotion with minimal description of the cognitive content of this state and with minimal explanation of its conceptual connection to morality. For example, Von Kreisler describes the emotion of compassion as a feeling of kindness that motivates an animal (or a person) to perform morally right actions. She adds that the person or the animal that is motivated by compassion understands how others should be treated. But because she does not specify what beliefs, judgments, or appraisals are relevant to understanding how others should be treated, we have no way of describing how compassion is distinguished from other emotions and why it is morally significant. Since there is relatively little specification of the cognitive content of this emotional state, I classify it as a *thin* definition.

By comparison, a thick account of the emotion of compassion supplies us with further specification about what an agent understands about the world and how this intentional state is morally significant. As Nussbaum describes it, the cognitive structure of compassion requires three necessary conditions: the judgment that the misfortune of another is serious, or has "size"; the belief that the sufferer is not at fault; and a judgment of similar possibility or a comparison of likeness between the person who has the emotion and the one who suffers misfortune. These necessary conditions explain how this emotion is morally laden. In order to say that anyone is *commendable* and *praiseworthy* for having compassion, this emotion must be appropriately directed at the right objects and displayed in the right circumstances. Not just any feeling by itself, even one of kindness, qualifies as an emotion that is praiseworthy.

Additionally, what a thick conception of compassion supplies us with is an account of its relation to moral goodness. In stories about animal compassion it is because compassion motivates the animal to right action that it is believed the animal deserves to be called virtuous. But what is missing so far is an account of what virtue is beyond merely stating that it is a commendable quality.

WHAT IS MORAL VIRTUE?

Because a number of writers are interested in crediting animals with moral virtues, it is important to be clear about what virtues are. While there are many philosophical and religious traditions that make reference to virtue, it is possible to say something about the core concept that cuts across many of these. Let's begin with a definition of *virtue* that is used by contemporary philosopher Linda Zagzebski, in her book *Virtues of the Mind*.[17] "A virtue, then, can be defined as a deep and enduring acquired excellence of a person, involving a characteristic motivation to produce a certain desired end and reliable success in bringing about that end."[18]

One central idea common to any virtue theory in ethics is that virtues are identified with inner traits of a person. While historically the list of traits that warrant being called virtues has varied, Zagzebski suggests that the traits most often identified as virtues include wisdom, courage, benevolence, justice, honesty, loyalty, integrity, and generosity.[19]

Von Kreisler and others are right in saying that anyone credited with virtue aims at morally right action, but more can and should be said about the relation between the inner traits of a person, like generosity or compassion, and the action that the agent performs. In any virtue theory the primary moral evaluation is of the person. Zagzebski calls a "pure virtue theory" one where the moral correctness of an action is not independent of our moral evaluation of the person but derivative of this evaluation. In other words, what determines the rightness or wrongness of the action is its relation to inner personal traits.[20]

One idea that is central to most conceptions of virtue—and to Aristotle's in particular—is that virtue is an *excellence* of a person. To say that a virtue, like honesty, is an excellence is to imply that a person credited with honesty is praiseworthy, but also that this feature of the person is an enduring quality of her identity. For example, I have a friend, Denise, who I believe has the virtue of honesty. I can cite particular occasions where she has acted honestly, such as when she told me with a clear eye how I could improve my life when I was trying to make painful decisions. But these individual instances do not exhaust what it means to say that she is an honest person. It is part of *who she is.* This feature is central to her disposition to act, not just on one occasion but over a longer stretch of time.

Characterizing a virtue as an excellence and an enduring quality of a person makes sense once we see that Aristotle distinguishes virtues from natural capacities. According to Aristotle, we are not born with virtue nor is virtue a natural instinct in a person.

> Hence it is also clear that none of the virtues of character arises in us naturally. For if something is by nature in one condition, habituation cannot bring it into another condition. . . . And so the virtues arise in us neither by nature nor against nature. Rather, we are by nature able to acquire them, and we are completed through habit.
>
> Further, if something arises in us by nature, we first have the capacity for it, and later perform the activity. This is clear in the case of the senses; for we did not acquire them by frequent seeing or hearing, but we already had them when we exercised them, and did not get them by exercising them. Virtues, by contrast, we acquire, just as we acquire crafts, by having first activated them. For we learn a craft by producing the same product that we must produce when we have learned it; we become builders, for instance, by building, and we become harpists by playing the harp. Similarly, then, we become just by doing just actions, temperate by doing temperate actions, brave by doing brave actions.[21]

Aristotle's view about how we acquire virtue through practice and habituation from an early age onward is the underlying presumption for our praising those who have developed generosity, loyalty, or honesty as part of their character. This kind of moral appraisal makes sense only if the agent herself is responsible for having those traits. One necessary condition for being responsible for having a trait of character is that it is acquired voluntarily. In other words, there must be a sense in which the agent might not have turned out to be loyal or honest, for example. She could have gone the other way. Our moral praise of a loyal or honest person reflects the assumption that she deserves moral credit for developing into a certain kind of person. As Zagzebski puts it, a natural capacity or faculty is not praised or blamed because it is involuntary, and the "completely involuntary is outside the moral realm."[22]

Additionally, Aristotle explicitly guards against the confusion that a person might receive moral credit for having a virtue when she merely performs a morally right action on a particular occasion. What is the difference?

> Moreover, in any case, what is true of crafts is not true of virtues. For the products of a craft determine by their own qualities whether they have been produced well; and so it suffices that they have the right qualities when they have been produced. But for actions in accord with the virtues to be done temperately or justly it does not suffice that they themselves have the right qualities. Rather, the agent must also be in the right state when he does them. *First, he must know that he is doing virtuous actions; second, he must decide on them, and decide on them for themselves; and, third, he must also do them from a firm and unchanging state.* (my italics)[23]

So in order to deserve moral praise for having the virtue of honesty, for example, a person must have developed this trait as a part of her character and display a kind of stability of disposition and action over time and in a variety of circumstances that require honesty as an appropriate feeling and response. We can now see why virtues of character deserve to be called "excellences."

It is useful here to distinguish between thin and thick conceptions of virtue in the same way that we distinguished between thin and thick accounts of compassion. Von Kreisler and others who conceptually link the emotional state of compassion with moral virtue are prepared to say that virtues are a commendable quality or trait of a person or an animal, and that being virtuous is sufficient for our moral commendation or praise of the agent who acts. I classify this kind of explanation of the concept of virtue as a thin definition because it fails to specify *why* those whom we credit with being virtuous deserve our moral praise, other than saying that they are commendable for having the virtue. By contrast, a thick conception of virtue is specific about why having a particular trait is morally good. Here the more traditional account of virtue originating in Aristotle is helpful. Virtues are excellences of a person that make up an enduring part of that person's identity. Virtues are states of character that are acquired gradually by practice and habit. They are not natural capacities, nor is an agent commended for having a virtue if she performs a good act on only one particular occasion. The additional requirement that Aristotle builds into what I am calling a thick concept of virtue is that the agent must have some cognizance she is performing a morally right act and is motivated by this reason.

WHY ARE THE VIRTUES MORALLY GOOD?

We might wonder why having a virtue is commendable or morally good in the first place. This question is not answered by merely saying that virtues lead to morally right action because, as we have seen, any virtue theory locates the primary moral evaluation on the person rather than on the action performed. What philosophical traditions such as Aristotle's supply us with additionally is an account of the relation between virtue and goodness. For Aristotle, this means that particular virtues acquired by a person and displayed in their activities are good *because* they contribute overall to a certain kind of flourishing life that is good in itself. Zagzebski calls such kinds of virtue theories "good-based." The virtues are constituents of the good life and the good life is explained by what Aristotle calls *eudaimonia*, or flourishing. Rosalind Hursthouse defines a virtue in this sense as "a character trait a human being needs to flourish or live well."[24]

There is another kind of virtue theory that Zagzebski calls "agent-based" or "motivation-based." According to this kind of theory, the virtues are not good because they contribute in fundamental ways to a flourishing life; they are good in themselves, in a foundational way. Zagzebski describes this by saying,

> Many of us have known persons whose goodness shines forth from the depths of their being. . . . If we then attempt to find out what it is about such a person that makes him good, we may be able to identify that goodness as involving certain feelings or motivations such as feelings of compassion or of self-respect or of respect for others, or motives of benevolence, sympathy or love, all of which are components of virtue. In each case we would not determine that his love, compassion or benevolence is good because of its relation to anything independently identified as good. We would simply see that these feelings or motivations are the states whose goodness we see in him.[25]

This description of motivation-based theories of the virtues is an important one for understanding what it would mean to say that some animals have moral virtue. Clearly animals do not have a conception of a flourishing life, so any theory about moral virtue that relied on this way of characterizing why the virtues are good would automatically rule out that animals have virtue. But if the virtues and the accompanying motivations that move a being to morally right action are good in themselves, then it will seem more plausible to attribute these kinds of morally laden emotions to animals.

In fact, a similar kind of distinction between "good-based" and "motivation-based" virtue theories is made by Steven F. Sapontzis in *Morals, Reason, and Animals.*[26] Here Sapontzis distinguishes between "virtuous acts that are done as part of fulfilling an ideal way of life," and "intentional, straightforward acts of kindness, courage, and the like."[27] The former he calls "fully moral agent-dependent (ad) acts." The latter are merely called "virtuous acts."[28] Only human beings perform *fully* moral acts, suggests Sapontzis, because a necessary condition for so acting is that the agent "believes it will contribute to attaining an ideal way of life," and "only rational [human] beings can project and dedicate themselves to attaining an ideal way of life."[29] While animals fail to be sufficiently rational to satisfy the conditions for performing fully moral (ad) acts, Sapontzis argues that they do perform acts that are virtuous and thereby meet a standard for moral agency. Since having the right motivational state is central to motivation-based accounts of virtue, we should take more care in explicating what kind of state this is.

WHAT IS THE RIGHT MOTIVATION?

We might begin by distinguishing between different kinds of motivations for action. Bodily events such as hunger motivate a person to action. Distinguished from these kinds of cases are "pure" motives of duty. But additionally there is the class of what one might call "emotional motives." For example, a generous person might be moved by the emotion of compassion or sympathy to share her own resources with someone in need. Aristotle makes the point that the motivation for an action matters to our moral appraisals of virtuous people. A politician who gives money to charity in order to win public esteem and gain votes in an election presumably would not have the motivation proper to virtue. But importantly, feelings or emotions themselves do not constitute praiseworthy motivations to act because these do not have the quality of being entirely voluntary. Praise and blame are attributed to those features of a person's inner life that are voluntary and, for Aristotle, these moral appraisals attach to how appropriate these feelings are in particular circumstances and to what or whom an emotion is directed given these circumstances. For example, if a person feels compassion toward a brutal murderer, one might argue that the emotion is misdirected. In a rather well-cited passage from *Nicomachean Ethics* Aristotle puts the point in the following way with respect to anger: "So also getting angry, or giving and spending money, is easy and everyone can do it; but doing it to the right person, in the right amount, at the right time, for the right end, and in the right way is no longer easy, nor can everyone do it. Hence doing these things well is rare, praiseworthy, and fine."[30]

Aristotle's remarks here remind us how much is involved when we are genuinely prepared to say that a person displays moral virtue. What is central to emotional motives like compassion is not merely that the agent is moved to perform morally right actions, but that she understands that the action is virtuous and performs that action for the sake of virtue and not for some other reason. Being able to specify what the agent understands about what she does and why she does it is crucial to identifying the motivational state proper to virtue. This is why the conceptual analysis of the emotional state of compassion supplied by a cognitive-evaluative theory, like Nussbaum's, is essential to describing how compassion is morally laden. Recall that as Nussbaum describes it, the cognitive structure of compassion requires three necessary conditions: the judgment that the misfortune of another is serious, or has "size"; the belief that the sufferer is not at fault; and a judgment of similar possibility or a comparison of likeness between the person who has the emotion and the one who suffers misfortune. In order to say that anyone is *commendable* and *praiseworthy* for having compassion, this emotion must be appropriately directed at the right objects and displayed in the right circumstances. This is why Aristotle remarks that performing virtue is "rare, praiseworthy, and fine."

Now that we have a clearer conception of how the emotion of compassion is conceptually connected to morality and a more complete understanding of what it means to have a virtue, we are better positioned to evaluate the claim that some animals are morally virtuous because they are motivated to act from the emotional state of compassion.

THICK AND THIN

We began this chapter with stories and anecdotes about animal compassion and virtue. I expressed my puzzlement about the concepts used in these stories and the inferences that readers are encouraged to draw from these; namely, that some animals are moral beings because they are motivated to act from compassion. My puzzlement was not about the literal truth or falsity of such stories but about what assumptions and meanings underlie the stories and what they purport to show. What I have tried to do is to bring the relevant philosophical ideas forward in such a way that the reader can appreciate the complexity of the question being asked, "Do some animals have moral virtue because they are motivated to act from compassion?" Because of its importance the question deserves to be clearly expressed. The distinction between thin and thick accounts of compassion and virtue allows us to do just that.

Thick characterizations of the central concepts described

in these stories about animal emotion and virtue reflect the depth and richness of the meanings that attach to our ordinary use of such expressions *compassion* and *virtue*. Thick concepts are not intended to replace our ordinary moral intuitions with philosophical abstractions. Instead they are employed in order to lend some precision to our practices of assigning moral credit and fault and our moral appraisals of people and what they do. For example, a thin conception of the emotion of compassion identifies this as a feeling of kindness that motivates a person or an animal to perform morally right action. But this narrow specification fails to capture the moral import of compassion since it fails to explain why we morally commend an agent for having this emotional state and what an agent must believe, judge, or appraise in order for compassion to be *appropriately* directed.

The same point can be made about the concept of virtue. Virtues are indeed morally commendable traits of a person, but a thin account of virtue only hints at what other concepts we are presupposing. Not just any commendable trait is a virtue, and not just any explanation for how virtues are acquired makes these morally significant. I have suggested that the core concept of virtue characterizes this as an excellence that makes up an enduring part of a person's character and who that person is—an integral part of one's identity. Virtues are distinguished from natural capacities because the latter are not voluntary, and it is voluntary actions and character traits gradually acquired by habit and practice that are the appropriate objects of moral praise and blame.

Writers who credit animals with compassion and virtue attempt to establish the ground-breaking conclusion that humans and animals share morality by operating with thin definitions of compassion and virtue. These definitions will not do the explanatory work these authors require of them and that is to establish that animals are moral kin with us because we share morally laden emotional states. To see that this is so, consider the following representation of the main argument we have identified in stories about animal compassion and virtue.

(1) *x* acts *compassionately.*

Usually *x* is the name of an animal, like Heart, whose actions can be described as "doing good." But, of course, the mere description of the action itself will not imply that an animal (or a person) has the trait of compassion and is praiseworthy because she is that kind of person. It must also be the case that

(2) *x* has *compassion* and is motivated to act for that reason.

What account of compassion is required in (2)? In Von Kreisler's story about Heart, it is not just that the emotional state attributed to Heart leads to right action but that compassion is an expression of Heart's moral virtue. So to specify how compassion is morally significant is to say that

(3) if *x* is motivated by *compassion,* then *x* is *morally virtuous.*

The conclusion of the argument is

(4) *x* is *morally virtuous.*

I have emphasized certain expressions in the argument because these are ambiguous concepts whose definitions may range from descriptions of animal behavior only, to "thin" references to the psychology of an animal, or to "thick" definitions of the intentional states necessary for the attribution of morally laden emotions as we have discussed in earlier sections of this chapter. But in order for the conclusion in (4) about our moral kinship with animals to be plausible, these concepts require a particular interpretation.

Indeed, not just any definition of *compassion* as this word occurs in premises (2) and (3) is consistent with the stories and anecdotes we have examined about animal compassion. These narratives illustrate that animals are like human beings in a particular respect. Recall Jeffrey Masson's remark about the pack of wolves that wait for their limping leader. "This act seems to illustrate the complex state we refer to as compassion. I would suggest that waiting for the animal is the same order of compassion as we witness among human beings."[31] In keeping with the concept of emotional kinship explained in chapter 2, we have seen that the theory of the emotions we choose generally should reflect how emotions are imbued with value. Since the moral significance of compassion, in particular, is explained by its connection to moral virtue, we should use a theory that reflects why and how this emotion is connected to virtue. Recall Aristotle's demand that the display of virtue be directed to "the right person, in the right amount, at the right time, for the right end, and in the right way." Nussbaum adds to this what the agent must understand in a praiseworthy and appropriate display of compassion—the judgment that the misfortune of another is serious, or has "size"; the belief that the sufferer is not at fault; and a judgment of similar possibility or a comparison of likeness between the person who has the emotion and the one who suffers misfortune.

If this *thick* account of compassion is used in premise (2) it must also be used in premise (3) in order to avoid a "fallacy of equivocation."[32] But when we substitute a thick conception of compassion into (3) we need to then explain what makes the entire statement in (3) plausibly true by specifying how and why being motivated by the emotional state of compassion implies that a subject is morally virtuous. We do not do justice to the concept of moral virtue used in (3) if we only describe virtue as a "commendable trait." Here a thick conception of virtue captures how we use this word to talk about human beings. Virtues are excellences of a person that make up an enduring part of one's identity. As states of character they are acquired gradually by practice and habit. They are not natural capacities, nor is an agent commended for having a virtue if she performs a good act on only one particular occasion. Additionally, the agent must have some cognizance that she is performing a morally right act and be motivated by this reason. Anyone who wishes to argue that animals are like human beings in sharing the capacity for virtue must employ a concept that for the most part captures the traditional understanding of what a virtue is that has persisted through time and through many philosophical and religious traditions.

In order to answer the question "Is Heart morally virtuous?" we need to explore the philosophical concepts that lie just below the surface of this question. The question now becomes "Does Heart have compassion in the thick sense of this word?" And, if so, "Does Heart have moral virtue in the thick sense as well?" Specifically, does Heart believe that the misfortune of Soul is serious, not brought about by Soul's negligence or through fault, and that Soul is relevantly similar to Heart in her capacity to suffer in this particular way? The question is not whether *we* have these beliefs and judgments; it is whether Heart makes these appraisals since it is only by satisfying these conditions that his motivation to act for Soul's sake is praiseworthy. Additionally, we will have to judge about something more comprehensive, and that is whether or not Heart's action is a consistent feature of his character by the acquisition of compassion by practice and habit. In other words, not just any correctly motivated action counts as a virtue or a trait of moral character. It doesn't for people, so the same conditions should apply to animals if we wish to extend the concept of virtue beyond the species border.

Given these more conceptually robust requirements for the attribution of compassion and virtue, I believe it is hard to justify that Heart or any other nonhuman animal has the morally laden emotional state of compassion. This is so because the justification for making this attribution involves attributing to animals what I am calling *thick* moral concepts. The kinds of intentional states connected to compassion in the morally relevant sense are more highly cognitive than any we are accustomed to attribute to animals. These involve, for example, judgments about fault or negligence. Additionally, once we see how moral character develops by habit and practice and is displayed by human beings whom we morally commend, it seems difficult to imagine how it can be true that animals have moral virtue where this is understood as an excellence of moral character.

Just in case we lose sight of the rationale for employing thick conceptions of compassion and virtue in the first place, let me remind the reader of two reasons for doing so. First, I have chosen a way of characterizing the nature of compassion that is sensitive to a particular sort of narrative context. Our first example was about a dog, Heart, who saves his daughter from hungry coyotes and is praised for his motivation to act and credited with being morally virtuous; the second example involves individual wolves that wait for their limping leader. In these cases the emotional state attributed to an animal is conceptually connected to morality by operating as a motivational state that is praiseworthy and expressive of what these authors identify as a moral virtue. It remains for us to fill in the background conditions about how to characterize the emotional state of compassion in such a way that makes this reading of the narrative coherent. As I have argued, not just any account of the nature of compassion or virtue will do this kind of explanatory work in such a way that captures our ordinary moral practices of assigning moral credit and fault. A thick conception of these moral concepts does explain our moral appraisals of agents and their actions.

Second, those writers who use stories and anecdotes as evidence that some animals have the morally laden emotional state of compassion suppose that animals are like human beings in this respect. This claim about our moral kinship with animals forces us to be fairly precise in how we understand what we share with animals. I have tried to carefully justify the choice of a thick definition of compassion and virtue by connecting these to the context of use. Even though there are alternative ways of defining particular emotions in the interdisciplinary study of the nature of emotion, I maintain that what fixes the particular kind of definition I am employing (a cognitive-evaluative one) is the context where animals are likened emotionally and morally to human beings. Von Kreisler, Masson, Sapontzis, DeGrazia, and others claim that humans and animals are alike both with respect to their capacity for emotion and with respect to moral virtue. If it is the likeness between animals and human beings that matters in narratives about animal emotion and moral virtue, then we should be precise about that very sense in which we apply and use the concepts of emotion and virtue in our moral practices involving human beings. In this setting, not just any definition of compassion and virtue will do, as I have tried to show.

My qualified remarks about these examples do not depend on assuming a particular interpretation about why the virtues are good, namely, because they contribute to a flourishing or to an ideal way of life. As Sapontzis and other commentators on virtue ethics have noted, motivation-based accounts of virtue construe particular virtues, like honesty or truthfulness, as foundationally good. In this way we can recognize the value of being motivated to perform morally right actions without attributing to the moral agent a conception of a flourishing life. But even if we understand virtues to be foundationally good, we still need to supply an explanation about how an animal might have acquired a virtue as part of her moral character, where the acquisition of virtue counts as an "excellence."

Sapontzis himself recognizes that in our ordinary moral practices involving human beings we must still know enough about why an agent acts in order to differentiate between virtuous actions and those that are not exemplifications of virtue, such as actions inadvertently performed, those in which the agent has ulterior motives, or those in which the agent fails to understand the morally salient features of the circumstances in which she finds herself. Sapontzis correctly acknowledges that there are additional constraints on actions performed as expressions of moral character. He writes,

> By "character," I mean the values a person holds, including his priorities among those values, and his readiness to act on those values and priorities.[33]
>
> An action is courageous only if it expresses the agent's commitment to moral value and his or her willingness to act on that commitment even when doing so has a significant chance of leading to serious personal loss or harm. . . . For an action to be courageous, it must be done in a dangerous situation, and the agent must believe the situation is dangerous for him or her.[34]
>
> Courage is not the only moral value of action that requires a certain kind of situation and a relevantly adequate understanding of the situation. There are similar requirements for acting loyally, kindly, temperately, honestly, compassionately, fairly, and so on.[35]

These conditions for acting virtuously are familiar to us because we have seen in earlier sections of this chapter how Aristotle insists that virtuous acts are done with the agent's knowledge that she is performing a virtuous action and are done for the sake of virtue. In order for the agent to "have an adequate understanding of the situation" in the morally relevant sense when she is motivated by compassion, for example, she must have beliefs, judgments, and appraisals about negligence, fault, and the seriousness of misfortune suffered. As I have described it, these judgments are part of the cognitive content of the emotional state of compassion.

So what should we say about the examples of animal virtue that are described by Sapontzis and others? Porpoises or dogs that save drowning human beings and a mother wolf that cares for her young perform morally right actions. But I do not agree that these animals display moral virtues since there is little warrant for saying that they have the intentional states that make courage or compassion morally significant motivational states or that express the animals' virtuous characters according to thick definitions of these terms.

CONCLUSION

I have not proven that it is, in principle, wrong to credit some animals with the morally laden emotional state of compassion or moral virtue. It is important to remember that such questions are not settled merely by conceptual analysis alone but also by an empirical investigation of the animal mind. My contribution here is to clarify the relevant concepts of compassion and moral virtue that are presupposed in particular anecdotes about animal emotion. This conceptual analysis is necessary for exploring further whether or not some animals are capable of having the relevant intentional states implicated by these concepts. But, admittedly, the attribution of compassion to an animal is now harder to justify once we have clarified the concepts necessary for characterizing how compassion is morally significant. Those writers who attribute thin definitions of compassion and virtue to animals have managed to strip these concepts from the moral background conditions in which they usually occur. These background conditions make sense of our ordinary human moral practices. By using thin conceptions of compassion and virtue we cannot explain how the emotional state of compassion is morally significant by being conceptually connected to a cluster of other moral concepts such as moral appraisal, moral character, and moral virtue. Consequently we are left with the impression that compassion is properly attributed to an animal even when it may make little sense to say that the animal has the cognitive competence necessary for making judgments or appraisals specific to the intentional content of compassion.

Now it might be objected that the conditions for having compassion or virtue are too stringent and difficult to satisfy. A critic might put the point this way: "We are only interested in establishing that animals have a *kind* of moral agency, or a sense of right and wrong. You misrepresent our position by implying that animals must be *exactly* like humans in having compassion and being moral." This criticism deserves a closer look. Maybe animals have "a little bit" of what humans have a lot of (emotion or morality). Perhaps moral agency or the property of being moral comes in degrees such that human beings have a generous helping of it and animals have quantitatively less. Most arguments of this type rely on a particular principle that I call the "Continuity Thesis." This thesis has a compelling rendering in Darwin, though a very similar principle about continuity can be found also in Aristotle. I devote the next chapter to explaining what the Continuity Thesis is and how it fails to support the conclusion that animals have morally laden emotions.

NOTES

1. Seton explicitly identifies moral virtues of character as properties additionally shared by humans and animals. He says, "Our kinship with the animals is shown by seeing in them the virtues most admired in Man. Lobo stands for Dignity and Love-Constancy; Silverspot, for Sagacity; Redruff, for Obedience; Bingo, for fidelity; Vixen and Molly Cottontail, for Mother-love; Wahb, for Physical Force; and the Pacing Mustang, for the Love of Liberty." Ernest Thompson Seton, *Lives of the Hunted* (New York: Charles Scribner's Sons, 1901), "Notes to the Reader."

2. Kristin Von Kreisler, *Beauty in the Beasts: True Stories of Animals Who Choose to Do Good* (New York: Jeremy P. Tarcher/Putnam, 2001), pp. 48–49.

3. Jeffrey Moussaieff Masson, *Dogs Never Lie About Love: Reflections on the Emotional World of Dogs* (New York: Three Rivers Press, 1997), p. 96.

4. Ibid.

5. Von Kreisler, *Beauty in the Beasts*, p. 50.

6. See David DeGrazia, *Taking Animals Seriously: Mental Life and Moral Status* (Cambridge: Cambridge University Press, 1996); Steven F. Sapontzis, *Morals, Reason, and Animals* (Philadelphia: Temple University Press, 1987).

7. DeGrazia, *Taking Animals Seriously*, p. 203.

8. Ibid., pp. 199–200.

9. Ibid.

10. Ibid., pp. 10–11.

11. Lawrence Blum characterizes the moral dimension of this emotional state in the following way: "Compassion is not a simple feeling-state but a complex emotional attitude toward another, characteristically involving imaginative dwelling on the condition of the other person, an active regard for his good, a view of him as a fellow human being, and emotional responses of a certain degree of intensity. . . . The imaginative reconstruction involved in compassion consists in imagining what the other person, given his character, beliefs, and values is undergoing, rather than what we our-

selves would feel in his situation." Lawrence Blum, "Compassion," in *Explaining Emotions*, ed. Amelie Oksenberg Rorty (Berkeley: University of California Press, 1980), pp. 509–10.

Alternatively, Justin Oakley argues that what is morally relevant about the emotional state of compassion is that the agent understands the plight of another person in distress and has insight into what that person needs to relieve their suffering, the agent feels or shares the pain of another to some degree, and the agent has a desire to help such a person. To leave out one component of Oakley's analysis is to fail to fully explain how this emotion is distinguished from others, but also how it is that compassion contributes to a morally good life. See Justin Oakley, *Morality and the Emotions* (London: Routledge, 1992), pp. 75–85.

12. Martha C. Nussbaum, *Upheavals of Thought: The Intelligence of Emotions* (Cambridge: Cambridge University Press, 2001), p. 301.

13. Ibid., p. 307. See Aristotle, *The Complete Works of Aristotle: The Revised Oxford Translation*, 2 vols., *Bollingen Series Lxxi.2* (Princeton, NJ: Princeton University Press, 1984), (86a–13).

14. This is why Blum does not get it entirely correct when he says, "The imaginative reconstruction involved in compassion consists in imaging what the other person, given his character, beliefs, and values is undergoing, rather than what we ourselves would feel in his situation." Blum, "Compassion," pp. 509–10.

Adam Smith reminds us that the point of view of the onlooker is central to determining that the misfortune is serious when he says, "But the poor wretch . . . laughs and sings perhaps, and is altogether insensible of his own misery. The anguish which humanity feels, therefore, at the sight of such an object, cannot be the reflection of any sentiment of the sufferer. The compassion of the spectator must arise altogether from the consideration of what he himself would feel if he was reduced to the same unhappy situation, and, what perhaps is impossible, was at the same time able to regard it with his present reason and judgment." Adam Smith, *The Theory of Moral Sentiments* (Oxford: Clarendon Press, 1976), p. 12.

15. Nussbaum provides the following example to illustrate how the point of view of the one who pities may be informed by the sufferer.

For example, a wind player whose lip becomes even slightly injured may judge the suffering to be of tremendous size, and I may have compassion for him on that account, even though I myself would find a similar injury trivial. But this is because, at a more general level, I validate the judgment of the sufferer: for I agree with him that it is a terrible thing to be deprived of one's career and one's mode of expression, whatever it is, and I see his injury as such a deprivation. My compassion revolves around the thought that it would be right for anyone suffering a loss of that sort to be very upset. On the other hand, the wind player will be right to laugh at me if I complain a great deal about a minor injury to my own lip; for the very thing that would mean loss of career to him means no such thing to me, and it is this general description that validates the judgment of "size." Human beings have different ways of specifying the content of the major constituents of human flourishing; but unless the onlooker can bring the suffering back to one of these major components, as she conceives of things, she will not have the emotion. (Nussbaum, *Upheavals of Thought*, pp. 310–11.)

16. Aristotle, *Complete Works of Aristotle* (1385b14–15, b24). Nussbaum parts company with Aristotle about this third cognitive condition for compassion. She insists that it is not the judgment of similar possibilities that is required but a *eudaimonistic* judgment. "Even when we feel compassion for animals, whom we know to be very different from ourselves, it is on the basis of our common vulnerability to pain, hunger, and other types of suffering that we feel the emotion." Nussbaum, *Upheavals of Thought*, p. 319.

Even though our assessment of what has value in a life (goals, projects, friends) are in the background as possible significant deprivations, I suggest that it is only when we imagine that such misfortunes have some applicability to a person or to an animal that we extend our compassion to that thing. In other words, it is *because* we imagine that animals can feel pain and are relevantly similar to us in that respect that we feel compassion toward them when they suffer pain. The judgment of similar possibilities is playing a central role in our determination that this being is one that deserves our compassionate attitude.

17. Linda Trinkaus Zagzebski, *Virtues of the Mind: An Inquiry into the Nature of Virtue and the Ethical Foundations of Knowledge* (Cambridge: Cambridge University Press, 1996).

18. Ibid., p. 137.

19. Ibid., p. 86.

20. Ibid., p. 79.

21. Aristotle, *Nicomachean Ethics*, 2d ed., trans. Terence Irwin (Indianapolis: Hackett, 1999) (1103a19–03b2).

22. Zagzebski, *Virtues of the Mind*, p. 103.

23. Aristotle, *Nicomachean Ethics* (1105a27–35).

24. Rosalind Hursthouse, "Virtue Theory and Abortion," *Philosophy and Public Affairs* 20 (1991): 226.

25. Zagzebski, *Virtues of the Mind*, p. 83.

26. Sapontzis, *Morals, Reason, and Animals.*

27. Ibid., p. 147.

28. A moral (ad) act is one in which the moral value of the act is assessed by reference to the agent's intentions and motivations for acting. This is the "agent-dependent" value of the act. In contrast, moral (ai) acts are those acts in which the value is assessed by reference to the value of the act itself, independently of the agent's reasons or motivations for acting.

29. Sapontzis, *Morals, Reason, and Animals*, p. 32.

30. Aristotle, *Nicomachean Ethics* (1109a27–30).

31. Masson, *Dogs Never Lie About Love*, p. 96.

32. The fallacy of equivocation involves using a word in two different senses throughout an argument. For example, the reasoning in the following argument is fallacious because we use the word *obtuse* to mean one thing in premise (1) and something else in premise (2).

(1) Some triangles are obtuse.
(2) Whatever is obtuse is ignorant.
(3) Therefore, some triangles are ignorant.

See Patrick J. Hurley, *A Concise Introduction to Logic*, 4th ed. (Belmont, CA: Wadsworth, 1991).

33. Sapontzis, *Morals, Reason, and Animals*, p. 19.
34. Ibid., p. 21.
35. Ibid., p. 22.

Chapter Four

EVOLUTIONARY CONTINUITY

It is common to see Darwin quoted when reading about animal emotion. This is not surprising since Darwin had quite a lot to say about the psychology of animals. In this chapter I want to focus attention on a particular thesis about the psychology of animals that has its origins in Darwin's work. I call this the "Continuity Thesis" because it depends on a more general tenet of Darwin's theory of evolution about the evolutionary continuity of traits across species of common descent. I will not argue that this thesis is false or that it is even especially controversial in how to interpret evolutionary continuity in the larger context of Darwin's theory. But I will recommend that we should restrict the use of the Continuity Thesis (CT). I suggest that (CT) is not appropriately used as evidence that animals have morally laden emotions or other kinds of psychological states when these are analyzed as having cognitive-evaluative intentional content. This conclusion does, I believe, undermine the plausibility of using Darwin's principle about evolutionary continuity as a rationale for attributing some psychological states to animals.[1]

Let's begin by looking at a few of the many stories and anecdotes that Darwin describes about the psychology of animals.

DARWIN'S STORIES

[T]he lower animals, like man, manifestly feel pleasure and pain, happiness and misery. Happiness is never better exhibited than by young animals, such as puppies, kittens, lambs, etc., when playing together, like our own children. Even insects play together, as has been described by that excellent observer, P. Huber, who saw ants chasing and pretending to bite each other, like so many puppies.[2]

Sir Andrew Smith, a zoologist whose scrupulous accuracy was known to many persons, told me the following story of which he was himself an eye-witness; at the Cape of Good Hope an officer had often plagued a certain baboon, and the animal, seeing him approaching one Sunday for parade, poured water into a hole and hastily made some thick mud, which he skillfully dashed over the officer as he passed by, to the amusement of many bystanders. For long afterwards the baboon rejoiced and triumphed whenever he saw his victim.[3]

Darwin's descriptions of the activities of mammals, birds, reptiles, and insects are a joy to read. These accounts are rich in detail and novel in the perspective they offer on the lives of nonhuman living things. But Darwin's account of the mental powers of animals also creates an interpretive puzzle. Some readers of Darwin, myself included, wish to know exactly how far to follow him in attributing a wide variety of emotions and other mental capacities to animals.

In *The Descent of Man* Darwin says, "The fact that the lower animals are excited by the same emotions as ourselves is so well established, that it will not be necessary to weary the reader by many details."[4] Nonetheless, he goes on to supply us with a wide assortment of examples. Darwin classifies jealousy, love, pride, shame, modesty, and magnanimity as complex emotions. These, he believes, are common to the "higher animals" and to us. We see this, for example, in some dogs when they display love for their masters. "[A] dog carrying a basket for his master exhibits in a high degree self-complacency or pride. There can, I think, be no doubt that a dog feels shame, as distinct from fear, and something very like modesty when begging too often for food. A great dog scorns the snarling of a little dog, and this may be called magnanimity."[5] Sympathy is evidenced by the case of a dog that "perseveringly" licked his mistress's face after she pretended to be beaten.[6] The following passage illustrates the range of mental powers that Darwin believed could be attributed to animals:

> It has, I think, now been shewn that man and the higher animals, especially the Primates, have some few instincts in common. All have the same senses, intuitions, and sensations, similar passions, affections, and emotions, even the more complex ones, such as jealousy, suspicion, emulation, gratitude, and magnanimity: they practice deceit and are revengeful; they are sometimes susceptible to ridicule, and even have a sense of humour; they feel wonder and curiosity; they possess the same faculties of imitation, attention, deliberation, choice, memory, imagination, the association of ideas, and reason, though in very different degrees.[7]

Historical and contemporary responses to Darwin's descriptions of the animal mind fall along a continuum from outright skepticism, to cautious agreement about a limited number of cases, to full-fledged endorsement that Darwin's descriptions establish facts about the mental powers of animals. Skeptics charge Darwin with poor scientific methodology because he describes unverifiable accounts of animal behavior that are largely anecdotal.[8] Michael Ghiselin postulates that Darwin intended his descriptions of animal emotion to be metaphorical.[9] Samuel Barnett calls this language anthropomorphic and offers a reinterpretation of Darwin's talk about animal "feelings" that makes reference to only those physiological properties of the animal that can be objectively measured and tested.[10]

In contrast, Daisie and Michael Radner defend Darwin's methodology and the attribution of those psychological states to animals that are closely related to physiology, such as sense experience.[11] In their view, the legitimate attributions of psychological states to animals include the "basic emotions," as illustrated by Darwin's claim that "[t]error acts in the same manner on them as on us, causing the muscles to tremble, the heart to palpitate, the sphincters to be relaxed, and the hair to stand on end."[12] But the Radners suggest that Darwin is less convincing in his effort to establish that dogs, for example, experience jealousy, pride, shame, modesty, and magnanimity.[13]

At the other end of the spectrum, James Rachels and Eileen Crist believe that Darwin's descriptions of animal emotion tell us something about what animals are actually like.[14] In a chapter titled "Darwin's Anthropomorphism," Crist notes that Darwin's narratives imbue animals with a kind of subjectivity that is missing from modern scientific language that characterizes the behavior of animals as the inevitable outcome of their instinctive natures and a set of environmental circumstances that "cue" an animal to action. Crist argues that Darwin's descriptions of the mental powers of animals are not intended to be a metaphorical extension of language from humans to animals but rather a powerful and realistic representation of animals as agents who author their lives. She also suggests that anthropomorphic depictions are preferred to conceptions of animals as mechanistic, a view that dominated behavioristic psychology in the more recent years since Darwin. However, Crist does not answer the reader who wonders whether Darwin has just gone too far in *literally* attributing a wide range of emotions and other mental states to animals.

Consider the following example that Crist quotes from Darwin about the common magpie. As Darwin describes it, the magpies assemble from all parts of the Delamere Forest to celebrate the "great magpie marriage," as reported by Rev. W. Darwin Fox. Darwin adds, "The whole affair was evidently considered by the birds as of the highest importance."[15] Crist remarks that Darwin's language encourages the reader to picture "[t]he birds' activities in light of the understanding and feeling that subjective meaningfulness invokes."[16] Even so, the question left unanswered by Crist is what we can legitimately and literally infer about the birds' activities. What does Darwin's language reveal, if anything, about the mental lives of the common magpie? Crist concedes that Darwin's descriptions are not necessarily "exact or incontestable representations of the birds' experience." Nevertheless, Crist believes that there is some fact of the matter about animal lives that is illustrated by Darwin's descriptions of animals. She remarks that "his understanding of animal life reflects his view of evolutionary continuity"[17] and that his "language for representing animals is a resounding affirmation of the evolutionary continuity between animals and humans."[18] This idea is worth exploring more carefully because it seems to suggest that what justifies attributing *complex* emotions to animals is a more general scientific thesis about evolutionary continuity. In the next section I examine more precisely what evolutionary continuity is, according to Darwin, and how this thesis might be used to argue that some animals have morally laden emotions.

THE CONTINUITY THESIS

The explanatory scope of evolutionary theory is comprehensive insofar as it accounts for how phenotypes of any species of plant or animal emerge by natural selection. Because human beings are part of the natural world, they too fall within the scope of evolutionary theory, and Darwin is at pains to demonstrate that this includes their psychology as well as their physiology. Because Darwin is interested in showing that the mental powers of humans can be explained by the gradual modification of traits found in their nonhuman ancestors, he advances a thesis about the evolutionary development of man's mental powers, in particular. A number of different formulations of evolutionary continuity can be found throughout *The Descent of Man.*

> If no organic being excepting man had possessed any mental power, or if his powers had been of a wholly different nature from those of the lower animals, then we should never have been able to convince ourselves that our high faculties had been gradually developed. But it can be shewn that there is no fundamental difference of this kind. We must also admit that there is a much wider interval in mental power between one of the lowest fishes, as a lamprey or lancelet, and one of the higher apes, than between an ape and man; yet this interval is filled up by numberless gradations.[19]

Evolutionary continuity follows from the general theory of evolution as Darwin implies by saying, "But everyone who admits the principle of evolution, must see that the mental powers of the higher animals, which are the same in kind with those of man, though so different in degree, are capable of advancement."[20]

There are two features of evolutionary continuity that Darwin seems to accept. First, the development of a mental trait as it is selected in those species of common descent is gradual. That is, there are no sharp discontinuities in emergent traits across species of common descent. Second, the mental powers of humans and nonhumans differ only by degree, though they are of the same *kind* of mental state. Writing about Darwin's contributions to the field of cognitive ethology, Allen and Bekoff characterize evolutionary continuity in the following way: "[F]or any trait T that is supposed to be an ancestral form of another sufficiently different trait T', the Darwinian idea of continuity presumes that there are viable intermediate forms between T and T'. . . . Whether one thinks that the sequence from T to T' was gradual or that it was punctuated by short periods of rapid change followed by long periods of relative stability doesn't matter. As long as one believes that *naturam non tacit saltum* (nature does not make jumps), one accepts a version of Darwin's continuity hypothesis."[21]

Although Allen and Bekoff's formulation of continuity captures the idea of incremental gradations between traits T and T', it makes no reference to that feature of continuity that is explicit in the quoted passages by Darwin, and that is the idea that T and T' differ only by degree and not by kind. By conjoining this claim to Allen and Bekoff's formulation, we can state the "Continuity Thesis" (CT) in the following way:

(CT) For any psychological trait T that is an ancestral form of another sufficiently different trait T', (1) there are viable intermediate forms between T and T'; and (2) T and T' are of the same kind.

Now we are in a position to see how (CT) might be used to imply that animals have emotions. Consider emotion states as a kind of psychological trait identifiable in humans. Call this psychological trait T'. The first conjunct of (CT) implies that the ancestral form of T' is T, where T' is separated from T by intermediate forms. But it does not follow from the first conjunct alone that emotion is a trait that is present in species of common descent, since the first conjunct specifies only that trait T' (the emotion state) in humans is separated from another "sufficiently different" ancestral trait T by incremental gradations. So T as it is present in a nonhuman ancestor may not be a trait that is describable as an emotion state.

However, the second conjunct adds to this that T and T' do not differ in kind. This conjunct guarantees that for any psychological trait T' identifiable in humans there is an ancestral trait T that can also be classified as the same *kind* of trait. So if (CT) is true, then for any emotion state identifiable in humans there will be an emotion state present as an ancestral trait in a species of common descent. Whatever differences exist between emotions in humans and emotions in nonhumans of common descent can be explained by saying that humans and nonhumans have different *degrees* of emotional states. By this reasoning we might come to believe that evolutionary continuity entails that some animals have emotions, including those that are morally laden.

CRITICISMS OF THE CONTINUITY THESIS

Darwin seems to have believed that the plausibility of evolutionary continuity is conditional on the general tenets of evolutionary theory. In particular, one might be led to accept the second conjunct of (CT) only if one presumes that when a new trait emerges in a more developmentally advanced species, that trait is a vestige of an ancestral trait in a species of common descent. This view is suggested by Darwin's detailed descriptions of physiology in chapter 1 of *The Descent of Man*, where he documents the claim that "the bodily structure of man shows traces, more or less plain, of his descent from some lower form."[22] Here Darwin remarks that every bone in the skeleton of a human has a corresponding bone in a monkey, bat, or seal. And every fissure and fold in the human brain has an analog in the orangutan.[23] So it should follow by the same reasoning that psychological traits identified by type or kind have their corresponding analogs in the animal ancestors of humans.

There are two substantive objections to evolutionary continuity formulated as (CT). First, Allen and Bekoff note that Darwin's examples of animal emotion and animal reasoning presuppose that the mental powers of extant species are separated by gradations along a continuum from lower to higher in complexity. This presumes that species are ordered along one line of evolutionary development reminiscent of the scale of nature. But this model of evolutionary development is one that Darwin explicitly disavows.[24] Allen and Bekoff remark that there is no justification for such a view, since "[a]lthough it is true that between any two extant species there must be at least one continuous sequence of relatively small modifications (through a common ancestor), it is not necessary that any such path pass through other extant species."[25]

Steven Jay Gould suggests a second objection to (CT) in an essay titled "Tales of a Feathered Tail."[26] One popular myth about evolution Gould is debunking in this essay is the idea that because birds evolved from dinosaurs, dinosaurs "didn't die out after all but remain among us twittering in the trees."[27] Gould explains that we are tempted to conclude this only if we conflate two different ideas: "[W]e must distinguish similarity of form from continuity in descent: two important concepts of very different meaning and far too frequent confusion. The fact of avian descent from dinosaurs (continuity) does not imply the persistence of dinosaurs (similarity in form and function). Evolution does mean change, after all, and our linguistic conventions honor the results of sufficiently extensive changes with new names. I don't call my dainty poodle a wolf or my car a horse-drawn carriage, despite the undoubted ties of genealogical continuity."[28]

The same distinction Gould makes between evolutionary descent and the persistence of a species (like dinosaurs) applies to traits as well. In 1894 Lloyd Morgan pointed out that the minor incremental modifications of psychological traits across species do not require that those traits be present in an attenuated form in less evolved species of common ancestry.[29] In other words, the basic gradual emergence of traits by natural selection does not necessarily entail psychological continuities, but rather, allows for "the possible psychological discontinuity within the biological continuity of Darwinian evolution."[30] One consequence is that evolutionary continuity may be true without it being the case that kinds of psychological states, like emotions, can be found in species all the way down an ancestral limb of common descent.

This critical point is illustrated by Morgan's identification of three different "methods" for the distribution of psychological states across species. The *method of uniform reduction* supports the truth of the second conjunct of (CT). This method implies that in three species, a, b, and c, where a is more highly evolved than b, and b is more highly evolved than c, all psychological faculties are represented in ratio across these species, but all are uniformly reduced. Perhaps it is this method that Darwin had in mind when he suggested that the mental powers of animals differ only by degree and not by kind. However, Morgan points out that the emergence of traits across species of common descent might be distributed according to the *method of levels*, which states that for any three species a, b, and c, higher psychological faculties emerge only when individuals of a species reach a certain level of complexity. This means that the most "highly evolved" species, in this case, a, may display some psychological states that ancestors of a, namely c, or perhaps even b fail to have. Neither the method of uniform reduction nor the method of levels requires relinquishing the first conjunct of (CT). But if psychological states are distributed according to the latter method, then it is not necessarily true that the psychological states of human beings differ only by degree and not by kind from the psychological states of other animals. This is so because the *kind* of psychological state identified in humans may be one that only human beings are capable of having.

Morgan's contribution to this issue is to remind us that although Darwin may have thought that evolutionary continuity entailed both conjuncts (1) and (2) of (CT), evolutionary continuity may merely entail the first conjunct of (CT) even while the second conjunct is false. If evolutionary continuity is taken to mean merely that there are viable intermediate forms between T and T', then kinds of psychological states in humans, such as emotion states, may not be present in species of common descent, although this kind of trait may have emerged by incremental gradations from a sufficiently different ancestral trait not describable as an emotion state.

Alternatively, suppose we believe that psychological traits are distributed across species according to what Morgan calls the "method of uniform reduction." Even so, (CT) does not imply that animals have emotions without considerable revision and refinement to this thesis. What is missing from the second conjunct of (CT) is some analysis of what counts as a *kind* of psychological trait and what might count as differences of *degree* in intermediate forms of psychological traits of the same kind.[31] I have been assuming that emotions do count as a kind of psychological trait but to really make sense of this idea we need to determine what kinds of states emotions are. This is a conceptual issue and one that is decided independently of any thesis about evolutionary continuity. We might make some progress in our thinking about this issue by considering another attempt to argue for psychological continuity between species.

THE UNITY OF PSYCHOLOGY

In an article titled "Animals and the Unity of Psychology," Gareth Matthews defines the "unity of psychology" as the idea that the "psychology of human beings is part of the psychology of animals generally."[32] Matthews notes that the unity of psychology is older than Darwin, having its origins in Aristotle's biological works, though it shares with Darwin's thesis about evolutionary continuity the idea that there is a population of "animated" or "ensouled" things such that there are psychological continuities holding between them and no strict psychological discontinuities. In this passage from the *History of Animals*, Aristotle is not arguing for *evolutionary* continuity, per se, but his account is nonetheless strikingly similar to what Darwin says about the psychology of animals.

> In the great majority of animals there are traces of psychical qualities or attitudes, which qualities are more markedly differentiated in the case of human beings. For just as we pointed out resemblances in the physical organs, so in a number of animals we observe gentleness or fierceness, mildness or cross temper, courage or timidity, fear or confidence, high spirit or low cunning, and, with regard to intelligence, something equivalent to sagacity. Some of these qualities in man, as compared with the corresponding qualities in animals, differ only quantitatively: that is to say, a man has more or less of this quality, and an animal has more or less of some other; other qualities in man are represented by analogous and not identical qualities: for instance, just as in man we find knowledge, wisdom, and sagacity, so in certain animals there exists some other natural potentiality akin to these . . . so that one is quite justified in saying that, as regards man and animals, certain psychical qualities are identical with one another, whilst others resemble, and others are analogous to, each other.[33]

Aiming for greater precision about Aristotle's position, Matthews formulates the unity of psychology as the Principle of Psychological Continuity (PPC). "(PPC) For any given psychological state, act or function, P, if a given animal belongs to some species other than the lowest one and that animal is capable of P, then there is an animal of some lower species such that the lower animal is capable of some psychological state, act or function, P', and P' is a model of P."[34] (PPC) implies that if there is some psychological state in humans, such as attentiveness, then there is an animal of some lower species, for example, a rabbit, such that the rabbit is capable of a psychological state that is a model of attentiveness in humans. Matthews claims that his use of the term *model* is meant to express the "working conception among psychologists and much of the lay public."[35] And the general intuition behind (PPC) is, as Matthews puts it, that "[i]f human beings can get angry . . . then so can some lower animals do either the very same thing, something similar, or at least something analogous."[36]

In order to use (PPC) to infer something specific about the psychology of animals, we must understand what is meant by one psychological state "modeling" another. Matthews himself does not offer a complete analysis of this concept but in an article titled "Evolution and Psychological Unity" Roger Crisp attempts to do just that in order to elucidate Matthews's principle (PPC).

Crisp asks us to imagine a refinement of the layperson's conception of a model. An example of a model in this sense might be a replica of a 1941 Spitfire airplane that is made this year and appears identical to the 1941 original. It is the same size as the original as well, the two differing only in their origins. According to Crisp, this way of modeling might be called a "model A" type. Imagine now that the replica of the Spitfire is made on a three-quarter scale to the original with plastic upholstery and no guns. This second type of model might be called a "model B" type. By varying the number of structural properties shared by the replica and the original, we end up with a conception of modeling that allows us to say that a model *x* of a thing *y* has a certain degree of similarity to *y*. Crisp describes the modeling of psychological states in the following way. Pain in a chimpanzee might be a model of type A of pain in a human being if each pain is brought about by similar circumstances and the only difference in psychological states is the difference in the origin of pain. Because of disanalogous physical structures and behavior between fish and humans, we might believe that pain in a fish is a model of type B (or C) of pain in a human, and so on.[37]

Crisp relies on a combination of criteria to specify model type: the structural properties shared by two animals, perhaps the similarities or differences in the neurology of their brains, and the relative similarities or differences in their behavior in contexts roughly similar.[38] Crisp also suggests that model type may vary depending on the particular psychological state being modeled. "It might be suggested that, say an Oedipus Complex is a counter-example to (PPC). For a chimpanzee is unlikely to experience a state which is a model of a human Oedipus Complex. But this ignores the possibility that a chimpanzee might experience a model B of an Oedipus Complex. A young male might find himself sexually attracted to his mother, and so feel envious of his father, but without developing a superego."[39]

But Crisp fails to acknowledge the general threat to (PPC) lurking behind this example. If developing a superego is *necessary* for having an Oedipus complex, then a chimpanzee will not experience a "model B" type of this psychological state or *any* model type, if the chimpanzee fails to develop a superego. The plausibility of (PPC) depends on the particular conditions of satisfaction of psychological states in humans that are being modeled. Of course, it is not just any psychological states that interest us, but those emotional states that imply something about the morality of the subject, or *morally laden* emotions. Recall that in chapter 3 I described how compassion, in particular, can be morally laden. I return to this example to illustrate how (PPC), even together with Crisp's analysis of modeling, falls short of establishing that animals have morally laden emotional states.

Recall that the cognitive-evaluative definition of emotion described by Nussbaum characterizes the moral significance of compassion by requiring three necessary conditions. First, the agent must judge that the misfortune of another is serious, or has "size." Second, the agent must believe that the sufferer is not at fault. And third, the agent must make a judgment or a comparison of likeness between herself and the one to whom compassion is directed. By characterizing compassion in this way we capture our reasons for morally commending those that are motivated from compassion. As I suggested earlier, not just any way of defining compassion will do this kind of explanatory work since not just any *feeling* attributable to a person (or any being whatsoever) qualifies as an emotion that is morally praiseworthy.

To illustrate this last point, suppose that Mary offers to work in a soup kitchen at her church serving Christmas dinner to homeless people who live in her community. She is motivated to do something good as suggested by her priest, but she harbors the additional belief that those who need to eat at the soup kitchen have not really applied themselves to finding housing and jobs. Moreover, she suspects that many of the clients who make use of this service are duping the church into thinking they have nothing to eat. Mary's helping behavior has all the trappings of being compassionate as long as she is quiet about what she really believes. However, if we come to find out that Mary believes that those she serves do not suffer any particular serious misfortune or that she believes their situation is brought about by not trying hard enough to provide for themselves, then we legitimately question whether or not she feels compassion and is motivated by this emotion. Specifically, what is missing are those essential defining ingredients of compassion that make this a morally commendable emotion; namely, the judgment that the misfortune of another is serious and the belief that the one who suffers is not at fault.

Keeping this example in mind, suppose we attempt to use (PPC) in the following way to show that some animals experience compassion, which in humans is the psychological state that is morally praiseworthy. Call this psychological state P. By (PPC) there is an animal of some lower species such that the lower animal is capable of some psychological state, act, or function, P', and P' is a model of P or compassion in humans. Without making too much of the distinction between "lower" and "higher" species in (PPC), let us use porcupines as our candidate for the sake of illustration. Suppose we see that a particular porcupine finds food for another one that has a broken leg. The psychological state in the porcupine appears to resemble the psychological state we call compassion in humans. Is it the very same emotion of compassion, something similar to it, or something analogous to compassion as this state occurs in humans? According to Crisp's analysis of what it means for one psychological state to model another, we may be tempted to infer that the porcupine's motivational state is a model of some type or other of compassion in humans. But what is additionally necessary to establish this conclusion is that the porcupine has the relevant intentional states that are required for compassion characterized as a morally significant emotion. So if the porcupine fails to judge that the animal he is assisting suffers from serious misfortune, or fails to believe that the animal he is assisting is not at fault, then the psychological state P' as it occurs in the porcupine is not a model of *any* type or degree of compassion as this emotion occurs in human beings.

This difficulty may not be immediately obvious if we are not specific about what kinds of states emotions are. We do, of course, talk about having a little bit of compassion or a greater amount of this emotional state. In the same way, we speak about feeling really angry or just a little bit frightened or jealous.[40] Because we are accustomed to speaking about emotions and other psychological states using quantitative language, we may not notice that some emotional states have necessary conditions of satisfaction that mark distinctions between what counts as compassion, for example, and what counts as another emotional state, such as jealousy or embarrassment. This distinction is made by reference to *what* is believed or judged to be the case when a subject has a particular emotion. The intentional content of compassion, for example, is specified by those beliefs, judgments, and appraisals about serious loss, blame, and likeness to the sufferer. But while it does make perfectly good sense to speak about having "a little" or "a lot" of compassion, this way of talking does not easily translate to the intentional content of compassion. The judgment that someone suffers undeservedly is not quantitatively divisible by degrees, though the evidence or warrant for this judgment may be stronger or weaker.

Recall that the rationale for using a cognitive-evaluative theory of the emotions in the first place is that it captures how particular emotions like compassion are connected to moral virtue (chapter 3). Characterizing compassion as a *thick* concept specifies how this emotion is morally laden. If in human beings the morally relevant sense of compassion requires judgments about serious misfortune, fault, and comparisons of likeness, then we ought to demand that attributions of morally laden emotions to animals have these conditions of satisfaction as well. However, once we acknowledge this we see how ill-suited the Continuity Thesis (CT) and the Principle of Psychological Continuity (PPC) are to this task. Both of these principles depend on the idea that psychological states come in degrees or gradations. But neither principle attempts to apply this to the intentional content of morally laden emotional states constituted by beliefs, judgments, and appraisals. The implausibility of grading particular psychological states like emotions is disguised because neither principle about psychological continuity offers an account of what emotional states are and what counts as an emotion of the same *kind*. Once we see that the conditions of satisfaction for morally laden emotions are met by particular beliefs and judgments, it becomes apparent that we are pursuing the inquiry about animal emotion in the wrong way. Rather than trying to answer the puzzling question "What does it mean for a porcupine to have a *lesser degree* of a belief, or a *little bit* of a judgment?" we should ask whether or not porcupines are capable at all of having beliefs and judgments about particular kinds of states of affairs, for example, misfortune and fault. But notice that the answer to this question will be decided independently of any thesis about psychological continuity across species of common descent. The negative conclusion I draw from this discussion is that neither (CT) nor (PPC), by themselves, establish that animals have morally laden emotions when these are analyzed as having cognitive-evaluative intentional content.

CONCLUSION

I began this chapter by remarking that Darwin's narratives about animal psychology pose an interpretative puzzle. How should we read Darwin's declaration that dogs feel modesty and that primates experience gratitude, vengefulness, wonder, and imagination? On the one hand, I am not entirely happy characterizing these examples as merely metaphorical as some critics of Darwin have suggested. Darwin's descriptions of the mental lives of animals suggest that he is recording and testifying about these events and behaviors as accurately as he can manage. Nonetheless, the scientific methodology leaves something to be desired, such as when Darwin describes a story about an animal as reported by a zoologist who is known for his "scrupulous accuracy." I defer a discussion about the literal truth of these narratives until chapter 8, where I discuss and compare fictional, scientific, and popular stories and anecdotes about animals. Nonetheless, in order to bring at least temporary closure to this issue, I recommend Elizabeth Knoll's charitable interpretation of Darwin's narratives about animal psychology.[41]

Without disavowing Darwin's varied attributions of psychological states to animals, Knoll suggests that Darwin intended for these descriptions to play an educative role. On Knoll's interpretation, Darwin's numerous anecdotes about dogs, in particular, were designed to make evolutionary theory more "friendly" to the general public. Darwin singles out dogs as having those complex emotions, such as nobility and even religious devotion, because dogs were familiar to Darwin's audience. Knoll writes,

> Many of Darwin's readers, even those who followed and intellectually accepted his argument, felt some unease and dislocation at the thought of being descended from, in the famous words of the conclusion, "a hairy quadruped, furnished with a tail and pointed ears, probably arboreal in its habits, and an inhabitant of the Old World ... classed amongst the Quadrumano, as surely as . . . the common and still more ancient progenitor of the Old and New World monkeys." All the canine comparisons could tame some of

the strangeness of this new idea. If Father Adam and Mother Eve had irretrievably vanished from a Darwinian universe, and we are brought face to face with our grandfather the baboon, at least we could still cling to Cousin Rover.[42]

This interpretation may explain Darwin's use of animal stories and anecdotes to illustrate the qualities of real animals. But we should not assume that contemporary writers who use Darwin's views about evolutionary continuity to argue that animals have emotions are also motivated to make evolutionary theory "friendly" to the general public. Our inquiry about animals, emotions, and morality will now focus on recent work in evolutionary ethics. In the next chapter I explore how primatologist Frans de Waal relies on Darwin's thesis about evolutionary continuity to explain the origins of morality.

NOTES

1. See, for example, Marc Bekoff, *Minding Animals: Awareness, Emotions, and Heart* (Oxford: Oxford University Press, 2002), p. 107; Marc Bekoff, "Wild Justice and Fair Play: Cooperation, Forgiveness, and Morality in Animals," *Biology and Philosophy* 19 (2004): 490–91; Frans B. M. de Waal, *Good Natured: The Origins of Right and Wrong in Humans and Other Animals* (Cambridge, MA: Harvard University Press, 1996); Frans B. M. de Waal, "Morally Evolved: Primate Social Instincts, Human Morality, and the Rise and Fall of 'Veneer Theory,'" in *Primates and Philosophers: How Morality Evolved*, ed. Steven Macedo and Josiah Ober, *University Center for Human Values* series (Princeton, NJ: Princeton University Press, 2006), p. 21; Frans B. M. de Waal and Jessica C. Flack, "'Any Animal Whatever': Darwinian Building Blocks of Morality in Monkeys and Apes," in *Evolutionary Origins of Morality*, ed. Leonard D. Katz (Bowling Green, OH: Imprint Academic, 2000), p. 73; David DeGrazia, *Taking Animals Seriously: Mental Life and Moral Status* (Cambridge: Cambridge University

Press, 1996), pp. 24, 114; Gary L. Francione, "Animals—Property or Persons?" in *Animal Rights: Current Debates and New Directions*, ed. Cass R. Sunstein and Martha C. Nussbaum (Oxford: Oxford University Press, 2004), p. 127; S. F. Sapontzis, *Morals, Reason, and Animals* (Philadelphia: Temple University Press, 1987), p. 34. For further discussion of Darwin on evolutionary continuity, see James Rachels, *Created from Animals: The Moral Implications of Darwinism* (Oxford: Oxford University Press, 1990), pp. 57–58; Daisie Radner and Michael Radner, *Animal Consciousness*, ed. Peter H. Hare, *Frontiers of Philosophy* series (Amherst, NY: Prometheus Books, 1996).

2. Charles Darwin, *The Descent of Man; and Selection in Relation to Sex* (Amherst, NY: Prometheus Books, 1998), p. 70.

3. Ibid., p. 71.

4. Ibid.

5. Ibid. pp. 71–72.

6. Ibid., p. 104.

7. Ibid., p. 80.

8. St. G. J. Mivert, "Darwin's Descent of Man," *Quarterly Review*, no. 131 (1871).

9. Michael T. Ghiselin, *The Triumph of the Darwinian Method* (Berkeley: University of California Press, 1969).

10. Samuel Barnett, "The Expression of Emotion," in *A Century of Darwin*, ed. S. A. Barnett (New York: Books for Libraries Press, 1958), p. 210.

11. Radner and Radner, *Animal Consciousness*, p. 126.

12. Darwin, *The Descent of Man*, p. 70.

13. Radner and Radner, *Animal Consciousness*, p. 124.

14. See Eileen Crist, *Images of Animals: Anthropomorphism and Animal Mind* (Philadelphia: Temple University Press, 1999); Rachels, *Created from Animals*.

15. Darwin, *The Descent of Man*, p. 419.

16. Crist, *Images of Animals*, p. 34.

17. Ibid., p. 12.

18. Ibid., p. 13.

19. Darwin, *The Descent of Man*, pp. 65–66.

20. Ibid., p. 632.

21. Colin Allen and Marc Bekoff, *Species of Mind: The Philosophy and Biology of Cognitive Ethology* (Cambridge, MA: MIT Press, 1997), p. 23.

22. Darwin, *The Descent of Man,* p. 6.

23. Ibid.

24. See Ghiselin, *Triumph of the Darwinian Method,* pp. 70–72.

25. Allen and Bekoff, *Species of Mind,* p. 24.

26. Steven Jay Gould, "Tales of a Feathered Tail," *Natural History,* November 2000.

27. Ibid., p. 36.

28. Ibid., p. 38.

29. C. Lloyd Morgan, *An Introduction to Comparative Psychology* (London: Walter Scott, 1894).

30. G. Gottlieb, "Comparative Psychology and Ethology," in *The First Century of Experimental Psychology,* ed. E. Hearst (Hillsdale, NJ: Erlbaum Publishing, 1979), p. 151.

31. For a discussion of this point, see Rachels, *Created from Animals,* pp. 57–58 and chap. 4.

32. Gareth B. Matthews, "Animals and the Unity of Psychology," *Philosophy* 53 (1978): 447.

33. From Aristotle, ed., *The Complete Works of Aristotle: The Revised Oxford Translation,* 2 vols., *Bollingen Series Lxxi.2* (Princeton: Princeton University Press, 1984), *History of Animals* (588a18–b3).

34. Matthews, "Animals and the Unity of Psychology," p. 437. Matthews acknowledges here that he makes "free use" of the idea that species can be ordered by reference to a single line of evolutionary development. He says, "I shall suppose that independent lines of development can be melded together sufficiently well to yield a good general placement of species on a single scale from lower to higher" (p. 437).

35. Ibid., p. 438.

36. Ibid.

37. Roger Crisp, "Evolution and Psychological Unity," in *Readings in Animal Cognition,* ed. Marc Bekoff and Dale Jamieson (Cambridge, MA: MIT Press, 1996), p. 316.

38. Ibid., pp. 310–11, 316.

39. Ibid., p. 316.

40. The strength of an emotion might be a function of the affective quality of that state or the feeling component of the emotion.

41. Elizabeth Knoll, "Dogs, Darwinism, and English Sensibilities," in *Anthropomorphism, Anecdotes, and Animals,* ed. Robert W. Mitchell, Nicholas S. Thompson, and H. Lyn Miles (Albany: State University of New York Press, 1997).

42. Ibid., pp. 15–16.

Chapter Five

THE GOOD CHIMP

In the last chapter we explored the Continuity Thesis (CT) and how it applies to kinds of psychological states like emotions. This was not entirely successful as a way of establishing that some animals have morally laden emotions. In this chapter we examine how evolutionary continuity is used by Frans de Waal to argue for the idea that the origins of morality can be found in our closest anthropoid relatives. Because stories and anecdotes about animals play an important role in the argument de Waal advances, we will explore several of these narratives more carefully. But first we need a sense of the intellectual terrain in order to say explicitly what part of de Waal's project intersects with our topic about animal emotion and morality.

Frans de Waal is a primatologist who has done much of his research at the Yerkes Regional Primate Center at Emory University in Atlanta, Georgia. His numerous publications, including popular books and articles intended for the general public, are testimony to his wealth of knowledge about primate behavior.[1] It is this fact, in addition to his appeal in the mainstream popular press, that justifies devoting a chapter to his views.[2] One recent contribution to the growing body of literature about evolutionary ethics comes in the form of the Tanner Lectures at Princeton University in 2003 and the invited commentary on these lectures by four philosophers.[3] Here de Waal revisits the position he articulated in *Good Natured*: that human morality can be explained by the evolutionary process of natural selection. Humans are by nature good, and the evidence for this can be found by looking at the behavior of our closest living ancestors: chimpanzees and other anthropoids more distantly related. De Waal reasons that if we discover that our closest relatives display tendencies that are central to human morality such as sympathy, empathy, and caring behavior more generally, then we will have discovered something very interesting about the origins of morality in human beings. A principle of parsimony guides us here in supposing that like behaviors displayed by evolutionarily close relatives should be given the same kind of explanation. We might then speculate from observing the good behavior of nonhuman primates that moral goodness is a natural property that is deeply rooted in our human nature.

De Waal does not argue explicitly that animals are moral beings, per se. Rather, he seeks to establish that some animals have the "foundation" or the "building blocks" of human morality. Nevertheless, he maintains that some animals are motivated to act from sympathy or empathy by their social instincts, and in this we see the evolutionary continuity of morality.

So there are two questions that overlap with the topic of animal emotion and morality that I will try to answer in this chapter. First, do nonhuman primates have emotions, like sympathy, that are in some sense morally significant? Using the concepts I have already developed, I might put this question in the following way: Does de Waal's research show that some chimpanzees have morally laden emotions? Second, does Darwin's principle about evolutionary continuity support de Waal's thesis that some animals have the "building blocks" of morality? Let's begin with two illustrative narratives that de Waal uses to make his case. I've chosen these particular narratives because they appear in more than one of de Waal's publications.

STORIES—LENDING A HAND

Readers may remember the "zoo rescue" story that was widely reported and discussed in mainstream newspapers in the United States.[4] In 1996 a three-year-old boy fell into the primate exhibit at the Brookfield Zoo in Chicago. Frans de Waal describes what happened next by saying, "The child . . . was scooped up and carried to safety by Binti Jua, a lowland gorilla. The gorilla sat down on a log in a stream, cradling the boy on her lap, giving him a brief back-pat before she continued on her way. Binti became a celebrity overnight, figuring in the speeches of leading politicians who held her up as an example of much-needed compassion."[5] While many scientists preferred to explain Binti's behavior by appealing to her "confused maternal instincts" or the possibility that she had been "trained to fetch objects," de Waal uses this example to illustrate how some animals "care for one another."[6]

Another anecdote is less sensational but is employed to the same end as an example of how animals help one another, displaying the capacity for empathy. De Waal reports that Kuni, a female bonobo, "adopted the point of view of a bird." He writes,

One day, Kuni captured a starling. Out of fear that she might molest the stunned bird, which appeared undamaged, the keeper urged the ape to let it go. . . . Kuni picked up the starling with one hand and climbed to the highest point of the highest tree where she wrapped her legs around the trunk so that she had both hands free to hold the bird. She then carefully unfolded its wings and spread them wide open, one wing in each hand, before throwing the bird as hard [as] she could towards the barrier of the enclosure. Unfortunately, it fell short and landed onto the bank of the moat where Kuni guarded it for a long time against a curious juvenile.[7]

Most important to our understanding of how to interpret this story is de Waal's remark, "What Kuni did would obviously have been inappropriate towards a member of her own species. Having seen birds in flight many times, she seemed to have a notion of what would be good for a bird, thus offering us an anthropoid version of the empathetic capacity so enduringly described by Adam Smith as 'changing places in fancy with the sufferer.'"[8]

What do these stories show about the origins of human morality? Some chimps behave in ways that are helpful and they seem to care for other animals as well as for human beings. But it is not only that these animals *behave* in ways that we might describe as caring. De Waal is interested in pressing the stronger claim that the caring behavior of chimpanzees observed in numerous settings is motivated by social emotions like empathy or sympathy that are themselves morally significant.[9] But crediting an animal or a person x with an emotional state y will have some relevance to morality only if two general conditions are satisfied: (1) emotion state y is situated in an account of morality that is sensitive to the contribution emotions make to the moral domain; and (2) the theory of emotions employed captures the moral significance of y. In what follows, I try to say more precisely how well de Waal's explanation of *the nature of morality* and *the nature of the emotions* satisfies these two conditions, as well as what more needs to be added to his explanation.

THE NATURE OF MORALITY

In a number of places de Waal describes morality in a metaphorical way as the sort of thing that is composed of building blocks or component parts, or as a tower made up of floors, the bottom floors occupied by animals and the top floors or the summit occupied by humans.[10] As he describes it in *Good Natured*, his project is to investigate whether or not the "building blocks of morality are recognizable in other animals."[11] Although de Waal does not argue for any particular moral theory, his views fall clearly into the tradition of David Hume and Adam Smith. Benevolence, he believes, "nourishes and guides all human morality. . . . Moral sentiments come first; moral principles, second."[12] The relevant sentiment, of course, in keeping with Hume and Smith, is sympathy.

De Waal's project is to explain how morality evolved. In this he claims to be following Darwin, who says, "Any animal whatever, endowed with well-marked social instincts, the parental and filial affections being here included, would inevitably acquire a moral sense or conscience, as soon as its intellectual powers had become as well developed, or nearly as well developed, as in man."[13] De Waal goes on to remind us that, according to Darwin, many animals express sympathy and "it is in this domain that striking continuities exist between humans and other social animals."[14] Elsewhere de Waal remarks that continuity between nonhuman primates and human primates can be located in the "powerful inclinations and emotions that bias our thinking and behavior."[15]

These emotional states are likely ones that humans share with other animals. "A chimpanzee stroking and patting a victim of attack or sharing her food with a hungry companion shows attitudes that are hard to distinguish from those of a person taking a crying child in the arms, or doing volunteer work in a soup kitchen."[16]

De Waal's overall argumentative strategy is first to identify those psychological capacities that he believes are relevant to human morality and then to argue that these capacities are recognizable in the behavior of nonhuman primates. Included in the list of tendencies or capacities necessary for human morality are "sympathy-related traits," "norm-related characteristics, such as prescriptive social rules," "reciprocity," peace-making, and avoidance of conflict."[17] We can see in this argumentative strategy how it is useful to appeal to evolutionary continuity. Recall how we stated the Continuity Thesis (CT) in chapter 4.

> For any psychological trait T that is an ancestral form of another sufficiently different trait T', (1) there are viable intermediate forms between T and T', and (2) T and T' are of the same kind.

(CT) can be revised in such a way that it applies not only to individual psychological traits but to a *set* of capacities or traits—those that are relevant to human morality. Let's call the property of being moral for humans the *M* property, and the set of capacities that are relevant to human morality the set of *M-capacities*, where $(T_1, T_2 \ldots T_n)$ are particular sympathy-related capabilities but will also include those more highly cognitive capabilities that de Waal believes are distinctive and unique to human beings such as judgment, reasoning, self-reflection, and logical inference.[18] Then let $m(t_1, t_2 \ldots t_n)$ stand for those morally relevant capacities such as sympathy, cognitive empathy, and a sense of fairness, that de Waal argues are recognizable in chimpanzees. Revised in this way, Darwin's principle of evolutionary continuity can be used to refer to the particular collection of psychological capacities or traits that interest us; those that we identify in advance as the ones that are conceptually connected to morality. The "Morality Continuity Thesis" (MCT) can be stated in the following way:

> (MCT) m $(t_1, t_2 \ldots t_n)$ is an ancestral form of M $(T_1, T_2 \ldots T_n)$ such that (1) there are viable intermediate forms between t_1 and T_1, t_2 and $T_2 \ldots t_n$ and T_n; and (2) t_1 and T_1, t_2 and $T_2 \ldots t_n$ and T_n are of the same kind.

Characterizing de Waal's position as (MCT) has several advantages. First, we can make sense of de Waal's remarks about the evolutionary continuity of psychological states. De Waal says, for example, that "social complexity and intelligence in monkeys, apes, and humans varies along a continuum and thus is distinguished by degrees and not categorically."[19] The first and second conjunct of (MCT) captures this idea by specifying that there are viable intermediate forms between particular cognitive capacities t_1 and T_1, t_2 and T_2, and so on, where these are of the same *kind* of state. But additionally by this principle we can clearly formulate de Waal's main idea about the origins of morality by singling out those capacities that are relevant to morality. This is guaranteed by selecting those capabilities in humans that are morally relevant (the set of *M-capabilities*), and by means of empirical observations of primate behavior identifying those same kinds of traits in non-human primates (the set of *m-capabilities*). Since the *m-capabilities* identified in nonhuman primates will be of the same kind—namely, the morally relevant ones—there is some justification for de Waal calling those traits that are properly credited to chimpanzees "moral sentiments."[20]

Another advantage to formulating de Waal's position as (MCT) is that we can clarify de Waal's metaphors about non-human primates having the "building blocks" of morality or occupying several of the "ground floors" of the tower of morality. As I understand it these remarks refer to a kind of gradualism of morality as a whole. De Waal identifies the simplest form of morality characterized by the moral sentiments; these are emotional states like sympathy and cognitive empathy. The most complex realization of morality is characterized by judgments, reason, universalization, and inferential reasoning.[21] This layered account of morality can be explained by supposing that in the set of *M-capabilities* that characterize human morality there are some *T* traits that are moral sentiments and some *T* traits that are more cognitively complex capacities. When de Waal additionally adds that his research does not show that chimpanzees are *moral*, what he might mean by this is that the property of being moral applies to the entire set of capabilities picked out by *M*. Chimpanzees don't have all of the *M-capabilities*, but even so, it does make sense to speak of chimpanzees having lesser degrees of at least some of these capacities, such as the cognitively simple states of the sympathy-related traits. These *m-traits* vary in degree but not in kind from the *M-traits*, so we can say about these animals that they have what is necessary for morality—the foundation or the ground floor of the tower of morality.

However, what is largely absent from de Waal's "building block" metaphor of morality is a precise account of what it means for these capacities to be conceptually connected to morality. For example, we might interpret this metaphor in any of the following ways. If *x* (a human being or an animal) has "sympathy-related traits," then perhaps:

1. *X* is a morally considerable being. This may imply only that *x* should be taken into account in our moral deliberations; or

2. *X* is a moral being. In this sense *x* has the property of being moral because our moral appraisals extend to *x* and what she does;[22] or

3. *X* can make moral judgments, and can reason to a conclusion about what it is morally right, wrong, permissible to do, say, and so on.[23]

Clearly these are overlapping concepts about which there is considerable philosophical debate. If, for example, *x* has the capacity for making moral judgments as asserted in (3), then it might be natural to assume that *x* has the property of being moral as asserted in (2), or at least that *x* has satisfied some plausible set of conditions necessary for acting morally, such as the ability to discern right from wrong and a grasp of moral concepts. So (3) probably implies (2). But does (2) imply (3)? Can an animal or a person be morally appraisable and *not* have the capacity for making moral judgments? There is no general consensus that being moral in this sense requires the capacity to make moral judgments or even exactly what making such judgments involves.[24] The answer to this question depends on how we specify the conditions for being morally appraisable and how we define other related moral concepts such as virtue, having the right motivational states, sympathy, empathy, or compassion. The topic I take up in the next section, "The Nature of Emotions," is how we should characterize sympathy and empathy in order to capture the moral significance of these kinds of emotional states.

Which interpretation—(1), (2), or (3)—best explains de Waal's building block metaphor? Because de Waal is prepared to attribute to nonhuman primates the capacity for moral sentiments, he appears to be stating something stronger about how emotions are connected to morality than what is expressed by (1). After all, as some philosophers have argued, a subject might be morally considerable by merely having the capacity for pleasures and pains.[25] So one might expect that the animals de Waal credits with sympathy and empathy have a more robust claim on being moral even if they cannot satisfy the more highly rational requirements necessary for making moral judgments. By this reasoning I infer that de Waal's view most closely approximates a commitment to (2), but this is only a guess. De Waal's brief references to Hume and Smith only hint that there is a philosophical tradition that characterizes emotions as morally significant. But without some specification of *how* sympathy-related emotions are morally significant, it is hard to decide which of these possible interpretations in (1)–(3) best captures de Waal's position.[26]

This unclarity leaves de Waal open to criticism by some philosophers that he has not articulated what is important to moral agency or moral reasoning, or to what is essential to any fairly comprehensive normative ethical theory. Christine Korsgaard, for example, denies that there is any sense in which animals are moral beings because she endorses a Kantian theory of ethics that requires self-consciousness, the capability to conceive of obligations and principles, and the freedom and capability to be guided by moral ideals as necessary conditions for moral agency.[27] Philip Kitcher suggests that the central role of judgment in Smith's "impartial spectator" or Kant's "inner reasoner" will make it unlikely that animals have those intentional states that are relevant to morality.[28] Richard Joyce argues that because animals do not have a language, they are incapable of entertaining moral concepts.[29] And Marc Hauser believes that since animals do not have self-awareness, they lack a moral sense and moral emotions.[30]

These objections get their impetus by the authors' respective articulations of what is distinctive about human morality, and that is the central role of rationality, judgment, and reason.[31] It is not a satisfactory response by de Waal to merely claim that we must reevaluate "the role played by rationality in moral judgment"[32] or that "emotions are our compass" in moral decision making.[33] A better strategy for de Waal is to supply us with a fuller account of morality that not only plausibly characterizes the depth and complexity of human moral practices but that also spells out more exactly how the emotions contribute to these human moral practices. What needs to emerge is a way of saying how attributing emotions to either humans or animals is morally significant, either by specifying a viable account of moral agency where emotional states figure prominently, or by specifying an account of the conditions for being morally appraisable where emotions play a central role. Not surprisingly, the best candidate is an ethical theory where our moral appraisals extend to assessing the motivations, dispositions, and intentions of the person or animal who acts rather than just the action itself. The normative theory that does include these kinds of appraisals should be paired with a theory of the emotions that characterizes how emotions can be morally significant. As the reader might anticipate, a cognitive-evaluative theory of the emotions does the explanatory work that is needed to say how emotion state concepts are morally laden.

There are two possible ways that de Waal might explain how sympathy-related traits are relevant to morality. We have already considered one of these in chapter 3. Emotions like sympathy and compassion are prime candidates for being connected to morality because they can be construed as virtues and as motivations to act for the sake of what is good or right. On an account of morality that is virtue-based, we take stock of emotions as part of an agent's moral character. Perhaps then de Waal could explain how sympathy-related traits are relevant to morality by identifying sympathy as a virtue. In chapter 3 we described how concepts such as compassion, virtue, motivation, and moral character require "thick" definitions in order to explain what it is that humans and animals share. But we concluded from this that the cognitive content of emotions, like compassion, when paired with what it means to acquire a virtue as part of one's moral character, makes it unlikely that animals have morally laden emotions in this way.

Alternatively, a more promising approach is indicated by de Waal, who sometimes writes as if the moral significance of the social emotions that he is prepared to attribute to some animals is captured by the appropriate attitudes of morally praising and blaming animals. For example, de Waal describes the case of the chimpanzee Georgia, who waits for visitors to walk by her enclosure and then sprays them with a mouthful of water as they pass. De Waal says, "But why let her off the hook that easily? Why would any human being who acts this way be scolded, arrested, or held accountable, whereas any animal, even a species that resembles us so closely, is considered a mere passive instrument of stimulus-response contingencies?"[34] When de Waal claims that "(h)uman moral judgment always looks for the intention behind the behavior," he has in mind the distinctions we make in moral practice when we morally praise or blame a person.[35] Our moral appraisals of a person depend on knowing the motivation of the agent who acts. "[P]erceived intentions are the stuff of moral judgment. . . . With praise and blame being meted out on the basis of our reading of other people's intentions, it is important to know if animals recognize knowledge or intention behind the behavior of others."[36] But here also de Waal only hints at the philosophical account that is relevant to specifying and explaining the moral significance of the emotions; namely, a theory about the conditions under which we morally appraise a subject and hold her morally responsible for what she does. There may be good reasons for *not* morally blaming Georgia for spraying visitors with water. But this determination needs to be made against the background conditions that any subject (either human or animal) should satisfy in order to warrant moral praise or blame. Since that is the topic of chapter 6, I postpone a more detailed discussion of this issue. In any case, if de Waal wants to convince us that some animals have emotions that can be described as *moral* sentiments, then he must specify the nature of emotion in a way that captures their moral significance.

THE NATURE OF EMOTIONS

The interesting and somewhat controversial claim that de Waal believes is supported by his observations and interpretations of primate behavior is that apes are capable of *cognitive* empathy.[37] The anecdotes "Zoo Rescue" and "Bird Toss" are presented as evidence that some animals can engage in cognitive empathy and are motivated to act for this reason. But what does this have to do with morality or, more precisely, the origins of morality? To answer this question we need to understand what cognitive empathy is and how it is morally significant.

De Waal distinguishes between three senses of the emotional state of empathy. In one sense an animal or a person may experience "emotional contagion." This is an automatic, involuntary "inner mimicry" of another's emotional state that activates the subject's autonomic responses such as heart rate, facial expressions, or bodily posture to match the "object's" emotional state. Because these reactions are immediate physiological responses, they are not necessarily conscious to the subject who has them.[38] De Waal refers to this kind of emotional state as a "simple, automatic Perception-Action Mechanism," or (PAM). But overlaid on this mechanism is a higher-order emotional state that de Waal classifies as "cognitive empathy." Subjects that are capable of cognitive empathy make "appraisals of another's predicament or situation." They assess the reasons for the object's emotional state by taking into account why the object behaves as she does relative to the situation or context, even in novel situations such as when Binti Jua "rescued" the child at the Brookfield Zoo in Chicago. The behavior of Binti Jua and Kuni are examples of "targeted helping," which, according to de Waal, reveal that the animal understands the specific predicament of the subject who needs help.[39] Last, de Waal identifies a third kind of empathy, "attribution," which he describes as the capacity to "fully adopt the other's perspective."[40] So on these ways of describing what empathy is, a subject might be empathetic in any of these senses that are graded along a continuum of cognitive complexity, from the simplest automatic empathetic response to a more complex appreciation of the particular features of another's situation.[41]

However, none of these definitions of empathy specify what is morally significant about this emotional state. We might expect that emotional contagion is not conceptually connected to morality since it is characterized as a physiological response. But what about cognitive empathy and attribution? Surely something more needs to be added here to explain how seeing, appraising, and adopting another's perspective matters to morality. One well-established explanation of how one might see and appraise the morally relevant features of a situation is Aristotle's account of "ethical perception." This idea may explain how emotions can be moral responses to particular circumstances.

For Aristotle, deciding how to act is secondary to perceiving, construing, or "reading the circumstances" of the situation one finds oneself in. In this sense we do not perceive what is uninterpreted or "given" in perception. What and how an agent sees is informed by how she characterizes the situation and how she describes the setting. In this way "[p]erception is informed by the virtues," since the agent is "responsible for how the situation appears as well as for omissions and distortions."[42] For example, if I see a long line of people waiting to be admitted to a housing shelter for the night, I might form the belief that they are all drug addicts, criminals, or lacking in initiative. Construing the situation in this particular way may prevent me from acknowledging that those who need housing may deserve my sympathy and help. Indeed, focusing on how unkempt they appear may obscure the fact that there are children and their mothers waiting in line to stay somewhere for the night. There may be more than one way of describing what matters ethically in a situation, and these different descriptions of a scene may contain equally compelling but competing ethical considerations. But this does not interfere with the main point that Aristotle is urging us to consider: there are some ways of perceiving that are more appropriate than others to recognizing what matters ethically in a situation. More importantly, we can develop our expertise in this way of perceiving. For Aristotle, acquiring ethical perception can be understood in the same way as the development and acquisition of the moral virtues. We come to see what matters ethically by being in conversation with others, by listening and understanding their point of view, and by other forms of collaboration. In this way, "[t]he agent comes to learn different ways of reading a situation and different questions to pose in order to see the picture with increased insight and clarity. How to see becomes as much a matter of inquiry as what to do."[43] One important characteristic of ethical perception is that it is not the kind of capacity that occurs automatically or naturally in a person. Like the virtues, it is a skill acquired through practice, habituation, and by reflection and attention to the agent's many direct experiences. Just as Aristotle says that each person is responsible for developing excellence of moral character, he also believes that each of us is responsible for how things appear. "Someone might say that everyone aims at the apparent good, but does not control its appearance; but the end appears to each person in a way that corresponds to his character. For if each person is somehow responsible for his own state of character, he will also be himself somehow responsible for its [*viz.* the end's] appearance [*phantasias*]."[44] Of course, according to Aristotle it is also the case that our emotional responsiveness to a situation is a way of marking what is morally relevant about that situation. Anger is appropriate to some situations and not to others depending on what the agent judges to be fair or unfair, cruel, undeserved, and so on.[45] Commenting on Aristotle, Nancy Sherman remarks, "The cognitions are essential concomitants for experiencing the emotion. As such, Aristotelian emotions are not blind feelings like itches or throbs, but intentional states directed at articulated features of an agent's environment."[46] Aristotle's conception of ethical perception explains what it means to be emotionally responsive to what matters ethically in a situation. Is cognitive empathy anything like ethical perception?

Characterizing cognitive empathy as the appraisal of another's situation is promising, but what is missing from this definition is the idea that the subject appreciates the *morally salient* features of a situation or predicament. If, for example, I see a homeless child begging in the street for food and my appraisal focuses only on the fact that he needs a haircut, then I have perhaps judged "precisely" but in a way that ignores what is morally pressing about the child's predicament. Merely defining cognitive empathy as appraisal is too vague to capture how this emotion is conceptually connected to morality.

Moreover, even though de Waal uses the expression "cognitive empathy" to characterize the behavior of Binti Jua and Kuni, he must also mean to attribute to them something like sympathy or compassion in order to describe this behavior as caring or targeted helping.[47] Empathy might allow a person or an animal to imaginatively reconstruct the other's situation, but what makes this capacity morally significant is the additional idea that the subject who has the capacity for empathy is motivated to alleviate the object's need or distress. So what must be added to cognitive empathy to capture its moral significance is the attribution to the subject of either sympathy or compassion, which involves the evaluative judgment that the object's distress is bad.[48]

By way of comparison, recall from chapter 3 how we specified compassion as a "painful emotion occasioned by the awareness of another person's undeserved misfortune."[49] This cognitive-evaluative definition of compassion allows us to see why as part of our ordinary moral practice we can and do morally commend a person for having this emotional state. But also by specifying the content of the subject's appraisal of another's predicament we see how this content is crucial for characterizing compassion as a moral concept. Judgments about need, serious loss, fault, and comparative likeness are what count as perceiving the moral particularities in a situation.[50] So, in order for de Waal to explain how cognitive empathy and other sympathy-related traits are connected to morality, there must be some further specification of the intentional content of these emotions beyond the claim that cognitive empathy involves appraisal of another's predicament.

Do Binti Jua and Kuni have cognitive empathy in the sense that matters to morality? What is missing from de Waal's interpretations of the anecdotes he describes is some reason for thinking that apes have the particular intentional states that capture their appraisals of the morally salient features of another's predicament, and that they are motivated to act to relieve the distress of the person or animal. De Waal describes Binti Jua's action as a "rescue," but he offers us no reason for thinking that this gorilla judged that the child *needed* rescuing. Remember Kuni, who spread the starling's wings and threw the bird from the highest point in her enclosure? De Waal says that "she knew what would be good for the bird." But again there are many psychological states that Kuni may have had that motivated her to throw the bird. Where is the evidence that Kuni grasped the concept "what is *good* for *x*" and acted for this reason? I am not suggesting that as a matter of principle non-human primates cannot acquire these intentional states. But once we demand that the definitions of emotion state concepts include judgments and appraisals about the morally salient features of a situation—in the case of compassion, a contextually rich collection of evaluations about need, fault, and serious loss—then it becomes a more difficult argument to make that animals do have these particular moral concepts.[51]

Establishing that animals have morally relevant emotional states requires more than merely pointing out that animals behave in ways that are similar to the ways in which humans behave when we extend to them moral praise or blame. At times de Waal seems to appreciate this point insofar as he recognizes that cognitive ethologists have an important contribution to make by investigating what "motivates" animals to act, whether they "realize" how their behavior affects others, and whether they "know," "want," or "calculate."[52] Nonetheless, de Waal ignores this issue when discussing actual examples, preferring instead to interpret the animal's behavior in such a way that the case is already made that animals have the morally relevant intentionality. For brevity I cite only two examples.

Attachment underlies sympathy, and the capacity for sympathy is a morally relevant intentional state, according to de Waal.[53] If so, then attachment to loved ones who have died will be evidenced by grief. Do animals have the emotional state of grief? De Waal explains that monkeys react to the death of another monkey in ways that are outwardly similar to human grieving. De Waal describes the following anecdote that was mentioned in chapter 1. The wild chimpanzee Flint, who was only eight years old, died three weeks after the loss of his mother. As quoted by de Waal, Jane Goodall suggests that perhaps Flint died of grief, since "[h]is whole world had revolved around Flo, and with her gone life was hollow and meaningless." De Waal suggests that there may be an alternative explanation; namely, that Flo and Flint fell victim to the same disease and that Flint merely held out a little longer. But de Waal goes on to add, "Seeing the termination of a familiar individual's life, chimpanzees may respond emotionally as if realizing, however vaguely, what death means—or at least that something terrible has befallen the other."[54] De Waal's interpretation seems to be that Flint's dying implicitly credits him with exactly those intentional states that capture what is morally relevant about the emotion of grief as experienced by humans. This is surprising since in the case described, de Waal provides the reader with no additional evidence to support the attribution of these intentional states to Flint beyond the fact that Flint died.

In chapter 3 of *Good Natured,* titled "Rank and Order," de Waal directs our attention to the group organization of primates. What is striking about bands of chimpanzees is the social regularity and hierarchies that govern the activities of individuals in such groups. What is morally relevant about the hierarchical organization of groups, according to de Waal, is that they are rule-governed. The sorts of rules we are interested in from a moral point of view are prescriptive rules, rules that specify how one *ought* to behave.[55] But to refer to behavior as rule-governed is ambiguous between two kinds of explanations of this behavior; one intentional, the other not. Chimps (or humans) may behave as if an individual of the group has transgressed a rule that we, as observers, believe is operative in the organization of that group. In this case, a rule to which individuals seem to conform is superimposed on the behavior by the observer herself in order to explain that behavior. It is in this sense, for example, that computers are said to follow rules insofar as they instantiate an algorithm in the program. But what is *morally* relevant to the notion of rule-governed behavior is that the individuals who appear to conform to a prescriptive rule do so by virtue of recognizing that there is a rule that *ought* to be followed. This is a very different kind of explanation because it makes reference to how a rule is represented in the mind of the rule follower. One might wonder additionally what sort of cognitive representation of the rule is required in order to say that one follows a moral rule as opposed to a rule of etiquette or a rule of prudence. De Waal does not tackle this difficult conceptual issue, but he does correctly remark that when we as observers judge that a rule is enforced in a monkey group, we do not know if the rule "exists as a rule" in the animal's head. This is just the sort of thesis that may be proven in the course of additional experimentation. But without bothering to supply the reader with a substantive reason for doing so, de Waal goes on to attribute these morally relevant intentional states to the animal described in the following anecdote.[56]

A high-ranking female, Puist, took the trouble and risk to help her male friend, Luit, chase off a rival, Nikkie. Nikkie, however, had a habit after major confrontations of singling out and cornering allies of his rivals, to punish them. This time Nikkie displayed at Puist shortly after he had been attacked. Puist turned to Luit, stretching out her hand in search of support but Luit did not lift a finger to protect her. Immediately after Nikkie had left the scene, Puist turned on Luit, barking furiously. She chased him across the enclosure and even pummeled him.

If Puist's fury was in fact the result of Luit's failure to help her after she had helped him, the incident suggests that reciprocity in chimpanzees may be governed by obligations and expectations similar to those in humans.[57]

De Waal does not provide the reader with warrant for describing Puist as a rule follower where this reflects her cognition of the rule's prescriptive character in the mind of the chimp. What de Waal should infer is that we do not yet know whether this incident illustrates that chimpanzees follow prescriptive rules that represent obligations in the same way that human beings follow rules representing obligations to act.[58]

ANTHROPOMORPHISM

De Waal carefully guards against the objection that he is anthropomorphizing animals when he attributes to them psychological states like emotions. Those scientists who work directly with chimpanzees, in particular, believe that it is natural to interpret their behavior in human terms. But these interpretations are then left vulnerable to the "wrath of philosophers and other scientists" who do not have this kind of firsthand experience with primates and who dismiss these descriptions of animal psychology as mistaken attributions of human traits to animals.[59] According to de Waal, the alternative to describing animal behavior in intentionalistic language is to view animals as merely passive objects whose behavior is shaped entirely by their environment. This is an unacceptable and "wildly uneconomic" explanation of animal behavior for the following reason. We should attribute to those primates who display caring behavior motivational states like empathy and sympathy, for example, because the principle of "evolutionary parsimony" demands this kind of explanation. According to this principle, "[i]f closely related species act the same, then the underlying mental processes are probably the same too."[60] For example, if we see similar behavior in dogs and wolves, we should not explain their similar behavior by resorting to different causes, since these kinds of animals are close evolutionary relatives. The same reasoning applies to similar behavior displayed by humans and chimpanzees. By this principle de Waal believes that we are justified in using a "shared language" in attributing cognitive empathy to both humans and chimpanzees when we observe targeted helping behavior in each species. De Waal adds that "this holds true regardless of whether we are talking about emotions or cognitions."[61] However, de Waal cautions that we should use intentional language to describe animal behavior if it is employed in a "critical fashion." In contrast, de Waal identifies a case of "uncritical anthropomorphism." The popular writer Elizabeth Marshall Thomas is prepared to describe canine virgin bitches as "saving" their virginity for future "husbands," for example.[62]

This one example of "uncritical anthropomorphism" is helpful, but it does not go far enough to spell out what kind of language we should avoid using to describe what animals do and why they do it. One difficulty with endorsing the principle of evolutionary parsimony is that we have few, if any, guidelines for applying it. Using a "shared language" to describe animal behavior is warranted in those cases where the animals are "evolutionary close relatives." But how do we decide whether or not a species is "close" enough to justify using an emotion state term like *cognitive empathy* or an explicitly morally laden emotion state term like *sympathy*? I am not suggesting here that using intentional language is never appropriate to describe animal behavior, but we still need to decide which intentional states are appropriate and warranted to attribute to kinds of animals as well as to individual animals. Our choice of intentionalistic language should be informed by an analysis of the concepts we are employing. Attributing *moral* emotions to some animals is one way of implying that human beings are not unique with respect to morality. This is a remarkable claim and one about which there is considerable disagreement. We should not accept the idea that some animals have morally laden emotions without carefully scrutinizing the grounds for doing so. De Waal writes,

> Animals, particularly those close to us, show an enormous spectrum of emotions and different kinds of relationships. It is only fair to reflect this fact in a broad array of terms. If animals can have enemies they can have friends; if they can cheat they can be honest, and if they can be spiteful they can also be kind and altruistic. Semantic distinctions between animal and human behavior often obscure fundamental similarities; a discussion of morality will be pointless if we allow our language to be distorted by a denial of benign motives and emotions in animals.[63]

It is only fair to remind the reader that attributing morally laden motives and emotions to animals may well function to disguise or gloss over differences between animals and humans; this is the other side of the coin. Clarifying what emotions are and how they are morally significant is not merely a "semantic waste of time," as de Waal suggests at times,[64] but a substantive analysis necessary for going on to explore the ways in which animals and humans are the same and how they are different.

CONCLUSION

We are now in a position to answer the two initial questions posed at the beginning of this chapter about de Waal's research into the origins of human morality. First, does de Waal have warrant to conclude that some chimpanzees have morally laden emotions? I think the answer to this is no. The two anecdotes we have examined are used to illustrate that Binti Jua and Kuni have the moral sentiment of cognitive empathy. But in these cases at least the behavioral evidence alone underdetermines the attribution of this morally laden emotional state for the following reasons.

De Waal fails to specify in the very definition of cognitive empathy what is morally relevant about this emotional state. Empathy may involve appraising another's situation precisely, but what matters to empathy understood as a moral concept is that the subject perceives what is morally salient about another's situation. Even this additional requirement doesn't quite capture what needs to be added to cognitive empathy to make it a morally significant concept, and that is its relation to sympathy or compassion. These states are genuine moral emotions in the case where they motivate a subject to help or to alleviate need, distress, or suffering when this is judged to be "serious" and undeserved. The moral significance of the emotional states of sympathy and compassion is explained by the presence of evaluative judgments as well as the motivations to act on these evaluations or appraisals. Once we appreciate what should be built into the intentional content of moral emotions like sympathy and compassion, it is easier to see that de Waal's examples of primate behavior fall somewhat short of establishing that chimpanzees have emotions that are morally laden. De Waal's case is made no more convincing by appealing to the principle of evolutionary parsimony, since we have little guidance about how to apply this principle or what counts as a *critical* use of anthropomorphism.

We now turn to the second question asked at the beginning of this chapter: Does Darwin's principle of evolutionary continuity support de Waal's thesis that chimpanzees have the building blocks of morality? The answer to this question is somewhat more complicated. The Morality Continuity Thesis (MCT) is a plausible rendering of Darwin's principle of evolutionary continuity that we have formulated to explain de Waal's metaphors about morality and his remarks about continuity. On this way of interpreting de Waal's project, chimpanzees are

not fully moral because they do not have the set of *M-capabilities*
that characterize human morality. But the claim that de Waal is
really interested in establishing is that chimpanzees have at least
the *m-capabilities* where these include sympathy-related traits
(such as cognitive empathy), prescriptive rule following, community concern, and so on. These we might describe as the
"ancestral forms" of the set of traits necessary for realizing
human morality. So, according to (MCT), chimpanzees may
have these *m-capabilities* that are less cognitively complex than
M-capabilities, differing only by degree and not by kind.

The difficulty with applying evolutionary continuity in this
way is that what counts as a kind of emotion state is left unspec-
ified altogether. When continuity applies to emotional states
that are defined so as to capture their moral significance, then
they must have intentional content constituted by appraisals
and evaluations directed to states of affairs in the world, or to
persons, animals, or projects, where these evaluations include
judgments about fault, negligence, need, loss, and so on. This
cognitive-evaluative intentional content characteristic of moral
emotions is not susceptible to the kind of quantitative gradualism that evolutionary continuity requires. We saw as much in
chapter 4 when (CT) was originally introduced and applied to
the morally laden emotion of compassion.

To see how this criticism applies to (MCT), suppose that
compassion is a T-trait of human beings, part of the set of *M-
capabilities*. Then (MCT) implies that there are viable intermediate forms between T and t, where t is an ancestral form of
compassion that differs by degree but not by kind from T. So,
if evolutionary continuity is expressed as (MCT) then, as de
Waal wants to argue, a chimpanzee might also have the
capacity for the moral sentiment of compassion though not in
the same degree as humans have this capacity. But for compassion to be a moral emotion for human beings there must be a
reference to evaluative judgments; those we have already

described. These are necessary conditions for compassion to be morally significant in the first place. The problem we are now facing is how to understand the attribution of some lesser amount or a quantitatively smaller degree of compassion where this emotional state has cognitive-evaluative intentional content. According to (MCT) a chimpanzee, for example, has a *little bit* or a *lesser degree* of the judgment that the suffering of another person is undeserved. What could this possibly mean?[65] Perhaps there is a way to apply this kind of gradualism to cognitive-evaluative intentional content, but one is particularly struck by how awkward it is to individuate judgments and evaluations by incremental degrees. This is, I believe, an indication that de Waal is on the wrong track.

It may be tempting to use evolutionary continuity in this way if one is less than clear about what makes emotions morally significant. I suspect that de Waal's description of morality as composed of distinct levels contributes to the unclarity about what makes emotions morally laden.[66] His preferred description of morality is one where the moral sentiments make a separate contribution at "Level 1," which he calls "building blocks." Judgment and reasoning make their entry to some degree at "Level 2," or "Social Pressures," but more obviously at "Level 3," enabling morality to be lifted to a higher "level of abstraction and self-reflection." De Waal also identifies two distinct factors that contribute to an understanding of what is good or virtuous. These are

(1) the emotional reaction and intuition of each individual that jump-start the moral process, and (2) the cognitive-rational evaluations that enable the individual to determine what is right.[67]

While he admits that it would be a mistake "to equate moral emotions with a lack of rationality and judgment,"[68] in these contexts de Waal strongly suggests that the moral emotions or moral sentiments are distinguished from rationality, judgment, and other cognitive attitudes. These descriptions of the distinct contributions that emotions and reason make to morality imply that emotions are neither evaluative nor cognitive. While this conception of the emotions is perhaps historically faithful, it is inadequate for explaining how emotions are conceptually connected to morality.[69]

So, I believe the answer to the second question is no, the principle of evolutionary continuity interpreted as (MCT) does not support de Waal's thesis that chimpanzees have the building blocks of morality. This is because morally laden emotions are not the kinds of psychological states that can be carved up quantitatively by increments or degrees and attributed in some lesser amount to any kind of subject, either human or nonhuman.

Before closing this discussion of evolutionary continuity it is fair to consider one appeal to my conclusions.[70] Perhaps the evidence that nonhuman primates have the building blocks of morality can be found in the comparison between children and animals. The argument might go roughly as follows. Moral development in children begins with the "simple emotions," like sympathy.[71] But some nonhuman primates are like children with respect to their caring behavior and their affective responses to others. It makes sense to explain these similar caring behaviors that we observe in children and chimpanzees by reference to simple emotional states that are morally significant.[72] So, since children and animals are *relevantly alike* in their capacity for sympathy, and since moral development in children begins with emotions like sympathy, then attributing sympathy to nonhuman primates can be considered the beginning, or at least a stage in the evolutionary development of morality in human beings. De Waal says,

Instead of our doing "violence to the willow," as Mencius called it, to create the cups and bowls of an artificial morality, we rely on natural growth in which simple emotions, like those encountered in young children and social animals, develop into the more refined, other-including sentiments that we recognize as underlying morality. My own argument here obviously revolves around the continuity between human social instincts and those of our closest relatives, the monkeys and apes, but I feel that we are standing at the threshold of a much larger shift in theorizing that will end up positioning morality firmly within the emotional core of human nature.[73]

In this way it might make sense to say that children have a little bit of morality or the "building blocks of morality" because they have affective capabilities, though not the intellectual and cognitive development to reason abstractly about moral matters. By analogy perhaps chimpanzees have a little bit of morality but not the intellectual and cognitive development to reason abstractly about moral matters. The plausibility of these claims depends, of course, on how we understand and characterize moral development in children as well as how we specify what it means to say that animals are like children in sharing "simple emotions." Some philosophers and developmental psychologists are prepared to say that children are not moral beings because they fail to have the rationality required for morality.[74] Explaining and evaluating this literature is clearly beyond the scope of the present work, but we can and should follow de Waal in his recommendation to examine the close conceptual relationship between children, animals, emotions, and morality. In the next chapter we explore the idea that children and animals are perhaps sufficiently similar to consider both moral beings because they are the proper subjects of moral responsibility ascriptions and deserving of moral praise and blame.

NOTES

1. Parts of this chapter were originally published in Beth Dixon, "Review Essay on *Good Natured: The Origins of Right and Wrong in Humans and Other Animals*, by Frans de Waal," *Human Ecology Review* 6, no. 1 (1999). Some of de Waal's popular writings include Frans B. M. de Waal, *Peacemaking among Primates* (Cambridge, MA: Harvard University Press, 1989); Frans B. M. de Waal, *Good Natured: The Origins of Right and Wrong in Humans and Other Animals* (Cambridge, MA: Harvard University Press, 1996); Frans B. M. de Waal, *Chimpanzee Politics: Power and Sex among Apes* (Baltimore, MD: Johns Hopkins University Press, 1998); Frans B. M. de Waal, *The Ape and the Sushi Master: Cultural Reflections of a Primatologist* (New York: Basic Books, 2001).

2. See, for example, Nicholas Wade, "Scientist Finds the Beginnings of Morality in Primate Behavior," *New York Times*, March 20, 2007.

3. Frans B. M. de Waal, "Morally Evolved: Primate Social Instincts, Human Morality, and the Rise and Fall of *Veneer Theory*," in *Primates and Philosophers: How Morality Evolved*, ed. Steven Macedo and Josiah Ober, *University Center for Human Values* series (Princeton, NJ: Princeton University Press, 2006).

4. See, for example, K. Davidson, "Scientists Debate Animal Motives," *San Francisco Examiner*, August 28, 1996.

5. Frans B. M. de Waal, "Anthropomorphism and Anthropodenial: Consistency in Our Thinking About Humans and Other Animals," *Philosophical Topics* 27, no. 1 (1999): 271.

6. Ibid. This anecdote is also discussed in de Waal, "Morally Evolved," p. 32; Lori Gruen, "The Morals of Animal Minds," in *The Cognitive Animal*, ed. Marc Bekoff, Collin Allen, and Gordon M. Burghardt (Cambridge, MA: MIT Press, 2002), p. 437.

7. De Waal, "Morally Evolved," p. 31.

8. Ibid.

9. Ibid., p. 48.

10. See de Waal, *Good Natured*, pp. 3, 211, 212.

11. Ibid., pp. 3, 39. See also de Waal, "Morally Evolved," p. 168.

Some commentators have complained that de Waal's use of these metaphors is too vague. See Philip Kitcher, "Ethics and Evolution: How to Get Here from There," in *Primates and Philosophers*, ed. Macedo and Ober, pp. 121, 123; Peter Railton, "Darwinian Building Blocks," in *Evolutionary Origins of Morality*, ed. Leonard D. Katz (Bowling Green, OH: Imprint Academic, 2000), p. 58; B. Thierry, "Building Elements of Morality Are Not Elements of Morality," in *Evolutionary Origins of Morality*, ed. Katz, p. 60.

12. De Waal, *Good Natured*, p. 87.

13. Charles Darwin, *The Descent of Man; and Selection in Relation to Sex* (Amherst, NY: Prometheus Books, 1998), p. 101.

14. De Waal, "Morally Evolved," p. 14.

15. Frans B. M. de Waal and Jessica C. Flack, "'Any Animal Whatever': Darwinian Building Blocks of Morality in Monkeys and Apes," in *Evolutionary Origins of Morality*, ed. Katz, p. 23.

16. Ibid.

17. De Waal, *Good Natured*, p. 211.

18. De Waal, "Morally Evolved," p. 168.

19. De Waal and Flack, "'Any Animal Whatever,'" p. 73.

20. De Waal, "Morally Evolved," p. 168.

21. Ibid., pp. 166–75.

22. This condition stands for a number of different claims. As we have seen in chapter 3, we might classify *x* as a moral being because she can act from virtue. But this condition might also be interpreted to mean that *x* can perform acts that are good or evil. What kinds of intentional states an animal (or a person) must have to qualify as a moral being in this sense is discussed later in this chapter and in chapters 6 and 7.

23. I borrow these formulations from Richard Joyce, *The Evolution of Morality* (Cambridge, MA: MIT Press, 2006), p. 76.

24. Joyce's discussion focuses on what conditions must be satisfied to make a moral judgment. See chapter 3 in Joyce, *Evolution of Morality*.

25. See, for example, Peter Singer, *Animal Liberation* (New York: Avon Books, 1975).

26. Philip Kitcher lodges a similar complaint in his commentary

on de Waal's Tanner lectures. See Kitcher, "Ethics and Evolution." Kitcher coins the expression "the Smith-Hume Lure" to refer to the oversimplification of the thesis to which de Waal and other evolutionary ethicists have succumbed.

> The lure consists in focusing on the central role of sympathy in the ethical accounts offered by Hume and Smith. So you first claim that moral conduct consists in the expression of the appropriate passions, and that sympathy is central to these passions. Then you argue that chimpanzees have capacities for sympathy, and conclude that they have the core of the psychology required for morality. If there are worries about what it means to talk about the "central" role of sympathy or the "core" of moral psychology, the primatologist or evolutionary theorist can shift the burden. Hume, Smith, and their contemporary champions sort out the ways in which sympathy figures in moral psychology and moral behavior; the primatologists demonstrate the sympathetic tendencies at work in primate social life; the evolutionary theorists show how tendencies of this type might have evolved. (p. 125)

The problem with such a strategy, Kitcher maintains, is that there are many different ways of characterizing psychological altruism "profiles." There is not only unclarity about determining which of these are properly attributed to either humans or animals, but additionally, there is unclarity about which of these profiles matter to morality. "Until we have a clearer view of the specific kinds of psychological altruism chimpanzees (and other nonhuman primates) display, and until we know what kinds are relevant to morality, it's premature to claim that human morality is a 'direct outgrowth' of tendencies these animals share" (pp. 129–30). Kitcher himself does not explain *how* emotion states like sympathy are relevant to morality, but this is indeed what de Waal needs to add to his explanation of the concept of emotion he is employing. In the next section of this chapter, I explain how the concept of sympathy should be explained in order to capture its moral significance.

27. Christine M. Korsgaard, "Morality and the Distinctiveness of Human Action," in *Primates and Philosophers*, ed. Macedo and Ober, pp. 116–17.

28. Kitcher, "Ethics and Evolution," pp. 133–34.

29. Joyce, *Evolution of Morality*, pp. 80–85.

30. Marc D. Hauser, *Wild Minds: What Animals Really Think* (New York: Henry Holt and Company, 2000), p. 224.

31. Lori Gruen criticizes some of these accounts of morality and moral agency, especially Korsgaard and Hauser, for their dependency on a single, highly rationalistic capacity for moral agency that appeals to duty and responsibility. She is right, I believe, to urge us to examine more carefully the normative assumptions that are sometimes relied on when some philosophers deny animals a share in morality. But the other side of the coin is to recommend, as I do here, that de Waal's emphasis on the emotions requires a normative framework that will make his remarks about the moral sentiments a viable contender to these alternative conceptions. See Gruen, "Morals of Animal Minds," pp. 439–40.

32. De Waal, "Morally Evolved," p. 55.

33. Ibid., p. 56.

34. Ibid., p. 61.

35. De Waal, *Good Natured*, p. 15.

36. Ibid., p. 73.

37. De Waal, "Morally Evolved," p. 40.

38. Ibid., pp. 37–38.

39. Ibid., p. 40.

40. Ibid., p. 39.

41. Ibid., p. 41.

42. I owe this account of Aristotle to Nancy Sherman, *The Fabric of Character* (Oxford, UK: Clarendon Press, 1989), p. 29.

43. Ibid., p. 30.

44. Aristotle, *Nicomachean Ethics*, 2nd ed., trans. Terence Irwin (Indianapolis: Hackett, 1999), (114b1–3) and (14b17). Quoted in Sherman, *Fabric of Character*, p. 32.

45. Aristotle, *Nicomachean Ethics* (1109a23).

46. Sherman, *Fabric of Character*, p. 45.

47. De Waal implies this in remarks he makes in de Waal, "Morally Evolved," pp. 28, 32. See also chapter 2 of de Waal, *Good Natured*.

48. I borrow Nussbaum's account of this distinction from Martha C. Nussbaum, *Upheavals of Thought: The Intelligence of Emotions* (Cambridge: Cambridge University Press, 2001), pp. 301–303. De Waal says that sympathy is a "mechanism" related to empathy. "Sympathy is defined as 'an affective response that consists of feelings of sorrow or concern for a distressed or needy other (rather than the same emotion as the other person). Sympathy is believed to involve an other-oriented, altruistic motivation.'" De Waal, "Morally Evolved," pp. 27–28.

49. Nussbaum, *Upheavals of Thought*, p. 301.

50. For more discussion of this point, see "The Discernment of Perception: An Aristotelian Conception of Private and Public Rationality," chapter 2 in Martha Nussbaum, *Love's Knowledge: Essays on Philosophy and Literature* (New York: Oxford University Press, 1990).

51. Richard Joyce reaches a similar conclusion but for a slightly different reason. Joyce argues that because evaluative concepts require a language, it follows that animals cannot make moral judgments. See Joyce, *Evolution of Morality*, pp. 80–85. I'm not entirely convinced that all evaluative concepts require linguistic ability. What I do agree with Joyce about is that moral emotions like guilt or shame are constituted by "thick" evaluative content that matches or approximates how we use such emotion state words. Joyce explains,

> Guilt seems most naturally to associate with the judgment that the person has performed a wrongful action for which amends might be made; shame seems to associate with a judgment that the person is "wrong in himself," and perhaps nothing can be done about it. One feels guilty for having told a lie, but one feels shame for being a liar. Guilt concerns transgressions; shame involves shortcomings. Guilt urges reparative action; shame encourages social withdrawal. One may feel shame about one's lowly upbringing,

or one's enormous nose, or one's accidental defeat at the hands of a lesser rival, but one would not feel guilt about such things. (p. 102)

What matters here is not that we should settle on this particular way of defining guilt and shame but that we come to appreciate how conceptually rich these moral emotions are. The plausibility of de Waal's position that some animals have moral emotions then depends on arguing that some animals have "thick" evaluative concepts that make reference to, for example, "wrongful action," "one's own shortcomings," "how to make amends," and so on. As I suggest in the main text of this chapter, I believe the empirical data does not support the claim that nonhuman primates have these intentional states.

52. De Waal, *Good Natured*, p. 3.

53. Ibid., p. 53.

54. Ibid., p. 55.

55. Ibid., p. 90.

56. I would make the same remark about an anecdote de Waal uses about prescriptive rule following in "Morally Evolved," p. 172.

57. Ibid., p. 97.

58. After carefully explaining the distinction between the *ought* and *should* of predication from the *ought* and *should* of evaluative judgment, Richard Joyce remarks, "The point of these pedantic observations is not to criticize de Waal, but rather to forewarn the reader that though it may be permissible to ascribe animals certain mental states whose contents involve the word 'ought' or 'should,' this may do nothing to establish the legitimacy of ascribing them *moral* judgments." See Joyce, *Evolution of Morality*, p. 78.

59. De Waal, "Morally Evolved," p. 60.

60. Ibid., p. 62.

61. Ibid., p. 167.

62. Elizabeth Marshall Thomas, *The Hidden Life of Dogs* (New York: Houghton Mifflin, 1993). Quoted in de Waal, "Morally Evolved," p. 64.

63. De Waal, *Good Natured*, p. 19.

64. Ibid., p. 212 and de Waal, "Morally Evolved," p. 181.

65. Of course, the evidence used in making a judgment might be inconclusive, doubtful, or conflicting. But the epistemic status of this evidence does not, in turn, produce degrees of the judgment itself, though we do speak of degrees of certainty (being more or less certain) that support a particular judgment.

66. See de Waal, "Morally Evolved," pp. 166–75; de Waal and Flack, "'Any Animal Whatever,'" p. 67.

67. De Waal and Flack, "Any Animal Whatever," p. 21.

68. Ibid., p. 20.

69. De Waal refers to the "Social Intuitionist" model of emotions approvingly in de Waal, "Morally Evolved," p. 179. But even this account of the emotions described by Jonathan Haidt allows for emotions to involve evaluations, appraisals, and judgments in how intuitions are formed. See Jonathan Haidt, "The Emotional Dog and Its Rational Tail: A Social Intuitionist Approach to Moral Judgment," *Psychological Review* 108, no. 4 (2001): 818.

70. I loosely attribute this reply to de Waal based on scattered passages in several of his publications. But nowhere does he articulate this line of reasoning exactly as I do here.

71. De Waal, "Morally Evolved," p. 23.

72. Ibid., p. 28. See also de Waal's claim that children and nonhuman primates are alike in their affective responses to nature in Peter Verbeek and Frans B. M. de Waal, "The Primate Relationship with Nature: Biophilia as a General Pattern," in *Children and Nature: Psychological, Sociocultural, and Evolutionary Investigations*, ed. Peter H. Kahn Jr. and Stephen R. Kellert (Cambridge, MA: MIT Press, 2002), pp. 20–21.

73. Ibid., p. 57.

74. See, for example, Jean Piaget, *The Moral Judgment of the Child* (New York: Free Press, 1965).

Chapter Six

CHILDREN AND ANIMALS

I concluded the last chapter by entertaining the possibility that chimpanzees are like children because they share "simple emotions" such as sympathy. Here and in chapter 7 I investigate the plausibility of this idea. First, I try to say more explicitly why emotional responsiveness in children is morally significant despite the generally accepted belief that their capacity to reason about moral matters is relatively undeveloped. The idea that children and animals are alike in their affective capacities has rather broad and intuitive appeal. Because this is so, it is worth exploring in more detail.

CHILDHOOD ANIMALITY

The Institute for the Advancement of Philosophy for Children (IAPC) publishes philosophical novels for the K–12 curriculum. These are intended to be read together with elementary schoolchildren to form the starting points for discussions of the philosophical ideas in these novels. One of my favorites is the novel *Lisa*, intended for grades 7–12 with a focus on ethical inquiry. In the first chapter, Lisa, who is probably twelve or thirteen years old, watches one of her new neighbors walk his dog down the street. Mr. Johnson's dog suddenly begins to pull and resist when he tries to chase a squirrel. Mr. Johnson shouts and then uses a branch from a nearby tree to hit the dog, "which crouched, motionless, absorbing the blows." "Lisa stared at the two in horror. She couldn't even cry out. Suddenly she sprang forward and tried to grasp the switch. 'You stop doing that!' She commanded furiously. Surprised, Mr. Johnson snatched the switch clear and turned, saying: 'What's it to you?' Beside herself in rage, she blurted out, 'I'm a dog too.'"[1] Lisa's reaction is understandable, but her comment "I'm a dog too!" is startling. Since her remark is not literally true, what could she mean by saying this? What Lisa says invites the reader to explain and interpret, especially in the context of the rest of the story where Lisa and her friends debate the reasons for and against vegetarianism and hunting animals. The teacher's manual that accompanies *Lisa* includes suggestions about how to continue to discuss with children the main ideas in the novel by supplying the educator with discussion questions and exercises. Some of these questions explore empathy in thinking and feeling, while others guide the inquirer to consider how children and animals are alike and how they are different. For example,

- Have you ever felt that other people didn't understand you, so that you turned to a cat or dog or horse for comfort and consolation?
- Have you ever felt that animals that like to play and have fun are closer to children than they are to adults?

- Do you think that young animals think about what they will be like when they grow up, the way young people do?
- Do you think kittens want to be cats and puppies can't wait to be dogs?
- Do you think that young animals ever want to be different animals—that a kitten might want to be a puppy, or a puppy might want to be a kitten?
- Do you think that young animals ever want to be able to read and write?[2]

These questions are invitations to the reader of *Lisa* to consider how children and animals might be alike—by their capacity to feel and play. And how they might be different in their expectations about the future; what they want to be able to do and be. Even though these are intended to be philosophically open-ended questions, the idea that children and animals are alike in certain ways is deeply embedded in our history and in our culture.

The term *childhood animality* has been used to refer to those associations between children and animals that are based on their affinities toward one another, their seeming psychological similarities, and also on the "cultural stories" of likeness that find their way into our philosophical, psychological, and political history.[3] Freud, for example, remarks, "Children show no trace of the arrogance which urges modern adult civilized men to draw a hard-and-fast line between their own nature and that of all other animals. Children have no scruples over allowing animals to rank as their full equals. Uninhibited as they are in the avowal of their bodily needs, they no doubt feel themselves more akin to animals than to their elders, who may well be a puzzle to them."[4]

Many photographs and paintings from the late 1800s pair children and animals in family settings. These are mostly portrait scenes that illustrate the emotional intimacy of a typical child and the family pet. These historical images represent attitudes about children and animals that persist even today; that children and animals are similar in their reasoning and emotional capabilities, that they are individuals that occupy a dependent but privileged place in the family, and that both have the potential to be "civilized" by education and training.[5]

While this cultural and historical background is fascinating in itself, focusing on the idea of childhood animality has a philosophical point. The close conceptual overlap between children and animals might lead us to predict that these kinds of beings will be characterized as occupying one and the same moral space as well. Indeed, some theories of moral responsibility have tended to treat children and animals as like cases.[6] Either the bar for moral accountability is set fairly low, allowing both animals and children to be morally responsible for what they do. Or it is set rather high, in which case neither children nor animals qualify as moral agents and as proper subjects for moral praise or blame.[7]

By closely examining our moral practices of ascribing responsibility we can disentangle what I believe is a mistaken assumption, which is that children and animals should be classified together as beings who are both properly credited with moral praise and blame, or who are together both exempt from being morally appraisable. But which theory of responsibility should we use to investigate this idea? Since our project throughout has been to explain the various ways in which emotions may be morally laden, we should use a theory of moral responsibility that most obviously accommodates the contribution that emotions make to our practices of moral praise and blame. P. F. Strawson's theory of the reactive attitudes is well-suited to our themes of emotions and morality. For Strawson, emotions play a starring role since it is our emotional responsiveness to one another that constitutes the practice of ascribing responsibility to a subject and assigning to her moral praise and blame.[8] When animals are likened to dependent children, or regarded as individuals who are the emotional equals of children and believed to be their intimate friends and loyal guardians, then where should animals and children be located in a theory of responsibility that takes as primary our practices and attitudes toward different kinds of subjects? Specifically, we might ask, what would P. F. Strawson's theory of the reactive attitudes imply about the moral culpability of animals and children?

A PUZZLE ABOUT THE REACTIVE ATTITUDES

The puzzle that I describe in this section is really just a question about where to locate children and animals in the moral and conceptual space described by Strawson in his influential article "Freedom and Resentment."[9] Strawson directs our attention to emotional states such as gratitude, resentment, forgiveness, shame, love, guilt, indignation, and hurt feelings. These represent the core of our moral engagements with other human beings. They are "commonplaces" that signal "what it is actually like to be involved in ordinary inter-personal relationships, ranging from the most intimate to the most casual."[10] The reactive attitudes are not merely emotional responses to another being. They express "the demand for the manifestation of a reasonable degree of good will or regard, on the part of others, not simply towards oneself, but towards all those on whose behalf moral indignation may be felt."[11]

Strawson identifies two primary conditions that typically reflect when it is "natural," "reasonable," or "appropriate" to adopt these reactive attitudes toward another human being. If we do feel resentment in response to some insult or injury, we may modify our attitude because of a certain kind of excuse offered: "It was an accident." "She didn't mean to." "She didn't know." These pleas make the attitude of resentment inappropriate because of extenuating circumstances even while acknowledging the injury that may have resulted from the action. Importantly, these excuses and the reactive attitudes that we adopt toward the agent entail that the agent is fully responsible for her actions and counts as someone to whom it is appropriate to have the reactive attitudes of resentment and forgiveness.

The second cluster of attitudes Strawson identifies as part of our commonplace practice characterizes the *kind* of person with whom we are dealing. This is not the temporary suspension of indignation or resentment because of extenuating circumstances that we believe are legitimately excusing at a time. It is a wholesale resistance to regarding this person as one to whom we have moral relations in the first place. We adopt the "objective attitude" toward a person as a response to excuses like "She's only a child"; or "He's a diagnosed schizophrenic"; or "That's purely compulsive behavior on his part." In other words, we are invited to view the agent herself as "psychologically abnormal" or "morally undeveloped," and by virtue of this as a person who is not morally responsible for her actions in general. As Strawson puts it, "To adopt the objective attitude to another human being is to see him, perhaps, as an object of social policy: as a subject for what, in a wide range of sense, might be called treatment; as something certainly to be taken account, perhaps precautionary account, of; to be managed or handled or cured or trained; perhaps simply to be avoided . . ."[12]

Strawson maintains that the practice of our reactive attitudes is a deep and natural feature of our ordinary interpersonal relations; as he says, "a part of the general framework of human life."[13] When Strawson characterizes the reactive attitudes in this way, he is making a point about the primacy of our practice of interpersonal relations and, additionally, that these attitudes are constitutive of moral responsibility ascriptions. These reactive attitudes just *are* what it means to hold a person morally responsible for what she does.

If we accept that the reactive attitudes are *constitutive* of moral responsibility ascriptions, then we might come to believe these attitudes apply more broadly than to adult human beings. We seem to express resentment or indignation toward animals as well as children in a variety of settings. Does this mean that these subjects are morally responsible for what they do and may be morally blameworthy for harms or injuries they inflict (providing that no temporary excusing conditions apply)? This would be so if it really is the case that animals and children express attitudes of moral ill will or good will in their conduct toward others or themselves and have a sufficiently complex grasp of moral matters to ascribe to them these moral attitudes. To be sure Strawson takes human adult relationships as the paradigm case of the participant reactive attitudes. Would Strawson say that our attitudes of indignation, resentment, hatred, or love, directed toward some animals and children are simply mistaken in their target? We will have to look closer to discern *why* Strawson believes that the participant attitudes single out moral relations between human adults.

We might initially believe that Strawson's characterization of the objective attitude captures our occasional regard for both domestic and wild animals as the sorts of beings that must be "managed or handled or cured or trained." Certainly some people regard animals, especially wild animals, as "objects of social policy" in the same way as a game manager of a wildlife habitat might ensure that populations of certain species are maintained at viable numbers. But even so, it is difficult to explain the deep and abiding love and respect that most people have toward their pets by reference to the objective attitude. Alternatively, as I will discuss in chapter 7, it is not unusual to call some animals "evil" or blame them for intentionally performing actions that harm human beings or even other animals. The problem about where to locate animals in Strawson's theory is created by our various conflicting and inconsistent practices and attitudes toward animals.

We may be equally puzzled about where to locate children in Strawson's scheme since they are beings who fall somewhere short of being full-fledged members of the moral community. Strawson says,

> Thus parents and others concerned with the care and upbringing of young children cannot have to their charges either kind of attitude in a pure or unqualified form. They are dealing with creatures who are potentially and increasingly capable both of holding, and being objects of, the full range of human and moral attitudes, but are not yet truly capable of either. The treatment of such creatures must therefore represent a kind of compromise, constantly shifting in one direction, between objectivity of attitude and developed human attitudes. . . . The punishment of a child is both like and unlike the punishment of an adult.[14]

Strawson admits here that while parents and guardians of children cannot adopt either the objective attitude or developed human attitudes in a "pure or unqualified form," the compromise position is to move back and forth between these attitudes.

Does Strawson's suggestion actually capture our practical regard for children? It seems quite likely that on some occasions a child may be genuinely deserving of moral praise or blame, but she may not yet be capable of the fully developed human attitudes that characterize our moral relations as mature adults. Similarly, even if she is not deserving of moral praise or blame on a particular occasion, we will not usually resort to the objective attitude in dealing with her; we will not regard her as the kind of thing that must be "managed or treated." Perhaps Strawson is only reminding us that we should make accommodations for her gradual transition to a full-fledged member of the moral community. But it is still unclear how, when, or even whether we should hold children morally accountable. Clearly we need more guidance on this issue than Strawson explicitly provides.

If neither children nor animals fit neatly into Strawson's schema of the reactive attitudes based on our various and sometimes conflicting practices and regard for these subjects, then we might wonder if we can use Strawson's theory at all to answer the question about whether these kinds of beings are morally responsible. Susan Dwyer describes this kind of difficulty about Strawson's approach in the following way:

> But something is amiss in thinking that an individual is morally responsible just in case others react to him in this way rather than that. Surely, there is something about *him* that makes him morally responsible or not. Moreover, taking the reactive attitudes to be constitutive of moral responsibility appears to allow no room for error: we feel indignant at A, and that is all there is to it. But aren't our feelings of indignation and resentment sometimes misplaced?
>
> The concerns can be addressed by articulating what it is to be a *proper* target of the reactive attitudes.[15]

R. Jay Wallace further develops Strawson's theory of responsibility by a careful exposition of what counts as a proper target of the reactive attitudes.[16] On Wallace's view both children and animals are exempt from moral responsibility because they fail to satisfy the conditions that he believes are necessary for being morally culpable.

THE RATIONALITY CONDITION—
REFLECTIVE SELF-CONTROL

Following Strawson, Wallace believes that the practice of holding a person morally responsible is one that takes place from the point of view of a "moral judge" rather than the agent of the act, where this practice is closely aligned with the moral sentiments of resentment, indignation, and guilt (a subset of the broader class of reactive attitudes that Strawson discusses). But Wallace adds to this that conditions of *fairness* demand that there be something about a person to whom we direct these attitudes that justifies our holding these attitudes toward him or her. It is this part of Wallace's project that I wish to appropriate, if only in an abbreviated way.

Certain agents may be exempt from moral responsibility because they lack capacities and abilities that make it appropriate, in general, to hold the agent responsible. Exemptions are different from excuses in this respect, since "excuses block responsibility for particular acts an agent has performed, [and] exemptions make it inappropriate to hold the agent accountable more generally."[17] According to Wallace, exempting conditions apply to young children, those who suffer from certain kinds of insanity or mental illness, and psychopaths, all by virtue of their failure to have "reflective self-control." More precisely it is only fair to hold a person morally responsible and blameworthy if the agent possesses:

(1) The power to grasp and apply moral reasons; and
(2) The power to control or regulate his behavior by light of such reasons.[18]

Wallace explains that grasping and applying a moral principle and the moral reasons behind it is a relatively complex task. What is required is a *participant understanding* of the contexts in which a principle applies. For example, understanding the principle that one should not deliberately harm other people (in the ordinary pursuit of one's own ends) requires knowing what counts as harmful in a variety of situations and understanding the different kinds of harms it is possible to inflict, such as emotional harm, physical harm, damage to a person's reputation, and so on.[19] It might be expected that participant understanding and grasping moral reasons admit of degrees. Although Wallace concedes that it is difficult to say exactly what level or degree of cognitive and volitional capacity is necessary for reflective self-control, he maintains that there is some level of reflective self-control that is required for moral responsibility.[20]

By Wallace's own account, animals are most certainly exempt from moral responsibility because they do not have the relevant degree of reflective self-control. Because animals lack the "general competence" to entertain moral reasons in support of obligations and to be motivated to act by these moral reasons, it would be unfair or unreasonable to hold an animal morally responsible for its actions. We may still sanction an animal's behavior that fails to meet our expectations of how the animal should behave, but this does not amount to moral blame.[21]

What is less clear is how Wallace's exempting conditions apply to children. Because children are learning how to use moral principles and moral concepts like fairness or harm, Wallace says they do not "completely lack the powers of reflective self-control."[22] This is what we would expect if possessing these cognitive and volitional powers comes in degrees of normative competence. The difficult part here is what we should say about the moral responsibility of children relative to their degree of possession of these powers. Wallace recommends that we treat children *as if* they are responsible agents because they have some degree of reflective self-control and because it is practically efficacious to treat them this way in order to encourage their development into full-fledged moral agents. The underlying assumption here is that by treating children "as if" they are responsible, it is presumed that they are not. We may get a child's behavior to conform to our moral expectations, but the behavior alone is not always indicative that she has grasped the relevant moral reasons or principles and has acted with this motivation. She may, Wallace notes, be acting from fear of punishment or the desire for her parent's approval. So, acting intentionally in a way that complies with moral obligations we accept is not always indicative of reflective self-control.

Since Wallace himself describes children's acquisition of reflective self-control as a gradual process, and fairly ascribing moral responsibility to anyone depends on a certain threshold level of reflective self-control, it is reasonable to want more precision about where to locate children in the development of this normative competence. After all, we may want to know if a child *deserves* the commendation of moral praise or the sanctions that accompany moral blame. In other words, treating a child *as if* she is morally accountable may be practical but not philosophically warranted in a particular instance. In the next section I suggest some reasons for thinking that children may deserve moral praise and blame even if they fail to have reflective self-control.

MORALLY APPRAISING CHILDREN

How should we decide whether or not to hold children morally accountable? A Strawsonian-type theory of moral responsibility takes as central our practical regard for children and how we respond to them in particular circumstances.[23] Consider the following anecdote that illustrates what teachers and parents of preschoolers have observed about children's interest and concern with fairness.

> Two four-year-olds were engaged in an increasingly acrimonious dispute over the possession of a large set of magic markers. A nearby adult pointed out that since there were 16 markers it would be *fair* if each child counted out 8 of them. Fascinated, the children not only forgot their quarrel, but even their drawings and devoted the next half hour to a very full and effective discussion generating and agreeing upon many further rules (e.g., if there are two of the same color, we each get one; if there is only one color, the person gets it whose favorite color it is; if both children like that color, or if neither does, they take turns using it).[24]

Gareth Matthews offers another example of children's moral thinking in his wonderful book, *Philosophy and the Young Child*.[25] "Ian (six years) found to his chagrin that the three children of his parents' friends monopolized the television; they kept him from watching his favorite program. 'Mother,' he asked in frustration, 'why is it better for three people to be selfish than for one?'"[26] Matthews later wrote a short story to read and discuss with children that posed a similar challenge to the idea that because three people were made happy and only one was disgruntled, the action of appropriating the TV programming was morally right. But as Matthews notes about the children who discussed the story, "they found [the principle of] utilitarianism unattractive, and they were not inclined to search for any similarly high-level principle or theory to replace utilitarianism."[27] Instead the children debated selfishness, hurt feelings, the ages of the children in the story, whether or not it was the *last* show televised in the series, the protocol of being nice to visitors, and so on.

The children described in these cases seem to be grasping the morally relevant features of the situations they find themselves in, but it is not so easy to say that they have a moral principle in mind that they are attempting to apply, or that they understand how to justify the moral considerations that they bring to bear in each particular case. In these examples we have what I think are genuine cases of children engaging in moral reasoning. Do they display what Wallace might say is the minimal degree of reflective self-control required for moral accountability? Probably not, based on the sophisticated concepts and cognitive abilities that Wallace builds into having "the power to grasp and apply moral reasons."[28] Ann Diller warns us that we must not make the idea of "having moral reasons" so complicated that it will turn out that children cannot have them at all. Because being hurt and hurting another person is in the domain of a child's experience, we can demand of a child, "Don't do that, *because* it hurts!" In such a case, "It hurts" is a moral reason that children can grasp and use as an explanation prohibiting some kinds of actions.[29] But this example of a moral reason is not very close to what Wallace describes as a general moral principle that agents apply in a thoughtful and circumscribed way as a result of deliberating about different kinds of harms and the reasons for or against the moral principle of nonmaleficence. Still, we may wonder what kind of theory of moral development allows that four-year-olds are moral reasoners. An answer is supplied by Matthews's description of moral development, one that he contrasts with the cognitive-developmental stage theories of Jean Piaget and Lawrence Kohlberg.[30]

> A young child is able to latch onto the moral kind, bravery, or lying, by grasping central paradigms of that kind, paradigms that even the most mature and sophisticated moral agents still count as paradigmatic. Moral development is then something much more complicated than simple concept displacement. It is: enlarging the stock of paradigms

for each moral kind; developing better and better definitions of whatever it is these paradigms exemplify; appreci-
ating better the relation between straightforward instances
of the kind and close relatives; and learning to adjudicate
competing claims from different moral kinds (classically the
sometimes competing claims of justice and compassion, but
many other conflicts are possible).[31]

Or imagine a young child who has only a few paradigms of the
moral concept of fairness, such as distributing an equal number
of cookies to his classmates. Compared to an adult's conception
of distributive justice this participant understanding is minimal.
But there is no denying that if this child has such a paradigm in
mind when he hands out favors to the class, then he is acting
from a moral reason *even if* he fails to understand anything
more about a general principle of distributive justice that would
justify his action. What should we conclude about the moral
agency of children and their moral accountability in particular
situations? Michael Pritchard puts it this way, "On this view
[Matthews's paradigm model of moral development] children
as well as adults can be acknowledged to share some ground
level understanding of morality. Although adults may typically
have the upper hand in regard to breadth of experience and
understanding, there is no warrant for entirely excluding children from the adult world of morality."[32]

What Wallace requires as a condition for *fairly* ascribing
moral responsibility to anyone is that she be capable of reflective self-control. Using this "rationality condition" has the consequence that children are exempt from moral responsibility.
But this may not be the right conclusion to draw. What I have
urged us to consider is that even though some children may
not have the minimal degree of reflective self-control to count
as a proper target of the reactive attitudes, it still makes sense
to morally appraise their actions. In some contexts children

may be legitimately deserving of moral praise or blame even though they may not employ moral principles, articulate moral justifications, or carefully consider alternative actions, among other indicators that Wallace cites.

If it does make sense to morally appraise children who do not have reflective self-control then we need a way of saying this in whatever account of moral responsibility we endorse. This is sufficient motivation for exploring the idea that there are conditions for being responsible that are more appropriate to capturing our moral appraisals of beings who are not full-fledged moral agents. For this reason I next consider Aristotle's conditions for acting voluntarily as one such possible account.

THE INTENTIONALITY CONDITION—VOLUNTARY ACTION

Aristotle recognizes that there is a kind of explanation that is common to the movements of human and nonhuman animals. These are intentional descriptions that refer to the desires of the animal and its selectivity of perception and attention and that explain the animal's object-directed behavior and the reaching out for something in the world.[33] In the *Nicomachean Ethics* Aristotle calls the common account of human and animal movement *voluntary action*. Although children and animals are classified as beings that act voluntarily, Aristotle is unequivocally committed to denying reason to nonhuman animals altogether. He also denies that children engage in deliberation and choice even though children, unlike animals, will develop their natural capacity for deliberate choice as they mature. This involves the recognition that human flourishing is the ultimate and proper end, and the capacity to deliberate about the most effective means for attaining this end.[34]

But what is it that children and animals share by virtue of

their capability to act voluntarily? In the *Nicomachean Ethics* Aristotle describes two conditions. First, the origin of the action must be internal to the agent. If, for example, a ship is blown off course by a strong wind, then we will say that the captain of the ship acted involuntarily (or did not act at all), because the origin of the ship's movement was the wind and not anything internal to the captain. Second, the agent of the action must have knowledge of the particular facts surrounding the action. If, for example, a soldier shoots his brother in war because he mistakes him for the enemy, then the soldier was ignorant in the relevant sense about the circumstances surrounding the action.[35] Consequently, the soldier's action is involuntary and he is not responsible. Ignorance of general moral principles is not excusable, according to Aristotle, and does not make the action involuntary.[36] We might then formulate Aristotle's conditions for acting voluntarily in the following way:

(V) A subject, *a*, performs an action *x* voluntarily if and only if the origin of *x* is internal to *a*, and *a* has knowledge of the particular facts surrounding *x*.

The capacity for voluntary action is central to our interest in the moral responsibility of children and animals because Aristotle goes on to explicitly connect voluntary action with moral praise and blame. He says, "Since virtue is concerned with passions and actions, and on voluntary passions and actions praise and blame are bestowed . . . to distinguish the voluntary and involuntary is presumably necessary for those who are studying the nature of virtue, and useful also for legislators with a view to the assigning of both honors and punishments."[37] These remarks seem to suggest the following condition for being morally responsible. I'll call this the *Intentionality Condition* (I).

(I) A subject, *a*, is morally responsible for an action, *x*, if and only if *a* does *x* voluntarily.

According to this reading of Aristotle, it is appropriate to morally praise or blame a child or an animal for an action on a particular occasion if that subject acts voluntarily. But is (I) a plausible principle of moral responsibility?[38] Richard Sorabji and Martha Nussbaum defend the plausibility of this principle.[39]

Consider Nussbaum's rationale for endorsing (I). She argues that applying moral praise and blame to beings that act voluntarily but who cannot deliberate and choose allows us to use such evaluations to aid in their moral development. In this way we can revise and modify the appropriate objects of a being's desire as she reaches out and aims for things in the world. This account is well suited to explain the transition from the pre-deliberative stages of a child's life to the point at which the child becomes a full-fledged moral agent who has values and strives for the ultimate good. "Praise and blame are from the beginning not just pushes, but appropriate modes of communication to an intelligent creature who acts in accordance with its own view of the good."[40] Nussbaum's reasons for defending (I) are convincing in the case of children since typically children *will* develop into full-fledged moral agents who deliberate and strive for the ultimate good. But what about animals? Unfortunately, Nussbaum's rationale for defending (I) does not apply obviously to animals since animals will never develop into beings that have values that we will try to shape by communicating our praise and blame. This does not mean that we will be in the business of using pushes or shoves to move animals in one way rather than another. This supposes wrongly that animals are like mechanisms in their movements. We may use intentional descriptions to appropriately characterize the behavior of animals and to capture the fact that they act voluntarily. But it is not so readily apparent that we should include animals in that class of things that are morally responsible. If Aristotle is right that both children and animals act voluntarily and, if principle (I) is at least an initially plausible condition for moral responsibility, then we need some additional reasons for thinking that animals, too, should be held morally responsible for their actions.

CONCLUSION

Childhood animality is a term I have borrowed to stand for the close associations between children and animals. The philosophical point I have pursued in this chapter is how the close association between children and animals is mirrored in several theories of moral responsibility.

Strawson's theory of the reactive attitudes has no precise location for either children or animals. We cannot characterize our various practices and complex relationships involving animals by either the participant attitude or the objective attitude. Likewise, our attitudes toward children cannot be neatly classified according to Strawson's scheme because children are on the way to becoming full-fledged members of the moral community. While Wallace's account of what it means to be a proper target of the reactive attitudes gives us more precision about whether or not it is fair to hold children and animals morally accountable, by my understanding of reflective self-control neither children nor animals have the minimal degree of these powers to be held morally responsible. Both are exempt according to this "rationality condition" for moral accountability. If children are believed to be like animals in their emotional capacities, their inability to justify or grasp moral principles, or their lack of volitional control, then we will not be surprised by their mutual exclusion as proper subjects of moral responsibility. But accepting such a popular *story* may result in our failing to identify genuine moral thinking and particular instances of normative competency in young children.

What I have urged us to consider here is that children are morally appraisable not because there are merely pragmatic reasons for treating them in this way but because our practical regard for children reveals that there are contexts where it is appropriate to extend to them moral praise and blame based on their limited grasp of moral concepts and their participation in moral practices connected to the understanding of these concepts. The prerequisites for doing so, at the very least, are that children understand the morally salient features of a particular situation.[41] In order to explain the moral culpability of children who are on their way to becoming full-fledged members of the moral community, we ought to employ a more liberal principle of responsibility. One plausible candidate is Aristotle's principle (I) that states that a subject is morally responsible if and only if she acts voluntarily.

In the next chapter we further explore the idea that both children and animals are alike in being morally responsible because they satisfy Aristotle's conditions for acting voluntarily. How we use the concept of blame to talk about animals, the differences between what wild and trained animals know, and comparisons between training animals and the moral education of children are topics that allow us to more closely examine the justifications for morally appraising animals.

NOTES

Sections of this chapter and the next are borrowed from my article titled "The Moral Responsibility of Children and Animals," forthcoming in the journal *Thinking*.

1. Matthew Lipman, *Lisa* (Montclair, NJ: Institute for the Advancement of Philosophy for Children, 1983), p. 2.

2. Matthew Lipman, and Ann Margaret Sharp, *Ethical Inquiry: Instructional Manual to Accompany Lisa*, 2nd ed. (Lanham, MD: University Press of America, 1985), p. 13.

3. Gene Myers coined the term *childhood animality* to refer to three contrasting cultural stories about children and animals that are familiar to most of us. First, that children are like animals in that both are closer to nature, where nature is understood to stand for wildness and what is untamed. One value judgment about this comparison is that the animal-like natural state is, as Hobbes would say, "Solitary, poor, nasty, brutish, and short." It must be overridden, controlled, and civilized. A second story linking children and animals casts these beings as natural but innocent and good. In the romantic tradition of Rousseau, children and animals have not yet become corrupted by society but live and act spontaneously and unrestrained. They are equally in need of protection by loving parents or guardians or by laws that prohibit cruelty. In the third kind of cultural story identified by Myers, children and animals occupy the same stage of evolutionary development. Based on the idea that "ontogeny recapitulates phylogeny," developing children, as well as members of primitive societies, represent an early evolutionary step. See Gene Myers, *Children and Animals: Social Development and Our Connections to Other Species*, ed. Mihaly Csikszentmihalyi, *Lives in Context* series (Boulder, CO: Westview Press, 1998); Paul Smeyers and Colin Wringe, "Adults and Children," in *The Blackwell Guide to the Philosophy of Education*, ed. Nigel Blake, Paul Smeyers, Richard Smith, and Paul Standish (Oxford, UK: Blackwell Publishing, 2003).

4. S. Freud, *Totem and Taboo: Some Points of Agreement between the Mental Lives of Savages and Neurotics*, trans. J. Strachey (New York: Norton, 1950), pp. 126–27.

5. Katherine C. Grier, *Pets in America: A History* (Chapel Hill: University of North Carolina Press, 2006), p. 172. In her fascinating book, Grier documents and discusses these points of similarity between children and animals.

6. See, for example, Harry Frankfurt's characterization of "wanton" agents who have first-order desires but no second-order volitions. Included in this category are nonhuman animals and all very young children. Harry Frankfurt, "Freedom of the Will and the Concept of a Person," in *Agency and Responsibility*, ed. Laura Waddell Ekstrom (Boulder, CO: Westview Press, 2001), p. 82.

7. Joel Feinberg makes a similar point about Aristotle's conditions required for "voluntary action" and those required for "deliberate choice." The standards for acting voluntarily, Feinberg says, diverge from "common sense" in that they fail to distinguish between "infants, mentally ill persons, mentally retarded persons, even animals." On the other hand, the concept of deliberate choice is "so elevated a test of voluntariness that relatively few acts could satisfy it." In this work I attempt to explain *why* in the case of children and animals we should seek a middle road between these two kinds of conditions for responsibility. See Joel Feinberg, *Harm to Self*, 4 vols., vol. 3, *The Moral Limits of the Criminal Law* (Oxford: Oxford University Press, 1986), pp. 114–16.

8. Some theories of responsibility may be ill suited to attempt to explain how children and animals are morally appraisable because they rely on rationalistic conditions. Theories that *may* be "rationalistic" in this sense include Frankfurt's "hierarchical" model of moral responsibility, Watson's evaluational requirement for free agency, and Susan Wolf's "Reason View," as well as Aristotle's condition for moral responsibility stated in terms of deliberate choice. See Aristotle, *Nicomachean Ethics*, trans. Terence Irwin, 2nd ed. (Indianapolis: Hackett, 1999) (NE III.2); Frankfurt, "Freedom of the Will and the Concept of a Person"; Gary Watson, "Free Agency," in *Agency and Responsibility*, ed. Ekstrom; and Susan Wolf, "The Reason View," in *Agency and Responsibility*, ed. Ekstrom. Typical of this kind of theory, R. P. Wolff writes, "It is quite appropriate that moral philosophers should group together children and madmen as being not fully responsible for their actions, for madmen are thought to lack freedom of choice, so children do not yet possess the power of reason in a developed form." See R. P. Wolff, *In Defense of Anarchism* (New York: Harper Torchbooks, 1970), p. 12.

My argumentative point does not depend on classifying these theories as *rationalistic*. We can certainly inquire about any account of responsible agency whether or not it accommodates the alleged normative competence of children and animals as kinds of subjects, as I do here in an illustrative way by looking at the details of R. Jay Wallace's theory.

9. Peter Strawson, "Freedom and Resentment," in *Perspectives on Moral Responsibility*, ed. John Martin Fischer and Mark Ravizza (Ithaca, NY: Cornell University Press, 1993).

10. Ibid., p. 50.

11. Ibid., p. 57.

12. Ibid., p. 52.

13. Ibid., p. 55.

14. Ibid., pp. 60–61.

15. Susan Dwyer, "Moral Development and Moral Responsibility," *Monist* 86, no. 2 (2003): 185.

16. R. Jay Wallace, *Responsibility and the Moral Sentiments* (Cambridge, MA: Harvard University Press, 1996).

17. Ibid., p. 154.

18. Ibid., p. 157.

19. Ibid.

20. Ibid., p. 160.

21. Ibid., p. 162.

22. Ibid., p. 167.

23. See, for example, Ann Diller, "Knowing Better," in *Thinking Children and Education*, ed. Matthew Lipman (Dubuque, IA: Kendall/Hunt, 1993).

24. Ibid., p. 709.

25. Gareth B. Matthews, *Philosophy and the Young Child* (Cambridge, MA: Harvard University Press, 1980).

26. Ibid., p. 28.

27. Gareth B. Matthews, *Dialogues with Children* (Cambridge, MA: Harvard University Press, 1984), p. 95.

28. For example, Wallace uses this rather specific description of what it means to have a participant understanding of the principle of nonmaleficence:

One will only be able to apply this principle to a wide array of situations if one has a sophisticated understanding of the concept of *harm,* knowing what kinds of treatment would count as harmful to another person (inflicting physical pain, causing psychic anguish or distress, damaging a person's reputation or interests, and so on). Furthermore, one must have some appreciation for the considerations that make it wrong to harm other people in these ways. These considerations need not take the form of a further justification for the principle of nonmaleficence itself—for present purposes, I should like to leave it open whether this principle requires or admits of a further justification. But if there are such further justifications available, one should have at least the ability to grasp the reasons that those justifications cite (perhaps as a result of the kind of reflection prompted by "hard cases"). And if there are no such justifications, so that the principle of nonmaleficence is itself basic, that too should be the sort of point one is able to understand. Otherwise one's deployment of the principle of nonmaleficence will have a wooden quality, rendering it ill-suited to guide one through the complexities of the moral life. Beyond this basic ability to appreciate the concepts and values involved in moral justifications, one will also need ancillary abilities of attention, concentration, and judgment, to bring moral principles accurately to bear on particular situations of action, and to focus effectively on the conclusions they support in deliberating about what to do. (Wallace, *Responsibility and the Moral Sentiments,* p. 158)

29. A child who acts in accordance with this kind of reason may be what John Martin Fischer calls "strongly reasons-responsive," which he says is a sufficient condition for moral responsibility. See John Martin Fischer, "Responsiveness and Moral Responsibility," in *Responsibility, Character, and the Emotions,* ed. Ferdinand Schoeman (Cambridge: Cambridge University Press, 1987), pp. 86–87.

30. See Lawrence Kohlberg, *The Philosophy of Moral Development:*

Essays on Moral Development, vol. 1 (San Francisco: Harper & Row, 1981); Jean Piaget, *The Moral Judgment of the Child* (New York: Free Press, 1965).

31. Gareth B. Matthews, "Concept Formation and Moral Development," in *Philosophical Perspectives in Developmental Psychology,* ed. James Russell (Oxford, UK: Basil Blackwell, 1987), p. 185.

32. Michael S. Pritchard, *On Becoming Responsible* (Lawrence: University Press of Kansas, 1991), p. 23.

33. See Aristotle, *The Complete Works of Aristotle: The Revised Oxford Translation,* 2 vols., *Bollingen Series Lxxi.2* (Princeton, NJ: Princeton University Press, 1984), *De Anima* III.9.

34. Aristotle, *Nicomachean Ethics* (*NE* 1111a25–26) (11b8–9) (44b8). See also Nancy Sherman, *The Fabric of Character* (Oxford, UK: Clarendon Press, 1989), pp. 160–62.

35. Aristotle, *Nicomachean Ethics,* III.1.

36. Richard Sorabji also adds that when voluntary action is discussed in *EE* 2.9, Aristotle qualifies the "internal origin" requirement so that, additionally, voluntary actions are those that are "up to the agent," where there is a genuine possibility of things turning out either way depending on the agent herself. See Richard Sorabji, *Animal Minds and Human Morals: The Origins of the Western Debate* (Ithaca, NY: Cornell University Press, 1993), p. 108.

37. Aristotle, *Nicomachean Ethics* (1109b30–35).

38. Standard challenges to (I) include cases where irresistible psychological impulses, such as beliefs and desires, are implanted in the agent causing her to act and cases where the agent may be inflicted with physiological cravings that are not caused by the agent herself. In these kinds of cases the cause of the action is in some obvious way "internal" to the agent, but we may be reluctant to hold her morally responsible for what she does. For a discussion of how philosophers have grappled with the "freedom-relevant condition," see John Martin Fischer and Mark Ravizza, eds., *Perspectives on Moral Responsibility* (Ithaca, NY: Cornell University Press, 1993); Ishtiyaque Haji, *Moral Appraisability: Puzzles, Proposals, and Perplexities* (New York: Oxford University Press, 1998). A challenge to the "cognitive condition" of principle (I) is considered in more detail in chapter 7.

39. Aristotle's apparent endorsement of (I) is controversial, since in the *Nicomachean Ethics* Aristotle complicates his earlier account by restricting the class of morally responsible beings to those who are capable of deliberation and choice. To be more precise,

(D) *a* is morally responsible for doing *x* if and only if (a) *a* does *x* voluntarily, and (b) *a* is capable of deliberating about *x*.

Terence Irwin argues that the more plausible account of moral responsibility Aristotle offers is really (D) rather than (I). The presence of both accounts is explained by saying that Aristotle makes several attempts to formulate one criterion for the ascription of responsibility, and (D) is the preferred criterion. On Irwin's interpretation, Aristotle is mistaken to initially extend moral praise and blame to children and animals, since moral responsibility more appropriately attaches to beings that are capable of deliberating and choosing how to act, as these reflect virtues and vices of moral character. I do not try to adjudicate between these different interpretations of Aristotle. About this issue see Terence Irwin, "Reason and Responsibility in Aristotle," in *Essays on Aristotle's Ethics*, ed. Amelie Oksenberg Rorty (Berkeley: University of California Press, 1980); Martha Nussbaum, *The Fragility of Goodness: Luck and Ethics in Greek Tragedy and Philosophy* (Cambridge: Cambridge University Press, 1986), pp. 282–86.

40. Nussbaum, *The Fragility of Goodness: Luck and Ethics in Greek Tragedy and Philosophy*, p. 286.

41. These features of moral thinking in children can be accommodated by Haji's theory of moral appraisability. On this account the necessary and sufficient conditions for being morally appraisable include, roughly, "having a non-culpable belief that one is doing something morally obligatory, right, or wrong"; having "appropriate responsibility grounding control in performing it"; and having "authentic actional springs, such as desires that are truly one's own." Haji suggests that on this view at least some children can satisfy all of these components, where some of these (authenticity and control) are matters of degree. Ishtiyaque Haji, August 2007. See also Haji, *Moral Appraisability: Puzzles, Proposals, and Perplexities.*

Chapter Seven

BAD WOLVES

In the last chapter we considered where to locate children and animals in Strawson's theory of the reactive attitudes. On such a theory of moral responsibility that takes our reactive attitudes toward other human beings as constitutive of moral responsibility ascriptions, it is at least plausible to imagine that our emotional relationships with animals signal our moral relationships with them. But we found that our conflicting practices did not settle the issue about whether our emotionally responsive attitudes toward animals are essentially reactions to moral beings, or whether these attitudes should be characterized as "objective attitudes," by regarding animals as "objects of social policy" to be "managed, handled, cured, or trained." Aristotle's principle (I) is a helpful contribution to our thinking about this issue since it implies that both children and animals are morally responsible because they have the capacity to act voluntarily. But is (I) a plausible principle of moral responsibility? Nussbaum's reasons for defending Aristotle on this point apply most naturally to children. But we have yet to see why it would make sense to say that animals, too, should be considered morally responsible beings.

In what follows I consider two possible reasons for allowing that some animals are the kinds of beings that should be held morally responsible and blameworthy for their actions. In the first section of this chapter I explain and evaluate the idea that children and animals are alike in their capacity for morally laden emotions. Following this, I investigate the idea suggested by Richard Sorabji that perhaps trained animals are morally responsible for their actions. As a way of beginning our inquiry consider the following fictional story about blaming wolves and what this might imply about our practice of holding actual animals morally accountable.

STORY—*THE LOOP*

A wolf creeps silently closer to a baby in a bassinet left unattended for a moment on the porch of a ranch house in Hope, Montana. While the mother is temporarily distracted, the wolf approaches the porch but leaves the baby unharmed after killing one of the farm dogs. This is the opening scene of *The Loop*, a novel by Nicholas Evans.[1] The story begins in this way by conjuring up a fear of what the wolf might do or be capable of. But as the story unfolds we see only this fearful possibility and never the realization of the threat and beastliness of wild wolves.

Evans's novel is about the politics, economics, and the emotional terrain of characters who take an interest and concern with wolves. The cast of characters includes Buck Calder, the wealthy and arrogant third-generation landowner who rides roughshod over his family and who is the public face of those townspeople who rally against wolves. Luke, his son, defies his father by virtue of his emotional sensitivity as well as his interest in living rather than dead wolves. Luke gravitates toward Helen, a biologist temporarily employed in Hope to track and radio-collar the local wolf population to verify whether or not these wolves are killing livestock. Other minor characters represent politically opposing stations; those employed by the Fish and Wildlife Service to monitor the Wolf Recovery Program, as well as local ranchers who defy the federal laws protecting wolves by hunting and killing any wolves they see. Their motto is "No wolves, no way, nowhere." The most interesting antiwolf character is Mr. Lovelace, the old wolfer, who is enticed out of retirement by Buck Calder and surreptitiously hired to trap and kill the local wolf population, including the pups that are born that spring. Mr. Lovelace has a reputation for "effective" wolf control because his father created the *Lovelace Loop*, a cluster of separately baited hooks designed to capture and kill wolf pups when they make their first venture from the den in their mother's absence. Initially Mr. Lovelace seems to neither despise nor care about the wolves aside from getting the job done. But he undergoes a transformation after he is hired by Calder. A conversation he has with his wife just before she died comes back to haunt Lovelace. She alludes to all the animals Lovelace has killed throughout his professional life and asks, "Do you think, Joseph, their life is the same as ours? I mean, what it's made of, that little flicker or spirit or whatever it is, inside them. Do you think it's the same as what we have inside us?"[2] As Lovelace considers using the loop, he recalls this question and begins to lament his killings. In the end Lovelace prefers to die rather than to continue his work.

The various attitudes toward wolves displayed by the characters in this novel are historically accurate. What these characters think and believe about wolves and how they variously justify their actions by these beliefs will be the focus of our philosophical attention.

Buck Calder is publicly concerned with the economic loss suffered by ranchers who lose livestock to predatory wolves. But Mr. Calder has only a passing interest in his poor neighbor whose livelihood really *does* depend on losing several calves. In contrast, Mr. Calder is the wealthiest ranch owner in Hope. Clearly he does not suffer the same, if any, economic threat by losing a few calves to predation. So his interest in resisting the federal agents and breaking the laws protecting wolves must lie elsewhere.

One striking feature of all the local ranchers is a clear commitment to their *right* to kill wolves even if it means breaking the law. They are, after all, landowners. And they insist on protecting their property against all intruders including wolves and government agents alike. The antipathy that the ranchers feel toward the Fish and Wildlife employees as well as the "overeducated biologists" goes beyond their disagreement with the wolf policy these individuals try to implement. It extends to any governmental intrusion. When a local rancher illegally kills a wolf and deposits it on a table during a town meeting, he is jailed and tried for breaking the federal law protecting wolves. "Abe" refuses legal representation because, as he says, "Lawyers are just wolves in suits."[3] But Calder is more complicated. Because he is a third-generation rancher he represents a long tradition of individualism, enjoying the fruits of his ancestors' efforts and hard work carving out a civilized oasis in the Montana wilderness. But he also represents the actual history of practices and attitudes that accompanied policies of wolf extermination that really did take place in the West from the 1850s until well into the twentieth century. In his mesmerizing book *Of Wolves and Men,* Barry Lopez documents and describes the actual killing of wolves in America and the ideology of this killing. Lopez notes that the rationale for the killing of wolves went far beyond predator control and the preservation of local economies.

> A lot of people didn't just kill wolves; they tortured them. They set wolves on fire and tore their jaws out and cut their Achilles tendons and turned dogs loose on them. They poisoned them with strychnine, arsenic, and cyanide, on such a scale that *millions* of other animals—raccoons, black-footed ferrets, red foxes, ravens, red-tailed hawks, eagles, ground squirrels, wolverines—were killed incidentally in the process. In the thick of the wolf fever they even poisoned themselves, and burned down their own property torching the woods to get rid of wolf havens. In the United States in the period between 1865 and 1885 cattleman killed wolves with almost pathological dedication. In the twentieth century people pulled up alongside wolves in airplanes and snowmobiles and blew them apart with shotguns for sport. In Minnesota in the 1970s people choked Eastern timber wolves to death in snares to show their contempt for the animal's designation as an endangered species.[4]

This is the legacy that the fictional Buck Calder inherits when he insists on a program of killing all the local wolves. Calder seems to be the perfect realization of those men who, according to Lopez, claim to have a right to kill other creatures and even consider it a "duty" to do so. By killing wolves these men rid the world of a "beast of waste and desolation." What makes this rationale plausible is a certain set of beliefs about what wolves are like.

The *character* of the wolf has been described historically in the following ways: the wolf is a loafer who doesn't work for his food;[5] the wolf is an "infidel" who must be eliminated altogether;[6] and the wolf is a coward who preys on defenseless animals like deer.[7] But what surely guarantees the righteousness of killing wolves is the idea that domesticated animals, such as sheep and cattle, are innocent while the wolf is innately evil; a being who deliberately murders and is cognizant of his brutality.[8] In 1904 William T. Hornaday, a respected naturalist accompanied by all the requisite scientific and educational credentials, published *The American Natural History* in four volumes. In the revised fifteenth edition there is this introduction to *carnivara* of the dog family: "Of all the wild creatures of North America, none are more despicable than wolves. There is no depth of meanness, treachery or cruelty to which they do not cheerfully descend . . . in the face of foes capable of defense, even Gray Wolves are rank cowards, and unless cornered in a den, will not even stop to fight for their own cubs."[9] Characterizing wolves as murderers who deliberately act in brutish ways allows for a certain kind of moral rationale for the destruction of all wolves. In this way retribution is justified.

BLAMING

In *Beast and Man* Mary Midgley acknowledges that our common way of talking includes calling animals evil even though we also sometimes revert to characterizing predators as "mechanical" or as "killing machines."[10] Midgley's opinion is that we are fundamentally confused when we describe animals as evil or when we attribute to them any virtue or vice because animals lack an understanding about what they do. Animals do not deliberate and choose to do harm when they kill or injure their prey. For Midgley, the real puzzle is not about the veracity of our ordinary talk about animals but rather *why* we feel compelled to describe animals as evil. Her answer is that by calling animals *evil* we can comfortably distance our human selves from the symbol of evil and all that it represents. When the idea of evil is realized in actual animals then evil is located outside of ourselves, and we can maintain our separateness from it by insisting on the differences between humans and particular kinds of animals, such as the wolf, the crocodile, or the shark. Midgley acknowledges that she is more interested in the "beastly" qualities that lurk within human beings rather than our attitudes toward those so-called evil "beasts without."

Nonetheless, not all animals that we commonly blame are symbols of evil. Gardeners blame rabbits and deer for eating lettuce and carrots from the garden plot, yet we can hardly explain our tendency to use the language of blame in these cases as a way of distancing ourselves from beastliness. Our ordinary talk about animals—both domestic and wild—includes the language of blame. Farmers blame insects for ravaging their crops. Homeowners blame squirrels for rearranging the insulation and for building nests in the attic. As we have seen in both fictional and actual settings, ranch owners blame wolves for killing livestock. Domestic animals are not exempt from the language of blame, although later in this chapter we will investigate the possible differences between blaming wild animals and blaming domestic trained animals. Dogs, for example, are sometimes blamed for dumping over the kitchen trash can and cats are blamed for ripping apart furniture with their claws. The list is quite endless, as anyone who has had much contact with animals knows. Yet how much of this ordinary talk about blaming entails that these animals are *morally* blameworthy for what they do?

Perhaps these uses of blame can be more correctly explained by saying that some animals are *causally* responsible (and causally blameworthy) for what they do. As Lionel Kenner points out in his article "On Blaming," we blame inanimate objects as well as human beings.[11] We blame bad weather for our arthritis, the car's brakes or the road conditions for the accident, and so on. In these cases, Kenner suggests, our blaming has nothing to do with moral disapproval.

What we mean by blame in these contexts is that there is an identifiable cause of an untoward event. By blaming the weather for my arthritis flare-up, I imply that the weather caused my ill health. This causal account of blaming extends to human beings as well. Kenner correctly points out that we can blame the driver of a car for an accident without necessarily implying that the driver was morally blameworthy. Perhaps she was a thoroughly proficient driver but lacked the necessary quickness of reflex to circumvent an obstacle. In an important sense she could not have displayed more skill than she actually had to avoid crashing the car, and for this reason we do not morally condemn the driver. Yet she was to blame because her driving was the cause of the accident.

Nonetheless, the nonmoral sense of blame will not adequately explain many of our examples that involve blaming animals. There is an important sense in which the rabbits who eat the lettuce plants in my garden *could have acted otherwise.* These rabbits might have desired and chosen some other type of vegetation on a particular day. This example is different from both the case of blaming inanimate objects (which don't choose or desire anything) and the case of blaming the driver who lacked the skill to avoid the accident and who couldn't choose to do anything but maneuver the car to the best of her ability. The problem is that a causal explanation leaves out any reference to intentions to act, and we do appropriately use intentional language (beliefs and desires) to explain some animal behavior.

Moreover, Midgley's charge that we are merely confused in our way of talking about animals underestimates the deep level of engagement that humans have with animals that sometimes expresses itself in emotional language. In particular, how should we explain our attitudes of adoration, love, respect, and compassion that we often take toward animals? These attitudes, as well as indignation, fear, and hostility, reflect an engagement with both domestic and wild animals that is normally reserved for our interactions with human beings. In fact, contrary to Midgley's claim that we use the concept of beastliness to distance ourselves from animals, the idea of childhood animality that I discussed in chapter 6 is an equally popular and compelling comparison that marks what is alleged to be a close similarity between children and animals. "What is an infant . . . but a brute beast in the shape of a man? And what is a young youth but (as it were) a wild untamed ass-colt unbridled?"[12] We now turn to evaluating the possibility that what children and some animals share are morally laden "simple" emotions. If this is so, we will have some justification for saying that both children and animals are alike in being morally appraisable.

SHARING "SIMPLE" EMOTIONS

Remember de Waal's remark about Georgia, the chimpanzee who sprays visitors with water when they walk outside her enclosure? "But why let her off the hook that easily? Why would any human being who acts this way be scolded, arrested, or held accountable, whereas any animal, even a species that resembles us so closely, is considered a mere passive instrument of stimulus-response contingencies?"[13] What de Waal believes we share with chimpanzees is our capacity for feeling and emotion, what he calls "cognitive empathy." In chapter 5 we speculated about whether or not cognitive empathy is a morally laden emotion. We concluded that de Waal does not specify his definition of this kind of emotion state completely enough to capture its moral significance. For de Waal, cognitive empathy involves appraising another's situation. But when we contrasted this definition with the Aristotelian idea of ethical perception, we saw what was missing from de Waal's definition to make cognitive empathy morally significant. Ethical perception is a way of seeing or construing a situation where the agent is cognizant of and sensitive to the *moral* particulars of that situation. Being able to "read the circumstances" is a kind of expertise that is developed like a skill as the moral virtues are developed, through experience, practice, and by interactions with others.

Even so, it might be argued that children who have not yet developed the virtues associated with mature ethical perception can still be emotionally responsive to others in a way that is morally significant. And perhaps it is these uneducated and "simple" emotions that are shared between children and some animals. After discussing how children can be morally appraisable in chapter 6 we are in a better position to evaluate the claim that children and animals are alike by sharing the capacity for morally laden emotions.

How should we characterize a child's capacity to be emotionally responsive in a way that matters to morality? Consider the following description by Nancy Sherman about how appropriate feeling in children is cultivated as part of the development of their moral character. Sherman is providing an account that she says is consistent with Aristotle's brief remarks on the habituation of character, including the emotions and the moral guidance that parents attempt to provide in order to bring this about.

> We should begin by asking how the perceptions constitutive of the emotions, and ultimately of moral responses, become refined. The parent, like the orator, is in the position of persuading. He or she makes prescriptions to the child and the child listens out of a complex set of desires (love of parents, the desire to imitate, fear of punishment, hope of reward, etc.). But the parent aims not simply to affect specific actions or desires; e.g. to thwart greed, to encourage com-

passion, to temper anger. Rather, part of what the parent tries to do is to bring the child to see the particular circumstances that here and now make certain emotions appropriate. The parent helps the child to compose the scene in the right way. This will involve persuading the child that the situation at hand is to be construed in this way rather than that, that what the child took to be a deliberate assault and cause for anger was really only an accident, that the laughter and smiles which annoy were intended as signs of delight rather than of teasing, that a particular distribution, though painful to endure, is in fact fair—that if one looked at the situation from the point of view of the others involved, one would come to that conclusion.[14]

The moral education of children and the developing degree of moral culpability that accompanies this education proceeds by asking the child to attend to the morally salient features of a situation, to "compose the scene in the right way." The child is directed to grasp moral concepts like fairness or kindness and is guided to feel in ways that are appropriate to particular situations. By this I mean to refer to more than the fact that children and adults have a facility for language that makes it possible to exchange ideas about concepts like fairness. The practice of morality opens out into myriad social settings where our emotions are judged to be sometimes appropriate or sometimes not because these are directed at the wrong person or informed by reasons that are not relevant. Learning to compose the scene in the right way is learning to make these evaluations so that our emotional responsiveness fits the situation. Ethical perception is directed to these particulars that matter morally in a wide range of activities and settings. Yet children are not born with ethical perception nor do they acquire this skill by merely learning rules about conduct. To borrow from Matthews's paradigm model of moral development, we might say that grasping a "simple moral paradigm," such as giving a toy away to be kind, involves a significant facility with human moral and social practices in general.

Consider how we might invite a child to explore the act of giving, as well as the simple presumption that giving is good. We might read a story together about giving or reflect on an event in the child's own experience (e.g., a birthday party where many gifts were given to a friend or classmate and "goody" bags were distributed to those who attended). What it means to give might then be examined together by discussing the following questions and possible scenarios:

- Is giving always the right thing to do?
- Can you give away something that doesn't belong to you?
- If you give someone a hug and you get a hug back, what does that mean?
- If you give your dog a hug and you don't get a hug back, what does that mean?
- If you give someone a gift, should you expect to get something back?
- If you give someone a kick, should you expect to get it back?
- If you have a cold, should you try to give it to other people?
- If I catch your chicken pox, does that mean you gave it to me?[15]

These questions illustrate how a simple moral paradigm like giving a present to a friend might, on closer investigation, open out into complex social settings that demand finely tuned assessments and evaluations. Grasping a moral concept and attending to those features that make it morally significant is really quite an intellectually complicated task. But even young children have the cognitive and affective capacities that make this kind of moral education possible, and because this is so they can be the subjects of moral praise and blame.[16]

We began this section by considering the possibility that chimpanzees and children share emotions, like sympathy, where these emotions play a role in the very early stages of the moral development of children. I believe this comparison between children and chimpanzees is not all that plausible once we closely attend to how the moral development of children emerges from the mutual emotional responsiveness between children and adults who are concerned with their upbringing. The mistake here is the idea that moral development in children begins with "simple" emotions, where the concept of emotion employed is stripped of its connection to those judgments and appraisals that children make about the morally relevant features of their experiences. Having a paradigm of a moral kind like *fairness* or *generosity* is not having a fixed or static feeling; it is a conceptual work in progress. For example, distributing an equal number of cookies to classmates may be the starting point for applying this concept of fairness to other settings, recording an adult's reaction of disapproval in one instance, and being sensitive to an encouraging smile on yet another occasion. This is just what it means to participate in a moral practice from the beginning stages of one's life, and not just for adult humans who have more highly intellectual reasoning abilities and skills. Can chimps acquire this expertise and facility with these kinds of moral practices? I have no argument that this is, in principle, impossible. But reflecting on exactly how children cultivate emotions that are responsive to moral particulars makes it seem improbable that chimpanzees are like children in this respect. For this reason I doubt that chimpanzees should be properly credited with the kind of emotional responsiveness that matters to moral responsibility, praise, and blame.

Even so, we should not be tempted by the false alternative that de Waal offers in the passage quoted earlier in this chapter. De Waal implies that if we fail to hold Georgia morally accountable for spraying unsuspecting visitors with water, then this is tantamount to considering her a "mere passive instrument of stimulus-response contingencies." There is no reason for thinking so. If we follow Aristotle's recommendation for classifying children and animals as beings that have desires, selectivity of perception, and attention that enables them to reach out for something in the world, then Georgia shares with children as well as adult human beings the capacity for acting voluntarily.[17] By virtue of this classification we may use intentional language to describe her actions and behavior. Denying her morally laden emotional states does not imply that she is a mere object whose movements are explained by internal and external pushes and shoves.

We have yet to consider another reason for thinking that animals may be morally responsible. Richard Sorabji also endorses Aristotle's principle (I) as a plausible interpretation of Aristotle on moral responsibility. And because he also accepts Aristotle's view that children and animals act voluntarily, he concludes that some animals may be the proper subjects of moral responsibility ascriptions. Sorabji says that "he sees nothing wrong" with the consequence that "non-rational animals can sometimes be held [morally] responsible."[18] A *trained* dog, Sorabji says, may be morally responsible for biting if it had the appearance that biting is wrong.[19] In support of this claim Sorabji refers to the work of Vicki Hearne, an animal trainer, who asserts about a particular dog that it had enough "moral sense to restrain the over-aggressive police handler for whom it was working."[20] Does a trained animal deserve our moral praise and blame by virtue of what that animal knows? An affirmative answer is strongly suggested by Hearne herself.

THE MORAL RESPONSIBILITY OF TRAINED ANIMALS

The striking feature of Vicki Hearne's books is the moral language she uses to describe the developing relationship between a trainer and an animal.[21] Both animals and their handlers become "responsible" and "mutually trustworthy" in the process of training. Good trainers respect what an animal knows. But respect sometimes breaks down, and in these cases animals are culpable for what they do or fail to do. "People who deliberately lead each other astray are considered culpable because it is assumed that they are capable of behaving well. (Chimps are not assumed to be capable of behaving well.) And dogs and horses, like doctors, teachers, and judges, don't necessarily get out of it when carelessness or some other lapse in concern is to blame rather than mischievousness or malice."[22]

Hearne's parenthetical remark that "chimps are not capable of behaving well" is worth explaining since we devoted part of chapter 5 to discussing whether or not the targeted helping behavior observed in chimpanzees may be motivated by morally laden emotions like sympathy. Hearne is making the point that domestication makes possible a certain kind of training of an animal. Of course, wild animals can be taught to behave in certain ways as we know from watching animal performances in circuses. But what is distinctive about domestic animals, she believes, is the way that they can and do acquire "social skills" and a "vocabulary" that mirror human practices and human expectations. The result of acquiring this vocabulary is that dogs and horses, for example, really do display a kind of trustworthiness and reliability that animal trainers recognize. A trained police dog "understands many forms of human culture and has his being within them. . . . He knows what belongs and what doesn't, sharing our community and our xenophobia as well."[23] Wolves that have been tamed or raised by human beings, and even chimpanzees that have been adopted by humans and raised as members of a family, are still wild, Hearne maintains. The best outcome for captive chimps that have grown too difficult to live with in proximity is that they be returned to the wild. They can be trained after a fashion but never find their way as participants in human culture.[24]

Hearne may be right about the differences between training wild animals and domestic animals. I'll leave that discussion for those who know and work with these kinds of animals. In any case, I believe she has articulated an idea that is crucial to our inquiry. We are trying to decide whether or not it is warranted to extend the language of moral praise and blame to subjects who are not human. But Hearne is reminding us that it is our human practices of expectation, obligation, and standards of behavior—our moral culture—that we are seeking to extend in this way. Given that we are testing the limits of our concept of moral appraisability, we might predict that the best nonhuman candidates who qualify for this status will be those subjects who most closely approximate understanding our normative standards. This involves understanding, for example, what is forbidden, discouraged, expected, hoped for, required, or celebrated. If Hearne is right that it is domestic animals that have the facility to be trained, and *good* training brings about an understanding of human culture, then our investigation about moral appraisability should focus on trained domestic animals.

The question I want to try to answer is whether or not the language of moral responsibility and moral blame applied to *trained* animals is warranted. The reason we might believe so is that trained animals do seem to know enough about the actions they perform in order for us to hold them to a standard of behavior. Hearne is exactly right to bring to our attention the intentional language used by those who work with animals to describe their actions. If we did not refer to the wants, desires, fears, or goals of a horse or a dog, we could not train them nor would we understand very much about them. Even so, I will argue that it is a mistake to extend the language of moral responsibility even to trained animals.

When Salty, a passionate but undisciplined young birddog, enters Vicki Hearne's life, she (the dog) is oblivious to the expectations that humans sometimes have for dogs. For example, she does not understand that it is inappropriate to jump through glass windows after birds, and so on. As Salty's training advances to retrieving, she comes to understand the seriousness of the command *Fetch* by repetition and by being corrected on the ear when she lies on the dumbbell or when she retrieves a stick or a cat instead. Her transformation into a dog that joyously retrieves on command is significant for both trainer and animal. What does Salty know when she learns how to retrieve in this way, and how has she acquired this knowledge?

While Salty may need a form of "convincing" along the way to learning the command *Fetch*, she herself does not need articulated reasons and explanations to obey. In fact, the training might just as well proceed with whistles, clicks, or hand signals, as it often does with dogs who work in the field hunting and pointing. This is not to minimize what has happened between trainer and dog, but it does reveal that Hearne's use of moral vocabulary to describe training is for our sake, as readers, and not for the sake of the animal. Salty knows nothing about the moral context of the work she does, but this makes no difference in how she learns to retrieve. When Salty is commanded to *Fetch* and she bounds forward to grab the dumbbell even in the presence of other playful dogs and birds flitting overhead, she knows enough about what she is doing for her trainer to hold her to a standard of behavior. The trainer does have an expectation that she retrieve in the presence of any or all of these distractions. And if Salty does not perform the retrieve correctly, her trainer is likely to be resentful or even indignant that Salty has violated these expectations. Does the trainer feel *moral* indignation or reactive moral emotions that are connected to moral responsibility and blameworthiness?

There are some considerations that count against this interpretation. I believe Salty is not cognizant of the morally relevant reasons for obeying the command *Fetch* if there are any.[25] She does not consider the moral consequences of acting one way rather than another, nor does she wonder whether or not she *deserves* the stern words from her trainer if she fails to bring the dumbbell back. Hearne might say that Salty is learning to participate in the human culture where dumbbells get thrown and trainers expect them to be brought back, but I think this falls significantly short of those ingredients that make up moral culture and moral practice. But perhaps more should be said about the differences between what Salty knows once she becomes an accomplished retriever and what young children know as participants in these moral practices. It is here that we can draw a rather important distinction between training animals and educating children.

In some sense both the training of animals and the education of children aim to develop the "critical capacities" of each. And even though I believe Hearne is right to say that some trained animals learn and acquire "human social skills," these animals do not have a facility with human moral practice as we have described it, even to a minimal degree. For example, we do not try to direct an animal's attention to understanding the reasons for her anger or fear, nor do we try to persuade an animal that we mean no offense when we laugh at her antics. Our relationship with even a trained animal does not involve investigating with that animal what it means to be generous by examining the kinds of situations where we give but expect nothing in return, and so on. Some philosophers might seek to explain this idea by saying that trained animals or even "good" chimps fail to have moral emotions or moral concepts because these can be grasped only by language users, and animals do not share with human beings this linguistic competence.[26] Perhaps this is part of it. But I can't help thinking that this difference is not measurable by only one kind of yardstick—the capacity for language. I want to draw our attention to the *thick* practice of morality. This is how moral matters proceed "on the ground" when we are trying to understand, for example, if we should blame ourselves when a friend declares hurt feelings or if she has been overly sensitive. So while I agree that a trained police dog probably is sufficiently cognizant of "human social skills" to refrain from biting the children it visits in the hospital, the dog does not possess an understanding of even very simple moral concerns that prohibit such an action. One way of putting this is to say that trained domestic animals do not participate in the practice of morality. This includes emotional responsiveness and ethical perception where these capabilities are informed by recognizing, judging, and evaluating the morally salient features of a situation. For this reason, trained animals are not morally responsible for their actions. Indeed, using Wallace's terminology, it would be "unfair" to hold them accountable in this way if they fail to grasp any of the morally relevant features of a situation, including those simple paradigms of moral concepts like giving, fairness, selfishness, or kindness that even young children use as starting points for ethical inquiry.

Now we can see what is wrong with Sorabji's defense of (I), Aristotle's condition for being morally responsible. (I) is too weak to capture what we ought to say about the moral responsibility of children and animals since it fails to distinguish the morally relevant differences in their cognitive and affective capabilities. Consequently (I) allows both children and trained animals to "meet the bar" for being morally responsible. Acting voluntarily does require that the agent knows the particular facts surrounding the action she performs. But this knowledge requirement does not distinguish between, for example, knowing not to bite children in a hospital and knowing the *moral* prohibitions against not biting. A trained dog acts voluntarily, but since the conditions for voluntary action do not explicitly require knowledge of moral reasons or even understanding what is morally salient about a particular situation, the dog is not morally responsible for her actions. Nor is she morally blameworthy if she violates our expectations about how she should behave. We might successfully train a dog to divide up cookies equally without eating them, but we will not instruct the dog to divide up the cookies this way because it is fair to do so.

In contrast, even young children can engage in ethical inquiry about moral concepts like fairness and what it means to be generous. They may begin such an inquiry by grasping a moral paradigm of fairness, such as distributing an equal number of cookies to classmates, and understand that this is an instance of fairness. Additionally, they can understand uncomplicated reasons for not harming one another. Because children can and do participate in these moral practices, they engage in moral thinking and action and can be held morally appraisable for some actions they perform.

In order to capture the genuine moral thinking and the normative competency of even young children by a principle of moral responsibility, we should adopt conditions that are less rationalistic than what Wallace identifies as "reflective self-control." Children as well as animals are exempt from responsibility by these conditions because they may not grasp moral principles or they may be unable to justify their moral beliefs in the way that Wallace describes. Alternatively, the weaker "Intentionality Condition" allows that both children and animals are morally responsible because they act voluntarily. This condition, I believe, obscures important differences in the capacities of these kinds of subjects. We can see this by comparing the practice of training animals to the practice of developing moral character and ethical perception in children. In order to explain the moral culpability of children who are on their way to becoming full-fledged members of the moral community, we should employ a kind of responsibility ascription in which the conditions of satisfaction fall somewhere in between voluntary action and reflective self-control. At the minimum, to be morally appraisable one needs to understand something about the concepts of morality in addition to being emotionally and cognitively responsive to moral particulars. Since even trained animals are unable to do this, they are exempt from this sort of minimal responsibility ascription.

CONCLUSION

I began this chapter by telling a fictional story populated by some characters who respect and even love wolves and others who detest wolves and insist on their right to kill any wolf they see. Hating the wolf and regarding him as treacherous, mean, and cowardly are historically accurate attitudes that led to the virtual extermination of the wolf in the United States. This is not merely a tragic incidental fact about our past. It is an occasion to scrutinize the meaning of our emotional engagement with animals both domestic and wild. In all these cases where we blame animals for what they do and our blaming is surrounded by the emotional attitudes such as resentment or indignation, what exactly do we presuppose about animals' capabilities, their freedom to choose, their agency, and their blameworthiness?

Wild animals are like trained domestic animals insofar as they act intentionally and with goals. They may have knowledge of the particular acts they perform. But they do not have ethical perception or moral knowledge. In other words, they do not participate in what we have described as a moral practice. Despite the fact that some people despise certain kinds of animals or regard particular animals as cowardly or deliberately cruel, animals are not morally culpable. Perhaps these attitudes reflect our unrealistic expectations about how animals should act. By examining the assumptions that underlie the idea of childhood animality, such as how children and animals differ in their cognitive and affective capabilities, we are in a better position to evaluate any theory of responsible agency by these "test cases," allowing us to be more precise about how children do partake in the domain of the moral as well as why animals do not.

What we have yet to talk about directly in our discussions about animals, emotion, and morality are the stories themselves. Most of us will agree that narratives that describe what animals think and how they act shape and inform our ideas about emotional and moral kinship. In the next chapter I examine what kind of contribution the animal story makes to our understanding of how we mark the boundary between humans and animals.

NOTES

1. Nicholas Evans, *The Loop* (New York: Dell Publishing, 1998).

2. Ibid., pp. 370–71.

3. Ibid., p. 309.

4. Barry Holstun Lopez, *Of Wolves and Men* (New York: Touchstone, 1978), p. 139.

5. Ibid., p. 138.

6. Evans, *The Loop*, p. 103.

7. Lopez, *Of Wolves and Men*, pp. 147–48.

8. Ibid., p. 146.

9. William T. Hornaday, *The American Natural History* (New York: Scribner's Sons, 1927), p. 22.

10. Mary Midgley, *Beast and Man: The Roots of Human Nature* (London: Routledge, 1978), p. 34.

11. Lionel Kenner, "On Blaming," in *The Spectrum of Responsibility*, ed. Peter French (New York: St. Martin's Press, 1991).

12. Keith Thomas, *Man and the Natural World: A History of the Modern Sensibility* (New York: Pantheon Books, 1983), p. 43.

13. Frans B. M. de Waal, "Morally Evolved: Primate Social Instincts, Human Morality, and the Rise and Fall of *Veneer Theory*," in *Primates and Philosophers: How Morality Evolved*, ed. Steven Macedo and Josiah Ober, *University Center for Human Values* series (Princeton, NJ: Princeton University Press, 2006), p. 61.

14. Nancy Sherman, *The Fabric of Character* (Oxford, UK: Clarendon Press, 1989), p. 171.

15. I owe these questions and the inspiration for making this point to the Institute for the Advancement of Philosophy for Children (IAPC). The IAPC publishes philosophical novels and teacher's manuals for the K–12 curriculum. These questions are from Matthew Lipman, *Getting Our Thoughts Together: Instructional Manual to Accompany Elfie*, 2nd ed. (Montclair, NJ: Institute for the Advancement of Philosophy for Children, 2006), p. 123.

16. Susan Dwyer surveys the empirical research about children's cognitive and affective development and concludes that there are psychological precursors to the reactive attitudes that can be discerned in even very young children. These are, for example, the capacity for empathy; the capacity to attribute emotions to others; the capacity to discriminate between intentional and unintentional harm, and to assign blame accordingly; and the capacity to distinguish between conventional rules and moral rules. See Susan Dwyer, "Moral Development and Moral Responsibility," *Monist* 86, no. 2 (2003); Richard A. Shweder, Elliot Turiel, and Nancy C. Much, "The Moral Intuitions of the Child," in *Social Cognitive Development*, ed. John H. Flavell and Lee Ross (Cambridge: Cambridge University Press, 1981).

17. Aristotle, ed., *The Complete Works of Aristotle: The Revised Oxford Translation*, 2 vols., *Bollingen Series Lxxi.2*, ed. Jonathan Barnes (Princeton, NJ: Princeton University Press, 1984), De Anima III.9.

18. Richard Sorabji, *Animal Minds and Human Morals: The Ori-

gins of the Western Debate (Ithaca, NY: Cornell University Press, 1993), p. 112. A very similar view is suggested by David DeGrazia. DeGrazia distinguishes between "full-fledged moral agency," which requires that the agent deliberate about moral reasons and justifications and a lesser degree of moral agency. DeGrazia makes two claims directly relevant to our study: (1) Moral responsibility of a lesser degree applies to animals that understand "rules of conduct" and (2) Holding animals morally responsible is like holding children morally responsible. For the reasons I give in this chapter, I believe that both of these claims are mistaken. See David DeGrazia, *Taking Animals Seriously: Mental Life and Moral Status* (Cambridge: Cambridge University Press, 1996), pp. 203–204.

19. Sorabji refers to Aristotle's use of *phantasia* to make this point. Though the exact interpretation of this term is complex and controversial, Nussbaum offers this, "*Phantasia*, then, is the animal's awareness of some object of desire. It can serve both to present the object of desire initially and later, to specify the object at hand as what is desired." Martha Nussbaum, *Aristotle's De Motu Animalium* (Princeton, NJ: Princeton University Press, 1978), p. 261.

Aristotle identifies two types of *phantasia*, the deliberative and the perceptual (433b28). Nonhuman animals, because they lack the ability to compare *phantasia* and to deliberate about which to choose, have *phantasia* related only to perception. Ibid., pp. 262–63.

20. Sorabji, *Animal Minds and Human Morals*, p. 112.

21. See especially Vicki Hearne, *Adam's Task: Calling Animals by Name* (New York: Vintage Books, 1987); Vicki Hearne, *Animal Happiness* (New York: HarperCollins, 1994).

22. Hearne, *Adam's Task*, p. 24.

23. Ibid., p. 21.

24. See chap. 2, "A Walk with Washoe: How Far Can We Go?" in Hearne, *Adam's Task*.

25. It may make more sense to speak of the moral reasons for not biting, rather than for not retrieving.

26. See, for example, Richard Joyce, *The Evolution of Morality* (Cambridge, MA: MIT Press, 2006), chap. 3; Robert C. Roberts, "Propositions and Animal Emotion," *Philosophy* 71 (1996).

Chapter Eight

STORIES

Not all stories that attribute emotions to animals are philosophically innocent. This we have seen in earlier chapters by examining how some stories may tempt us to conclude that animals are moral beings but without sufficient justification. Does this mean we ought to abandon the use of animal stories and anecdotes as empirical data about the animal mind? Not at all. But those who wish to use animal narratives as a way of discovering what is true about animals need to be mindful about what is problematic about this methodology and seek to correct for these difficulties. What complicates the use of stories is that they may function in a variety of different ways. Good animal stories can entertain us while they contribute to our understanding of what animals are like, and they certainly have the power to move us emotionally and sympathetically to adopt a philosophical conclusion or an ethical position about animals. As Ralph Lutts writes, "Animals are ideas as well as living, breathing creatures."[1] It is the blurring of the *idea* of animal and the *literal* animal that I hope to shed some light on by focusing on how such stories can be used to discern the real qualities of animals.

By this time the reader may have already formed an opinion about which of the animal narratives read and discussed here depict what real animals are like. Perhaps the following distinction can be made. If we merely want to be entertained, then we should read fictional stories about animals. But if we want to further investigate whether or not *real* animals have emotions then we should confine our attention to those stories that are scientific, plausibly true, or not excessively anthropomorphic. Of course, the problem is to skillfully identify those narratives that are truthful, plausible, or scientific. Martha Nussbaum and Bernard Rollin suggest some criteria for distinguishing between plausible and excessively anthropomorphic narratives, but I believe these criteria are too narrow in their focus and too difficult to apply in particular cases. Instead I recommend that stories about animal emotion be subjected to the kind of analysis I have used throughout this book. This involves clearly defining emotion state concepts and the sense of emotional kinship in the story itself in such a way that we may precisely explain the contribution that emotions make to morality. However, "vetting" a story about animal emotion in this way for its philosophical credibility does not necessarily exhaust its meaning. By paying attention also to the social context of such stories and how they may move us to adopt an ethical position about animals, we can begin to see how stories about animal emotion and morality contribute to an understanding of the value of animals.

THE PROBLEM OF METHODOLOGY

How should animal stories, narratives, anecdotes, or case studies be used to investigate the psychology of animals? While there are surely skeptics who believe that anecdotes have no role to play in descriptions of real animals and how they think, I will not argue against using anecdotes and narratives, per se.[2] As I see it, the problem of methodology is not whether stories and anecdotes should be used at all but *how* and what *kind* of contribution they make to our understanding of the animal mind.

The problem of methodology is well illustrated by the variety of scholarly responses to Darwin, who skillfully employed anecdotes and stories about animals as evidence for his scientific views.[3] But as I have already described in chapter 4, Darwin's stories and anecdotes about the emotions of animals, in particular, are controversial. Recall that some critics charged Darwin with using poor methodology because he relied at times on merely anecdotal accounts of animal behavior. Others have called his descriptive language of animals anthropomorphic.[4] In contrast, there are readers of Darwin who believe that his descriptions of animal emotion tell us facts about what animals are actually like.[5]

Likewise, contemporary writers about animal emotion who use stories and anecdotes struggle with how to mark the distinction between factual descriptions of the animal mind and those that are anthropomorphic or excessively fanciful. *The Smile of a Dolphin: Remarkable Accounts of Animal Emotions* is an anthology of stories about the emotions of animals with contributions by animal ethologists, behavioral ecologists, psychologists, sociologists, and anthropologists.[6] In the preface for this collection, Steven Jay Gould heralds the reinstatement of the "anecdote" or "case study" in science and history, but he is clearly aware of the limitations of this methodology.

Finally, while the scientific experts of this volume present their case studies to pursue their lover's quarrel with conventional limitations upon our understanding of the rich (and highly functional) emotional lives of animals, I must mention my own lover's quarrel with many of the stories in this book—a sure sign of a volume's vibrancy when the writer of a preface must engage the authors in his own dialogue of doubt amidst his prevailing pleasure. Bravo for case studies, and bravo for the inevitable "subjectivity" within any product of this genre. But all the more reason—given the dubiety, even the hostility, of many colleagues—for taking special care to avoid the genuine and serious pitfalls that led the doubters to their exaggerated reactions of pure dismissal in the first place. Yes, we are human and cannot avoid the language and knowledge of our own emotional experience when we describe a strikingly similar reaction observed in another species. But anthropomorphism remains a genuine barrier to understanding these different worlds, and I really doubt that Kierkegaard's issues can bear any more than the most distantly metaphorical (and almost surely misleading) relation to a whale's concern.[7]

Gould only hints that we must take special care to guard against the "genuine and serious pitfalls" inherent to case studies and anecdotes in the study of the animal mind. Bernard Rollin is more explicit, urging us to weed out the "outrageous" and "outlandish" stories from those that are reasonable and plausible.

Once one has in principle allowed the possibility of anthropomorphic, anecdotal information about animal mentation, one must proceed to distinguish between plausible and implausible anecdotes, plausible and implausible anthropomorphic attributions, remembering that even if we are right to be skeptical, implausible accounts may turn out to be true. Many people tell outrageous anecdotes, or interpret them in highly fanciful or unlikely ways, and even publish such non-sense. This should no more blind us to the plethora of plausible anecdotes and reasonable interpretations forthcoming from people with significant experiences of the animals in question, than should the presence of outlandish stories about or outrageous interpretations of human behavior cause us to doubt all accounts of human behavior.[8]

What these authors have in common is a certain view about what counts as the problem of methodology created by animal stories and anecdotes; namely, how to classify the story as literally true or excessively anthropomorphic, metaphorical, implausible, and so on. The role of the story is to *realistically* represent what animals are like psychologically. And the challenge for interpreters of the story and case study is to identify what parts or features of the story are literally true about the animal and which parts are merely fanciful.

There are several things wrong with this way of characterizing the role of animal stories as methodology. First, the implied assumption is that when animal stories and anecdotes are used in the context of scientific inquiry, they have only one kind of meaning—realistic or factual meaning. On the contrary, even in these settings many stories substitute factual content for normative value and encourage readers to embrace these values. I discuss this sense of meaning of the animal story in the last section of this chapter, "The Value of Animal Stories." Second, merely judging that animal stories are realistic representations of what animals are like psychologically ignores altogether how the literary style of the narrative impacts us, the readers, and by doing so how it contributes to our understanding of the animal mind. The positive contribution that narrative and storytelling makes in scientific inquiry is not sufficiently explored even by those authors who endorse the use of the animal narrative as methodology. An exception to this is Martha Nussbaum, who has written extensively about the role of narrative in philosophy and, in particular, about the importance of narrative for investigating both human and animal emotion.[9]

In the next section I explore the idea that using stories and anecdotes to investigate animal emotion is not merely accidental or supplemental data to be vetted only for its literal truthfulness. Rather, the study of animal emotion requires or demands narrative to do justice to the inquiry. William Long, writing in the early 1900s, argues that narrative is the appropriate form for scientific descriptions where the objects of study are nature and animals. Martha Nussbaum argues that understanding the emotions, per se, depends on narrative to capture our experiences of these states. For Nussbaum, what is fanciful in a story does not need to be eliminated but rather put to use by the reader to inspire her imagination.

THE ROLE OF FANCY

When the "Nature-Faker" controversy captured the attention of the popular press during the early part of the twentieth century it was most obviously a debate about the literal truthfulness of the wild animal story. What emerged from nature writers such as William Long, Ernest Thompson Seton, Charles Roberts, and Jack London during this period was a new literary genre: the "realistic animal story." These stories showcased individual animals as the main characters. They were often written from the animals' point of view and made transparent their mental lives, including how they learned, reasoned, and felt emotionally. Even though these stories were wildly popular, they were not intended to merely entertain readers but also to educate. As Thomas Dunlap puts it, the realistic animal stories were "presented not as fiction or fable but as the fruits of nature study backed by science."[10] What made these stories especially controversial was their declared truthfulness. Seton begins his "Notes to the Reader" in *Wild Animals I Have Known* by saying, "These stories are true. Although I have left the strict line of historical truth in many places, the animals in this book were all real characters. They lived the lives I have depicted, and showed the stamp of heroism and personality more strongly by far than it has been in the power of my pen to tell."[11] John Burroughs led the attack on Seton and Long when he published "Real and Sham Natural History" in the *Atlantic Monthly* (March 1903). "[I]n Mr. Thompson Seton's *Wild Animals I Have Known,* and in recent work of his awkward imitator, the Rev. William J. Long, I am bound to say that the line between fact and fiction is repeatedly crossed, and that a deliberate attempt is made to induce the reader to cross, too, and to work such a spell upon him that he shall not know that he has crossed and is in the land of make-believe."[12]

A salient feature of this controversy was about the *form* that scientific descriptions should take. What kinds of descriptions are best for understanding not only what animals are like but our relations to them? Although Burroughs himself was well known as a literary naturalist, his ideas about how to combine subjective, poetic descriptions of animals and nature with objective, scientific accounts were in sharp contrast to writers like Seton and Long.[13] Burroughs believed that science and poetry should go "hand in hand." They each have a contribution to make to our understanding, but the task of each discipline is distinct.

> Science is impersonal and cold, and is not for the heart but for the head. The heart symbolizes so much for us, it stands for the very color and perfume of life, for the whole world of sentiment and emotion—a world that lies outside the sphere

of science. Science may and does beget emotion, because we are emotional beings; it may and does awaken the feeling of the beautiful and the sublime, but this effect is incidental: its office is to enlighten the reason and the understanding. It would not have us sigh or tremble or fear, or worship; it would have us see and understand. To this extent it is the enemy of literature, it cuts out the personal equation and the play of fancy and emotion which is the life of literature.[14]

John Burroughs would have us believe that seeing and understanding what animals are like is distinct from, even an "enemy" of, literature and narrative. But this presupposes that understanding animals is a narrow kind of investigation; one where we might merely record the number of legs on a beetle or the wingspan of a butterfly. The contrasting position is William Long's recommendations to the nature student to use her insight, imagination, and human sympathy in order to really *see* animals as "luminous" living things as opposed to "stuffed specimens."

Long distinguishes between science, or "the world of description," and storytelling about animals characterized as "the world of appreciation."[15] Scientific descriptions of animals classify and catalog these according to general principles. For example, we might classify a mouse as a "long tailed" or a "jumping" variety. But what is left out of such descriptions, Long reminds us, are the individuals. The individual mouse's actions may be interpreted by poets, prophets, and thinkers who will reveal more truth about this particular mouse than science can reveal, "as emotions are more real than facts, and love is more true than economics."[16]

Long is suggesting here that a more accurate and truthful depiction of animals is captured only by a certain kind of narrative, one that singles out individuals as actors going about their daily lives. Scientific descriptions provide us with accounts that are true of kinds of animals; for example, their eating and hunting habits and whatever behavior is common to all members of a species. But such accounts fail to capture the idiosyncratic truths about individual animals. Imagine if we were to write about a human life by resorting to generalized descriptions that are true of all or most human beings; for example, that human beings walk on two legs, eat meat or vegetables but not stones, and so on. Of course, we would concede that such a description is factual, but, additionally, we can see how much is left out. What is missing is an account of how it is for an individual person to live a human life that includes *her* experiences, what motivates her, and what fears, loyalties, hopes, and loves figure into the living of her particular life. According to Long, the stories that we tell about individual animals are crucial to the authenticity of the account and crucial to capturing the real qualities of individual animals. Long puts the point eloquently in this way:

> There is one other thing that the modern nature-writer has learned, namely, that in this, as in every other field of literature, only a book which has style can live. And style is but the unconscious expression of personality. Not only may the personal element enter into the new nature-books; it must enter there if we are to interpret the facts truthfully. Every animal has an individuality, however small or dim; that is certain. . . . And the nature-student must seek from his own individuality, which is the only thing that he knows absolutely . . . to interpret truthfully and sympathetically the individual before him. For this work he must have not only sight but vision; not simply eyes and ears and a note-book; but insight, imagination, and, above all, an intense human sympathy, by which alone the inner life of an animal becomes luminous, and without which the living creatures are little better than stuffed specimens, and their actions the meaningless dance of shadows across the mouth of Plato's cave.[17]

What is striking about Long's recommendations to the nature student is the demand for narrative style in the articulation of *authentic* descriptions of animals. Because the subject of inquiry is an animal, a living thing; we are in danger of getting it wrong about what animals are like if we do not employ narratives that are infused with imagination and sympathy. How can this be so? In what way do stories and the fancy of our imagination bring us closer to understanding the animal mind? For Long, the role of fancy in narrative is to bring us face to face with the *living* animal. By telling or listening to a story about the life of an animal, we achieve an intimacy of description that is meaningful and truthful and, according to Long, more authentic than other kinds of descriptions that merely "catalog" the behavior of an animal. "The truth is, that he who watches any animal closely enough will see what no naturalist has ever seen. This is the simple secret of the wonderful cat story, or the incredible dog story, to be heard in almost every house. It means that, after you have catalogued dogs perfectly, you still have in every dog a new subject with some new habits. Every boy who keeps a pet has something to tell the best naturalist."[18]

Martha Nussbaum finds a role for the fancy of our imagination by characterizing the emotions as lived experiences. For Nussbaum, we are in danger of getting it wrong about what the emotions are like if we do not employ narrative descriptions of these that are infused with imagination and sympathy.

We might begin by asking why narrative is particularly well suited to the study of the emotions, whether it is human or animal emotion. As we have seen in earlier chapters, the general theory that Nussbaum favors and argues for in her book *Upheavals of Thought* is a eudaimonistic theory. According to this view, the emotions are "suffused with intelligence and discernment" and "contain in themselves an awareness of value or importance" directed upon objects, people, and events in the world.[19] Nussbaum maintains that if we are to properly investigate particular emotions such as anger, love, or fear, we must see these in the context of our own attachments to things in the external world and our valuing of these things. Narratives or stories can function so as to bring these attachments before us vividly, and by doing so they will encourage us to imagine our own emotional lives with more clarity and understanding.[20]

An important feature of the methodology Nussbaum employs is the idea that we should begin our investigation into the study of the emotions with our own experiences. Since Nussbaum is attempting to shape a general theory of the emotions, she argues that we need to establish correlations between the science of emotion and at least a common core of the phenomena of emotion that is part of our familiar experience. This approach assumes the "general ability of the reader to identify and classify instances of emotion, such as grief, fear, envy . . ."[21] This way of studying the emotions has a "methodological analogue" when applied to animal emotion. Scientific accounts of human emotions must square with the kinds of descriptions we employ to characterize our human emotional lives. And in the same way the scientific accounts of animals' emotions should be tested against "our best interpretive accounts" of animals' emotional lives or the behavior they display indicative of emotional experience. Since animals themselves cannot speak about their emotional experiences we rely on the story or the narrative about the animal to inform us about the phenomena science can investigate.

But not just any commonsense description of an animal's behavior in a story can function appropriately in this way. What matters is that the author is in a position to know the animal described and can report about the animal's behavior in a way that is empathetic and sensitive to the context surrounding the animal's actions. In this way we can avoid what

Nussbaum refers to as the "twin pitfalls" of either reduc-
tionism about animal mentality (Behaviorism and Materi-
alism) or anthropocentrism.[22]

To illustrate this methodology Nussbaum uses a story by
George Pitcher titled *The Dogs Who Came to Stay*. As the story is
told, Lupa is a distrustful and fearful wild dog who has found
refuge in a shed owned by George Pitcher and Ed Cone. She
initially avoids all attempts to lure her out to be fed by hand
and petted. But eventually Pitcher wins Lupa's trust and she is
welcomed into the family. As Nussbaum describes it the details
of this story illustrate that Pitcher is correct in attributing certain emotions to Lupa. When she initially ducks and hides, it
is because she is fearful of humans. When she eventually, cau-
tiously, wags her tail in Pitcher's presence, the explanation of
her behavior is captured by this description: "although most
humans are to be avoided, you seem to be different."[23] The
details of Lupa's life after she comes to live with George and
Ed demonstrate Lupa's unconditional love and devotion as
well as her loyalty to both men. According to Nussbaum, the
narrative itself supports the idea that animals have emotions
because it is consistent with the scientific data, and it is told by
a person who has intimate knowledge of a particular animal
and who can speculate in an empathetic way about why Lupa
acts as she does. The attributions of emotional states to Lupa
square with her subsequent behavior.

> As the narrative progresses, indeed, it is precisely the inter-
> weaving of reaction and counter-reaction that convinces the
> reader that Pitcher has gotten it right about the dog: he is
> not just standing at a distance, he is involved in an emo-
> tional relationship. Again and again, a tentative hypothesis
> is confirmed by further behavioral interactions, and the
> closeness and responsiveness of the relationship the two
> dogs (mother and son) ultimately develop with Pitcher and

Cone itself permits the dogs to cultivate complex positional emotions that researchers sometimes ascribe only to primates. The reader sees that Lupa and Remus feel love for their human friends, and even something of compassion when they suffer—as well as fear, anger, and joy of various types, associated with various specific goals and projects.[24]

Nussbaum reminds us that attributing emotions to other human beings goes beyond the evidence, involving a projection to the minds of others. It is with a "sympathetic imagination" that we construct the mental lives of human beings and so it should be with animals. "All of our ethical life involves, in this sense, an element of projection, a going beyond the facts, a use of '*fancy*.'"[25]

For Nussbaum, the role of fancy in narrative allows us to "cross the species barrier" to construct the inner emotional lives of animals. This happens in two ways. In the first place the story reveals what is required to get the emotional attribution right. George Pitcher's empathy and intimacy with the dogs is central to the correct attribution of love to Lupa and Remus. But additionally the story has the power to influence the reader to "mine his or her own experiences for similar examples" of animal emotion. By allowing the story to inspire our imaginations about the mental lives of particular animals we may gain a more perspicuous representation of what animals are like; they are beings with complex emotional lives.

But the issue of truthfulness can still intrude, as it did in response to the realistic animal stories of the early 1900s. Even though we may believe that our sympathetic imagination contributes in some way to an "authentic" understanding of animals, we are also right to insist that there be limits to our imaginative understanding of animals as this is shaped by narrative. In other words, it is a real possibility that storytelling may at times cross the line between fact and fiction and deposit us in

the "land of make-believe" as Burroughs warned. Our immediate task then is to try to locate and describe the limits of
fancy in stories about animal emotion.

THE LIMITS OF FANCY

Nussbaum herself raises the possibility that the story *The Dogs
Who Came to Stay* is "suspiciously anthropomorphic," where the
account of love attributed to the dogs is too similar to the
sense of love that Pitcher laments was missing from his own
childhood. But in Nussbaum's opinion what makes Pitcher's
account trustworthy are these features of his story:

- [The author] pursues no theoretical agenda;
- He displays observational capacity to a good theoretical
  end;
- He neither withholds imaginative speculation, nor uses
  it loosely;
- He is keenly aware that the animal has specific capacities
  but is nonverbal;
- He gives an account of the emotions of *dogs*, and not a
  fanciful human projection of emotion.[26]

What is dissatisfying about at least some of these suggested
methodological constraints on narrative is that we are missing
a reliable criterion of application. For example, in order to
decide whether Pitcher (or any other author) "neither withholds imaginative speculation, nor uses it loosely," we must
already have an opinion about the veracity and plausibility of
the story itself. Similarly, our judgment about whether or not
Pitcher has given a "fanciful human projection of emotion"
depends on what we think is plausible about the emotional
attributions made in the story. In other words, our reference

point for assessing the limits of fancy in any given animal story is just our intuitive reaction to that story. Since many people disagree about this very issue—what is to count as plausible or excessively fanciful in characterizing the animal mind in the context of a story or otherwise—these criteria do not help us all that much.[27]

To illustrate how we might struggle to apply Nussbaum's criteria, think back to the three animal narratives we used in chapter 3: Ernest Thompson Seton's story about Lobo, the wolf; E. B. White's children's story *Charlotte's Web*; and Jane Goodall's narrative about Flint, the chimpanzee who seemingly lost the will to survive after his mother died. Of these stories *Charlotte's Web* is, perhaps, most easily ruled "suspiciously anthropomorphic" because the author attributes to spiders, pigs, and other farm animals the capacity to speak and write. But what about the attribution of the emotion of grief and sadness credited to Wilbur, the pig, when his spider friend dies? Is attributing grief to a pig a "fanciful human projection of emotion"? As we have seen by examining animal narratives about emotional kinship, virtue, and moral blame in earlier chapters there might be genuine disagreement about how to answer this question. Of course, this story is not about an actual pig and his friendship with an actual spider, but perhaps the story makes a more general recommendation for attributing emotional sensitivity to real animals.

The story of Lobo is more difficult to classify as obviously anthropomorphic since Seton himself declares that his stories are true. Suppose there was no actual wolf whose life story matched the one that Seton tells in "Lobo: The King of Currumpaw." Would this fictionalization seriously undercut the claim that a wolf might experience grief when he loses his mate? We might be tempted to say that this story has greater plausibility in capturing the real qualities of wolves because Lobo is not depicted as having linguistic competence, unlike the characters in *Charlotte's Web*. But we know that a controversy swirled around nature writers Seton and Long. Not everyone who reads the story of Lobo will agree that the emotional state of grief attributed to a wolf is appropriate and warranted, and there will probably be no consensus about whether or not Seton has used "imaginative speculation . . . loosely."

Nussbaum admits that the attribution of emotions to Remus and Lupa in *The Dogs Who Came to Stay* is a "highly human story," though she maintains that this is no more unreliable than Pitcher's self-report about his own emotional life.[28] But if the story about the love and loyalty that is attributed to Remus and Lupa is a *human* story, then quite rightly it will seem plausible since it will coincide with our own experiences of love, fear, and our attachments and valuing of persons, objects, and goals in the world. When the reader of such a story is encouraged to "mine his or her own experiences for similar examples" of animal emotion, she will have no trouble supplying these since it is the reader's own experience of these emotions that she is using to make sense of the story.

By way of illustration consider again the anecdote by Jane Goodall that we have discussed in earlier chapters. Nussbaum uses this story about Flint, the chimpanzee, as an example of an animal that is properly credited with emotional states. Goodall writes that when Flint lost his mother his life became "hollow and meaningless," and that when she last saw him alive "he was shallow-eyed, gaunt and utterly depressed, huddled in the vegetation close to where Flo had died."[29] Nussbaum suggests that by the use of "fancy" and our sympathetic imagination we can "cross the species barrier."[30] This is not difficult to do when presented with a story like this since we only need to imagine what grief is like in the human case and then imagine that this concept applies to Flint. How do we decide if this application of the concept of grief is excessively fanciful? Goodall's credentials as an observer of chimpanzees certainly qualify her to report about Flint's behavior in a way that is empathetic and sensitive to the context surrounding Flint's actions—one of the features that Nussbaum insists is necessary for getting the story right. But surely being situated in this way does not automatically guarantee that Goodall has correctly applied the concept of grief in this case.[31] We should be open to the possibility that even those who live, work, and play with animals may not correctly attribute emotions to them; not because they are uninformed about animal behavior but because the very concept of emotion employed may not be carefully explained or defined. Ultimately I believe we must be prepared to follow Nussbaum's advice when she suggests that "[p]hilosophy should be responsive to human experience and yet critical of the defective thinking it sometimes contains."[32] This cautionary remark guides Nussbaum's construction of a general theory of the emotions, but it is also good advice when applied to stories about animal emotion.

Alternatively, consider Bernard Rollin's recommendations for how to distinguish between plausible and implausible anecdotes. "Does the anecdote cohere with other knowledge we have of animals of that sort? Have similar accounts been given by other disinterested observers at other times and in other places? Does the interpretation of the anecdote rely upon problematic theoretical notions (such as imputing a grasp of "birthday" to a dog)? How well does the data license the interpretation? Does the person relating the anecdote have a vested interest in either the tale or its interpretation?"[33] Rollin's suggested criteria for the plausibility of stories are, like Nussbaum's, difficult to apply. For example, what should count as a "problematic theoretical notion"? This is the heart of the issue about animal emotion because some, maybe most, pet owners will insist that their dogs, cats, or horses feel a wide range of emotions including jealousy, embarrassment, and compassion. The fact that this is a widespread popular belief, of course, doesn't make it true that animals have these psycho-logical states. So how, exactly, will we decide whether or not a concept is problematic to attribute to a particular animal or even to a kind of animal? Moreover, what if we decide that the author of a story or anecdote *does* have a "vested interest" in the tale or its interpretation? What is the relation between this interest and the truthfulness of the story? If all such stories were ruled implausible for this reason there would likely be no stories or anecdotes to consider.

One main difficulty with both Rollin's and Nussbaum's cri-teria for identifying legitimate narratives about the animal mind is that they underestimate the persuasive quality of a good story. In his article "Anthropomorphic Anecdotalism as Method," Robert Mitchell describes why we should be cau-tious in our interpretations of animal mentality when we are presented with descriptions of animal behavior in the form of stories or anecdotes.[34] Mitchell draws on the work of Bennett and Feldman, authors of *Reconstructing Reality in the Courtroom*, who argue that stories constitute the most effective vehicle for presenting evidence about criminal activities in the court-room.[35] Their research indicates that what can sway judg-ments of the jury is a "well-constructed" story—one that is con-sistent with the main theme and that is internally consistent. Such a story will influence how juries regard the defendant and their judgments of guilt or innocence *even when the evi-dence is relatively minimal.*

This research forms the basis for Mitchell's own empirical studies that examine how animal stories persuade readers. In one study designed by Mitchell, undergraduates were pre-sented with a short description of animals interacting with one another.[36] Subjects were then asked to interpret the behavior of one of the animals described when six different species were depicted: people, chimpanzees, elephants, bears, dogs, and otters. The author reports, "There were no major differences in how the animals were ranked. Subjects described the animal as jealous, protective, neglected, left out, and wanting attention, regardless of the species."[37] Mitchell believes that these results indicate that when an animal is depicted as an actor in a story, it is the consistency and plausibility of the story itself that influences what subjects believe about the mental capabilities of the animal described in the story, rather than how physically similar the animal is to human beings, how phylogenetically close the animal is to human beings, how familiar the kind of animal is, and so on. Mitchell remarks, "Our narrative depictions of animals in stories, cartoons, and films powerfully influence us in our anthropomorphizing and empathizing with animals. . . . Overall, these data suggest that what animals *do* [in a story] may be the most important determinant for people's perception of their psychology."[38] Mitchell's research suggests that a good story may distract us from what else is needed to establish a conclusion about the real qualities of animals. If so, how should we correct for the persuasive influence of a "well-constructed" story to locate the limits of fancy?

By now it should be clear how I would recommend answering this question. The conceptual analysis of narratives about animal emotion that I have undertaken in earlier chapters reveals serious difficulties in justifying those theoretical commitments needed to establish that humans and animals share morally laden emotions. In chapter 2 I asked what concept of emotion is presupposed in narratives that declare our emotional kinship with animals. To understand what it is assumed we share with animals in these narrative settings we needed to employ a theory of emotions that characterizes emotional states as having cognitive-evaluative content that is connected to valuing things in the world. But in some stories about emotional kinship the kinds of emotions attributed to animals are morally laden emotions; they are connected to morality in a particular way that implies that animals and humans are moral kin as well. In those narrative settings that we considered in chapters 3 through 7, animals are described as being morally virtuous, motivated by the right intentional state to perform morally right actions, morally appraisable because they are emotionally responsive to the needs of others, or as the kinds of beings that are likened to children in the early stages of moral development. In all of these cases I have argued that something more is necessary beyond the story itself to establish that animals and humans are moral kin because they share emotions. This something more is a precise account of the moral framework that surrounds the ideas of moral virtue, the development of moral character, perceiving the moral particulars of a situation, the conditions under which we morally praise and blame, and what it means for children to participate in a moral practice. Those who wish to make the case that some animals have morally laden emotions by telling us a story or an anecdote must also be prepared to supply an account of how the concept of emotion employed in the story is morally significant by the way emotions contribute to these particular moral background conditions. Deciding whether or not a particular story, anecdote, or narrative that attributes morally laden emotions to an animal is a "fanciful human projection" is not simply answered without this conceptual lens that focuses on what emotions are and how emotions are connected to morality in the various ways we have explored. I offer just one more example to illustrate why we need to aim for a deeper analysis of emotion state concepts used in narratives about animal emotion.

In the introduction to *The Smile of a Dolphin*, Marc Bekoff writes that most of us believe emotions are "feelings," such as love, hate, fear, joy, happiness, grief, despair, empathy, jealousy, anger, relief, disgust, and so on. But Bekoff tries for a more robust definition by saying, "For our purposes, let's say that emotions are psychoneural processes that express themselves as mood."[39] While Bekoff is careful to warn us that it would perhaps be a mistake to assume that animal emotions are exactly like ours, he is optimistic about the possibility that "feelings" are not limited to mammals alone. "There is increasing evidence that birds, reptiles, and even fish experience some emotions."[40]

Consider, for example, Bekoff's own story that he tells about his dog, "Jethro." Jethro arrives at Bekoff's front door one day with a baby rabbit in his mouth. "Bunny" is still alive but needs care and attention. The entire time that Bunny recuperates in a box in the house and even when he is released and takes up residence in a nearby woodpile, Jethro keeps a watchful eye but never attempts to eat Bunny. Bekoff remarks, "I think Jethro is a truly compassionate soul." This attribution of compassion to the dog is confirmed by Jethro's subsequent behavior of bringing another wet animal home, a young bird. Bekoff concludes, "Jethro has now saved two animals from death. He could thoughtlessly have gulped down either one of them with little effort. But you don't do that to friends."[41]

There is a kind of playfulness about this passage. But since it is Bekoff's interpretation of his dog's behavior that carries the explanatory weight of the story, we should take seriously what he says. Jethro is *compassionate* in his dealings with small defenseless animals. Not only does he bring them to a human to be looked after, he also anxiously watches over their recovery and, most importantly, he doesn't eat them because they are his friends. Compassion is not a value-neutral emotional state. As we have seen in chapter 3, attributing compassion to a human being is typically a way of morally commending her. This moral commendation is explained by analyzing this emotional state so as to include evaluations about what another person or animal needs, the seriousness of this need, and whether or not the object of compassion is blameless for her undeserved suffering. So if Jethro deserves our moral praise for being motivated by compassion it will be because he has some cognizance of these states of affairs.

Notice that if we use Bekoff's own definition of emotion we can make no sense of the story that Bekoff tells about Jethro. By Bekoff's account it is hard to tell what "moods" are supposed to be. But certainly "psychoneural processes" do not need to manifest themselves as moral motivations to act. What is missing from the story and its interpretation is the rationale for attributing a morally laden emotional state to Jethro. Without this readers are left with the idea that what Jethro shares with us are the moral motivations of compassion and the moral connotations of friendship that hold between those who act for the sake of one another. If we haven't bothered to be precise about the concept of compassion, for example, then we may not notice that a significant philosophical move has been made. Once we have specified how compassion is morally significant and why we are disposed to morally praise anyone for having this emotional state, then we can go on to investigate what kinds of creatures have the cognitive capacity for just these moral concepts. In the absence of the supporting conceptual and empirical evidence we may have a fanciful idea only about what animals are really like.

Because I have been critical about how to interpret many narratives about animal emotion surveyed throughout this book, the reader might surmise that I am recommending we do away with these kinds of stories altogether. I *am* urging readers of the animal story to guard against unsupported conclusions about our moral kinship with animals. But if we only confine our attention to the literal truthfulness of stories about animal emotion we may fail to do justice to the positive contribution that stories make to our understanding of the animal mind, and that is to allow us to see animals with "insight, imagination, and intense human sympathy."

READING FOR CONTEXT

When Bernard Rollin recommends a method for distinguishing plausible from implausible animal stories and anecdotes, he is partly right to ask whether or not the person relating the animal anecdote or story has a vested interest in either the tale or its interpretation. This suggestion reminds us about the larger context surrounding the story and what may shape and influence its interpretation. Rollin may have in mind cases where there is a deliberate attempt by the author or reporter of the story to mislead readers. In this case if we know what "vested interest" is present we can try to correct for bias. But there is another way in which context can be relevant to storytelling. Stories may be responsive to social and cultural contexts where these factors find their way into how the characters are depicted and the story line itself. What sometimes makes a particular story, or even a whole genre, popular is whether or not it satisfies the interests of a wider community of readers who share the same cultural space. By way of example, consider again the realistic animal story.

Explicitly the nature-faker controversy was about the literal truthfulness of the animal story. But there was another dimension to this debate. The prevailing science of the late 1800s was dominated by Darwin's theory of evolution, and popular reactions to Darwin's theory were by and large pessimistic. Characterizing these attitudes, Lisa Mighetto writes, "The darker implications of Darwinism had produced despondency among intellectuals on both sides of the Atlantic. 'We are crushed and trampled on remorselessly by the movement of nature,' mourned one Victorian, 'and our feelings count for nothing.' Another noted gloomily that 'Nature means one vast whirlpool of war, death, and agony.' . . . At the end of the century, literary naturalists on both sides of the Atlantic reinforced this view, depicting man as a helpless, inconsequential creature, subject to the whim of natural forces."[42] Moreover, many believed that if humans and animals are linked by evolutionary continuity then the bestial natures of animals are, by extension, character-izations of human nature as well. This was an unflattering and unacceptable conclusion about human beings.

Enter the realistic animal story where animals are digni-fied, courageous, and beneficent. A world inhabited by these wild animals is a world that the ordinary reader can identify with and imagine herself a part of. This is not surprising, because the animals in these stories are very much like us in all *important* respects. Specifically, in Seton's stories animals are depicted as moral exemplars who display the virtues of compassion, altruism, courage, fidelity, parental love, and so on.[43] Evolutionary theory may have threatened the exalted status of human beings by subsuming them into the "vast whirlpool of war, death, and agony," but writers of the realistic animal story discovered morality in nature by characterizing animals as model citizens who shared the same kinds of moral motivations and emotional lives as human beings.

The scientific culture of the early twentieth century rekin-dled an interest in the fundamental question: Where do we locate human beings, as a part of nature or outside of this domain? The realistic animal story answers this question by implying that human beings are a part of nature. But the qual-ities of humans that some might say matter the most—namely, our moral agency, virtuous moral character, freedom to choose, and responsibility for our actions—can be found also in those animals that inhabit nature.[44] If animals and humans are moral kin, then human beings are not unique with respect to morality. Our moral kinship implies that we are located alongside animals in the natural world rather than distinct from animals and nature.

It is one thing to observe that the nature writers of the early twentieth century may have written stories that are responsive to the cultural chaos created by Darwin's theory of evolution. But it may be more difficult to make this claim about contemporary animal narratives. Are there social and cultural phenomena before us now that inspire stories about animal emotion and morality? Consider the following possibility that may explain the recent surge in the popularity of animal narratives and, in particular, those that mark how similar animals are to human beings.[45]

Admittedly we are surrounded by a large amount of moral failure. We read daily about morally corrupt elected officials, corporate managers, police officers, sports heroes, and even entire governments. Against this background, stories about the moral goodness of animals seem absolutely refreshing. Perhaps we are psychologically prepared to read about heroic rescues by apes and porpoises, sympathetic chimpanzees, and dogs that manifest virtues like compassion. In the foreword of Kristin Von Kreisler's book *Beauty in the Beasts: True Stories of Animals Who Choose to Do Good*, Jeffrey Masson remarks that "[t]here is a hunger in the general public for true stories of the positive things that animals do." Since there is a "scarcity of human heroes," he urges us to look to animals "for our moral lessons, [and] for our ethical education."[46] If Masson is right that the public is looking for moral heroes, then there is no shortage of contemporary animal stories that satisfy this interest.

Elizabeth Marshall Thomas tells the following anecdote about her dog, "Ruby," in a story titled "A Friend in Need."[47] On an outing with four dogs, the smallest, a shih tzu named "Wicket," got left behind because he was too small to cross a stream on the trail. As Marshall Thomas looked on, Ruby stayed back to coax Wicket over the water to no avail. Eventually Ruby led him to another smaller crossing and eventually enticed the small dog over by crossing back and forth several times. Ruby and Wicket ran to catch up to the other hikers, but Ruby continued to stay close to Wicket. The author concludes by saying, "I was moved by this because Ruby is a very humble dog, low on our totem pole, and so is Wicket. Quietly, all on her own, with no aid from people, she helped the little guy."[48]

We easily recognize Ruby's moral qualities because we understand that when humans help those who are disadvantaged in one way or another, they act in a way that is morally commendable. Do stories like this one pass the test for being literally true? This question seems to miss the point. Perhaps many stories that mark our moral kinship with animals can be grouped together as narratives that satisfy a cultural demand for moral clarity. It may not be merely accidental that animals serve as our moral exemplars in many stories since I suspect we are still fascinated by the question, Where do we locate human beings in relation to animals and the natural world? While stories about animal emotion and morality rarely argue for the conclusion that animals and humans are moral kin, they vividly *describe* this commonality, making it easy for us to identify where to locate animals in relation to humans. These stories recommend an answer to the question about how human beings fit into the natural world by emphasizing our continuity with animals and what we have in common rather than our discontinuity with animals and how we are different.[49] By emphasizing our commonality with animals we make a choice about what matters to how we see ourselves. Stories about animal emotion and morality illustrate how we *want* to answer the question about where to mark the boundary between humans and animals. In this way they can be vehicles for the articulation of normative value.

THE VALUE OF ANIMAL STORIES

We should find a place for evaluative meaning in narratives about animal emotion, even if it interferes with our interest in reading the story literally to discern the facts about real animals. To see why, consider Linnda Caporael and Cecilia Heyes's commentary about why humans anthropomorphize.[50] It is their third "tentative" explanation that interests me. The authors suggest that "attributing human characteristics to animals is a way of changing the values we place on them and how we can behave toward them. . . . Anthropomorphism may be an important means for connecting values to action for environmental preservation, and too important to discourage, whatever its foundations, *whether or not animals really do have mental states*" (my italics).[51] Perhaps when we attribute to animals emotional states in the context of a story it is one way of negotiating the value of animals. By doing so we may alter how human beings perceive the natural world and the ways in which we imagine it is possible or desirable to act toward animals and the natural environment at large. The important role that animal narratives, anecdotes, and stories can play is to capture a commonsense view of animals that the authors describe as "value-making talk," and "value-making perception." Ascribing to animals emotional states is one way of articulating the worth of animals in opposition to technology and a mechanization of the world.[52]

We may be convinced that animals should not be mistreated because they are *actually* like us psychologically. But just as effectively we may become motivated to take up the cause of animal rights and animal welfare because we *believe* that animals are like us. Eliciting our sympathies may involve simply circumventing the issue about the literal attribution of emotion to animals. Finessing the truth in the animal story can still move us to adopt an ethical position about animal welfare because our moral imaginations are triggered by the idea of heroic, compassionate, and courageous animals in such a way that we sympathize with their plights. Is there a problem with this? Only if we are tempted by these attributions to endorse the philosophical conclusion that animals are moral beings.[53]

Consider this story by Anne Innis Dagg titled "A Furious Complaint." The author accompanied a caravan of camels on safari in the Sahara Desert to research camel physiology under conditions of extreme heat.[54] The author's indignation about how the camels were treated is obvious. She notes that they were loaded down heavily with gear, ordered to lie down and get up, and refused water so that they would not wander off into the desert. The loud bellowing of the camels is their "anger at their hard lives." The kind of anger, the author feels, is *moral* indignation about how the camels are treated. But she is prepared to attribute to the camels this moral indignation as well. The camels decline to be petted on the nose and feel outrage *for a reason*. "Many desert travelers scorn the camel, objecting to the noise it makes and to the superior expression on its face. Perhaps it annoys them that camels seem so independent and aloof, declining to have their noses or necks stroked in the way that horses seem to enjoy. But then life for a camel is unbelievably hard. No wonder they're impervious to friendly approaches from humans. No wonder they protest the outrage each day of being hungry and thirsty and laden with heavy packs they must carry for long hours."[55] Here it seems entirely beside the point to insist that camels may fail to be capable of the kind of anger describable as moral indignation. What is striking about this short narrative is that we discover a point of view, not necessarily the camel's own point of view, but a moral point of view nonetheless. We imagine what it might be like to do hard burdensome work in extreme heat and to be deprived of water. Rightly so we feel justifiable anger at such conditions.

Eliciting our sympathies may be crucial to bringing us around to a certain way of valuing animals and the natural world. This goal may take precedence over the aim of literally depicting the real qualities of animals. We may not begin reading these stories with the idea that animals are deserving of a certain kind of treatment, but when we are finished, our sympathies are aroused and we may bring our normative judgments into line with this emotional reaction about what counts as fair, kind, or respectful treatment of animals.[56]

CONCLUSION

I have argued here that determining whether or not animals literally do have emotions is complicated by the methodology of storytelling. If we employ narratives and stories as observational windows that reveal what animals are literally like, we may be unduly influenced by the compelling quality of the story itself. Or, the story may inadvertently disguise the concept of emotion used and applied to animals. This leaves us in a skeptical position with regard to discovering the real psychological qualities of animals. I have expressed my dissatisfaction with the use of some stories for these reasons. But I have also tried to make what I hope is a constructive contribution to the research about animal emotion in order to correct for these methodological problems. Throughout our examination of narratives about animal emotion I have recommended to the reader that we need to engage in a conceptual analysis of emotion state terms and descriptions as well as to investigate how emotions are morally significant. Not all stories about animal emotion are philosophically benign. This is so because some stories encourage us to conclude that animals are moral beings. A story that implies this may seem plausible yet fail to advance a philosophical argument that warrants this conclusion.

But not all stories that attribute emotions to animals are intended to be read as conveying factual information about the animal mind. In many cases the story itself may be a vehicle for articulating normative value because it is vivid and emotionally compelling. Such a narrative can recommend an ethical position for humans to adopt, not only about how animals themselves should be regarded and treated, but also about how to understand the value of animals and nature when there are competing conceptions that degrade and impoverish this domain.

NOTES

1. Ralph H. Lutts, "The Wild Animal Story: Animals and Ideas," in *The Wild Animal Story*, ed. Ralph H. Lutts (Philadelphia: Temple University Press, 1998), p. 2.

2. For a survey of some of the issues connected to "anecdotalism," see Richard W. Byrne, "What's the Use of Anecdotes? Distinguishing Psychological Mechanisms in Primate Tactical Deception," in *Anthropomorphism, Anecdotes, and Animals*, ed. Robert W. Mitchell, Nicholas S. Thompson, and H. Lyn Miles (Albany: State University of New York Press, 1997); Robert W. Mitchell, "Anthropomorphic Anecdotalism as Method," in *Anthropomorphism, Anecdotes, and Animals*, ed. Mitchell, Thompson, and Miles; Bernard E. Rollin, "Anecdote, Anthropomorphism, and Animal Behavior," in *Anthropomorphism, Anecdotes, and Animals*, ed. Mitchell, Thompson, and Miles; and Paul S. Silverman, "A Pragmatic Approach to the Inference of Animal Mind," in *Anthropomorphism, Anecdotes, and Animals*, ed. Mitchell, Thompson, and Miles.

3. See especially Charles Darwin, *The Descent of Man; and Selection in Relation to Sex* (Amherst, NY: Prometheus Books, 1998).

4. See especially Samuel Barnett, "The Expression of Emotion," in *A Century of Darwin*, ed. S. A. Barnett (New York: Books for Libraries Press, 1958); and Michael T. Ghiselin, *The Triumph of the Darwinian Method* (Berkeley: University of California Press, 1969).

5. See Eileen Crist, *Images of Animals: Anthropomorphism and Animal Mind* (Philadelphia: Temple University Press, 1999); and

James Rachels, *Created from Animals: The Moral Implications of Darwinism* (Oxford: Oxford University Press, 1990).

    6. Marc Bekoff, ed., *The Smile of a Dolphin: Remarkable Accounts of Animal Emotions* (New York: Discovery Books, 2000).

    7. Ibid., pp. 16–17.

    8. Rollin, "Anecdote, Anthropomorphism, and Animal Behavior," p. 131. Marc Hauser is sympathetic to using stories and anecdotes in science, but he also expresses some frustration with Jeffrey Masson's view. In his book *Dogs Never Lie about Love*, Masson says,

> I am aware that most of the "evidence" I have presented for the reality of emotions to dogs consists of stories—what scientists call, dismissively, anecdotal evidence. With their restricted sense of valid criteria, most scientists want to be able to test, probe and replicate data. You cannot do that with a single story. Scientists seem to think that whereas a story can be either true or false, something that takes place more than once in a laboratory has to be true. There is no reason to believe this to be the case. Data can be faked, forged, or misrepresented as easily as can a story, and what we learn from some laboratory experiments . . . does not tell us anything we could not have known without experiments. (p. xxi)

Hauser goes on to remark, "Masson's criticisms are replete with disturbing and confusing assertions. Scientists think that anecdotes are unsatisfying, but not useless. They may provide clues or stimulate hunches, but scientific curiosity ultimately leads to further exploration, additional observations, and experimental tests. And yes, scientists can fake data, which is precisely why replication is so important." Marc D. Hauser, *Wild Minds: What Animals Really Think* (New York: Henry Holt and Company, 2000), pp. 5–6.

    9. Martha C. Nussbaum, *Upheavals of Thought: The Intelligence of Emotions* (Cambridge: Cambridge University Press, 2001).

    10. Thomas R. Dunlap, "The Realistic Animal Story: Ernest Thompson Seton, Charles Roberts, and Darwinism," in *The Wild*

Animal Story, ed. Ralph Lutts, *Animals, Culture, and Society* (Philadelphia: Temple University Press, 1998), p. 238.

11. Ernest Thompson Seton, *Wild Animals I Have Known* (New York: Charles Scribner's Sons, 1911), p. 9.

12. John Burroughs, "Real and Sham Natural History," in *The Wild Animal Story*, ed. Lutts, p. 132.

13. Ralph Lutts notes about Burroughs that "[b]etween 1889 and 1906 more than 300,000 copies of his school reader were sold, introducing a generation of children to nature." Ralph H. Lutts, "Will the Real Wild Animal Please Stand Up! The Nature Fakers," in *The Wild Animal Story*, ed. Lutts, p. 269.

14. John Burroughs, "Science and Sentiment," *Independent*, February 15, 1912, p. 360.

15. William J. Long, "The Modern School of Nature-Study and Its Critics," in *The Wild Animal Story*, ed. Lutts, p. 144.

16. Ibid., p. 145.

17. Ibid., pp. 147–48.

18. Long, "Modern School of Nature-Study and Its Critics," p. 146.

19. Nussbaum, *Upheavals of Thought*, p. 1.

20. Ibid., p. 2.

21. Ibid., p. 9.

22. Ibid., pp. 119–20.

23. Ibid., p. 122.

24. Ibid., pp. 122–23.

25. Ibid., pp. 124–25.

26. Ibid., p. 120.

27. Nussbaum references Wise (2000) for "both good and bad" examples of narratives, but she does not indicate which stories in Wise are to be classified in this way and why.

28. Nussbaum, *Upheavals of Thought*, p. 122.

29. Jane Goodall, *Through a Window* (Boston: Houghton Mifflin, 1990), p. 196.

30. Nussbaum, *Upheavals of Thought*, p. 125.

31. This is also true of Nussbaum's remark that because she personally *knew* the dogs Remus and Lupa she can attest to the correct application of emotions to them (p. 121).

32. Ibid., p. 11.

33. Rollin, "Anecdote, Anthropomorphism, and Animal Behavior," p. 131.

34. Mitchell, "Anthropomorphic Anecdotalism as Method."

35. W. L. Bennett and M. S. Feldman, *Reconstructing Reality in the Courtroom: Justice and Judgment in American Culture* (New Brunswick, NJ: Rutgers University Press, 1981).

36. In one study subjects were presented with this description: "Dr. Gallagher studies nonverbal behavior of people and their dogs. She observed the following interaction. M, a male, and F, a female, sit on the ground. M reaches his arm to touch F, and M's dog H rushes up to them and moves between M and F, facing and staring at M [or F] while touching him [or her]." See Mitchell, "Anthropomorphic Anecdotalism as Method," pp. 165–66.

37. Ibid.

38. Ibid., p. 167.

39. Marc Bekoff, "Mixing Science and Emotion," in *The Smile of a Dolphin*, ed. Bekoff, p. 21.

40. Ibid., p. 25.

41. Marc Bekoff, "A Nurturing Nature," in *The Smile of a Dolphin*, ed. Bekoff, p. 41. One reader of this manuscript wondered if Jethro was a retriever.

42. Lisa Mighetto, *Wild Animals and American Environmental Ethics* (Tucson: University of Arizona Press, 1991), pp. 9–10.

43. Seton himself says, "In my previous books I have tried to emphasize our kinship with the animals by showing that in them we can find the virtues most admired in Man. Logo stands for Dignity and Love-constancy; Silverspot, for Sagacity; Redruff, for Obedience; Bingo, for Fidelity; Vixen and Molly Cottontail, for Mother-love; Wahb, for Physical Force; and the Pacing Mustang, for the Love of Liberty." From "Notes to the Reader," in Ernest Thompson Seton, *Lives of the Hunted* (New York: Charles Scribner's Sons, 1901). See also Robert H. MacDonald, "The Revolt against Instinct: The Animal Stories of Seton and Roberts," in *The Wild Animal Story*, ed. Ralph H. Lutts (Philadelphia: Temple University Press, 1998).

44. As Seton puts it, "[W]e and the beasts are kin. Man has

nothing that the animals have not at least a vestige of, the animals have nothing that man does not in some degree share." From Seton, *Wild Animals I Have Known*, p. 12.

45. In a recent article in the *New York Times*, Dwight Garner inquires about the recent flurry in popular publications about animals. The article surveys what a number of authors believe explains the appeal of such books, but the answers are various and rather inconclusive. Tellingly, the article begins with this sentence, "Four legs good, two legs bad." See Dwight Garner, "Ideas and Trends; Best Sellers That Woof and Meow," *New York Times*, July 15, 2007.

46. Kristin Von Kreisler, *Beauty in the Beasts: True Stories of Animals Who Choose to Do Good* (New York: Jeremy P. Tarcher/Putnam, 2001), p. xii.

47. Elizabeth Marshall Thomas, "A Friend in Need," in *The Smile of a Dolphin*, ed. Bekoff.

48. Ibid., p. 184.

49. Philip Kitcher remarks, "As Steve Gould saw so clearly, in any evaluation of our evolutionary history you can emphasize the continuities or the discontinuities. I think little is gained by either emphasis. You do better simply to recognize what has endured and what has altered." Philip Kitcher, "Ethics and Evolution: How to Get Here from There," in *Primates and Philosophers: How Morality Evolved*, ed. Stephen Macedo and Josiah Ober, *University Center for Human Values* series (Princeton, NJ: Princeton University Press, 2006), p. 139.

50. Linnda R. Caporael and Cecilia M. Heyes, "Why Anthropomorphize? Folk Psychology and Other Stories," in *Anthropomorphism, Anecdotes, and Animals*, ed. Mitchell, Thompson, and Miles.

51. Ibid., p. 70.

52. By way of illustration, consider what Seton says in response to those "tender hearts" that distressed over the outcome of the story about Lobo.

> To this I reply: In what frame of mind are my hearers left with regard to the animal? Are their sympathies quickened toward the man who killed him, or toward the noble creature who, superior to every trial, died as he had lived, dignified, fearless, and steadfast?

In answer to a question many times put, I may say that I do not champion any theory of diet. I do not intend primarily to denounce certain field sports, or even cruelty to animals. My chief motive, my most earnest underlying wish, has been to stop the extermination of harmless wild animals; not for their sakes, but for ours, firmly believing that each of our native wild creatures is in itself a precious heritage that we have no right to destroy or put beyond the reach of our children.

I have tried to stop the stupid and brutal work of destruction by an appeal—not to reason: that has failed hitherto—but to sympathy, and especially the sympathies of the coming generation.

(Ernest Thompson Seton, "On His Animal Stories,"
in *The Wild Animal Story*, ed. Lutts, p. 47.)

Seton's stories may well have had the intended effect on his readers to move them to an ethical position about animal welfare.

53. Ralph Lutts writes that the movie *The Bear* (Columbia, 1989) used trained bears, animation, and Jim Henson puppetry in addition to live "actors." But the film was criticized and called a "nature fake" by some because it anthropomorphized bears. In a review of the film Pauline Kael wrote, "It's saying that we shouldn't kill bears, because they're so much like us—after it fakes the evidence that they are." Pauline Kael, "Current Cinema," *New Yorker*, November 13, 1989. Most likely the film is susceptible to this criticism not because it intentionally tries to deceive but because it displays an ambiguity of purpose; on the one hand depicting what bears are like (literally) and on the other hand recommending an ethical stance for viewers to adopt.

54. Anne Innis Dagg, "A Furious Complaint," in *The Smile of a Dolphin*, ed. Bekoff.

55. Ibid., p. 105.

56. It is also possible to read some of Jane Goodall's animal narratives in this way. In a chapter titled "Our Shame," Goodall details how chimpanzees are hunted by humans, chimpanzee mothers

killed, and the offspring captured and transported by disreputable dealers to live in captivity. The captured chimpanzees experience abuse, ill health, boredom, and death. At one point Goodall compares these dealers who illegally capture and transport chimpanzees to slave traders who became rich by trading human slaves. She compares the chimpanzee survivors to survivors of the concentration camps of the Third Reich. What makes our empathy and moral indignation possible is that chimpanzees are characterized as beings that have the same emotional responsiveness as us. We cannot be indifferent to how chimpanzees are treated given our emotional kinship. In this way, attributing emotions to some animals moves us to regard them as *morally considerable* and perhaps to reevaluate how we should treat animals. Classifying some animals as morally considerable implies that they are the kinds of creatures that may make moral demands on us. In this way by attributing emotions to some animals we may reassess how to draw the boundaries of the moral community, i.e., "who should matter, how they should matter, and why." See Goodall, *Through a Window*; Lori Gruen, "The Morals of Animal Minds," in *The Cognitive Animal*, ed. Marc Bekoff, Colin Allen, and Gordon M. Burghardt (Cambridge, MA: MIT Press, 2002), p. 437.

Chapter Nine

MARKING THE BOUNDARY

*Man is of a far different structure in his guts from ravenous crea-
tures as dogs, wolves, etc., who, minding only their belly, have their
guts descending almost straight down from their ventricle or stomach
to the fundament: whereas in this noble microcosm man, there are in
these intestinal parts many anfractuous circumvolutions, windings
and turnings, whereby, longer retention of his food being procured, he
might so much the better attend upon sublime speculations, and prof-
itable employments in Church and Commonwealth.*[1]

Claims about human uniqueness have a sorrowful history. At one time or another philosophers, intellectuals,
and scientists have declared that what distinguishes human
beings from the natural world and animals, in particular, is that
humans have a deliberative, intellectual, or rational soul; that
they are featherless bipeds, political animals, laughing animals;

239

or that they have the capacity to use tools, the ability to cook, reason, speak, and use language, the ability to choose freely, form opinions, have a conscience, possess private property, and that humans alone cannot wiggle their ears.[2] What is lamentable about these intellectual efforts is that almost every attempt to identify what is unique to human beings has been accompanied by explicit assertions of inferiority about what is *not* human. Where humans are characterized as civil, refined, rational, and good; animals are characterized as fierce, gluttonous, wanton, brutal, lascivious, lustful, and governed by beastly impulses, bodily appetite, and passions.[3] The category of *beast, brute,* and *animal* has also been used to stand for human members of our society thought to be inferior. At one time or another blacks, American Indians, Irish, infants and children, women, the poor, and common people have all been characterized as primitive, wild, and savage.[4]

One way of correcting for such misplaced views about human uniqueness and superiority is to closely examine the concepts used to characterize animal nature and human nature. Because the emotions are often contrasted with what is thought to be unique to humans, namely, intellect, rationality, or deliberation, there is an obvious need to specify what we mean when we attribute emotions to either humans or animals. If, for example, emotions are construed as bodily passions, feeling states, irrational, and beyond the control of the subject who has them, then attributing emotions to animals can be a way of marking our difference from animals (and all those who are thought to be *animal-like*).

In this work I have focused rather narrowly on animal narratives and anecdotes that are used as evidence for our emotional kinship with animals. But even here where it is claimed that we are *like* animals instead of *different* from animals, there is still a need to clarify the nature of emotion relied on in those argumentative contexts that imply humans and animals share emotions. What we have discovered is that many narratives about emotional kinship typically characterize the emotions as states that signal our attachments to persons, projects, and goals that are of central importance to the subject who has these emotions. A eudaimonistic theory of emotions can plausibly capture how emotions are imbued with value. Using this kind of theory of the emotions allows us to supply a deeper analysis of emotional kinship, illustrating what is common to both animal and human lives while still adjusting the theory, as Nussbaum recommends, for the ways in which animal emotion is different from human emotion.

Using a eudaimonistic theory of the emotions to characterize claims about our emotional kinship with animals does not settle whether or not humans and animals share what I am calling *morally laden* emotions. Emotions are morally laden in particular contexts by how they are connected to moral virtues or as motivational states that invite our moral appraisal of the animal itself. Investigating whether an animal shares with humans morally laden emotions is both an analytical and an empirical project.[5] The analytical part of this project requires a precise account of morality and of the moral concepts and emotion state concepts that operate as background conditions for saying how emotions can be morally significant. The empirical research about the cognitive capacities of animals will include an investigation of whether or not some animals do, in fact, have the morally relevant intentional states necessary for explicating how emotions are morally significant.

The reader will know by now that it is the first of these tasks that I have undertaken by examining particular animal narratives that are used to show that some animals share with us morally laden emotions. I have not tried to approximate the kind of research that ethologists and animal behaviorists typically do by going into the field to observe wild animals or even by collecting data from my own pets about how they act in particular circumstances. What I have undertaken is a conceptual analysis of what some philosophers, ethologists, and popular writers must mean when they attribute morally laden emotions to animals. Writers who attribute particular kinds of emotions to animals are typically interested in establishing our moral kinship with animals. A conceptual analysis of emotion and the ways in which emotions are morally significant reveals what underlying assumptions are required to make this idea plausible. What we have seen is that for emotions to be connected to morality they must be understood as having cognitive-evaluative intentional content. Emotions cannot be merely defined as "feelings" or even as "neurophysiological states" if emotions are to do the explanatory work that some authors demand of this concept. It may still be true that emotions have an affective component or that they are at least partly defined as physical states of the brain. Defining emotions as intentional states does not preclude characterizing them in either of these ways. But once we see how the concept of emotion is being employed in particular narrative settings that attribute morally laden emotions to animals, we can explore what conceptual commitments are entailed when we make these attributions. I have argued throughout that the conclusion that some animals have morally laden emotions is underdetermined by the evidence. This is not a *proof* that establishes that it is necessarily wrong to attribute to animals these kinds of emotions. But in my opinion this conclusion about what animals share with humans should not be treated as obviously true, requiring no justification whatsoever. Those that disagree can and should take up the challenge to explain with more precision how they are using emotion state concepts as well as those moral concepts that are relevant to the particular way in which emotions are morally significant. This may be the place to briefly review what has gone wrong with some attempts to establish that animals have morally laden emotional states.

SUMMARY OF THE ARGUMENT

In chapter 3 I examined a number of narratives that attribute compassion and moral virtue to animals. I described the concepts of compassion and virtue used in these settings as *thin* definitions. Thin definitions strip the concepts of compassion and virtue from other morally relevant concepts that surround our use of these expressions. So if we want to explain why being motivated from the emotional state of compassion is morally praiseworthy, we will need to say something more about what cognitive and evaluative intentional states are necessary for having this emotion. Moreover, if we follow the recommendations for those who credit some animals with moral virtue because they have compassion, we also need to specify how such motivational dispositions develop as part of a subject's moral character in order to deserve our moral commendation for being that kind of person or animal. In other words, thick definitions of concepts like compassion and virtue lend precision to our moral practices of assigning credit and fault, and our moral appraisals of people and what they do. But once we specify the conditions that operate ordinarily in our use of thick moral concepts like compassion and virtue, we see how improbable it is to apply these concepts to animals. The cognitive-evaluative intentional content of compassion involves judgments about fault or blameworthiness of those who suffer and about what counts as a serious loss. Acting from virtue requires knowledge of the morally relevant circumstances of one's action. And developing virtue as a part of one's moral character involves practice and habituation over a lifetime (among other things). The mistake made by those writers who attribute compassion and moral virtue to animals is failing to analyze the way in which these ideas are connected to other moral concepts that are necessary for understanding how and why compassion is morally significant.

In chapter 4 I considered one way of responding to this conclusion. It might be thought that while some animals do not have compassion and virtue in the *thick* sense characteristic of human beings, some animals may have a little bit of those morally laden emotional states like compassion by comparison to human beings. Darwin's principle about evolutionary continuity is sometimes used to make the case that some animals have emotions that differ by *degree* but not by *kind*. One primary objective in this chapter was to explain more precisely what Darwin meant by *evolutionary continuity*. To that end, I formulated the Continuity Thesis (CT) as a way of understanding this basic idea. The Principle of Psychological Continuity (PPC) was also presented and explained as an Aristotelian version of Darwin's principle. I believe both principles suffer from the same kind of difficulty. Both principles seem applicable to emotions as psychological states identifiable in human beings. From this it is initially plausible to infer that some animals are capable of emotions of the same kind, model, or type that we attribute to humans. But nowhere do we find a specification of what counts as a kind of emotion. What is missing here is an account of what emotions are, such that we will be able to individuate states of this kind quantitatively or by degree as (CT) and (PPC) require. The particular problem is revealed by characterizing emotions so as to capture their moral significance. How we differentiate compassion from other emotional states depends on *what* a subject believes or judges about. But intentional content (judgments, appraisals, beliefs) do not lend themselves to quantitative individuation. While there may be such a thing as having a "little bit of compassion," gradualism applied to beliefs, judgments, or appraisals is not intuitively plausible. Even though the principle of evolutionary continuity is often invoked to explain why it is correct to say that animals have emotions, the right conclusion to draw is that such a principle has limited applicability. As formulated here neither

(CT) nor (PPC) justify the inference that some animals have morally laden emotional states.

Chapter 5 investigated the possibility that chimpanzees have emotions like sympathy or cognitive empathy. Here we explored how a particular ethologist, Frans de Waal, applies his considerable research data about chimpanzee behavior to explain the evolutionary origins of morality in human beings. One kind of evidence that de Waal uses to conclude that morality evolved is the identification of those emotional states that motivate primate behavior. De Waal refers to these as moral sentiments that occupy the "ground floor of morality." My critical remarks about the success of this project apply most directly to the conceptual analysis de Waal uses to establish his conclusion. As de Waal describes it, *cognitive empathy* is a moral sentiment that we have warrant to attribute to some chimpanzees based on observations about how they act. This emotional state is defined so as to include the "appraisal" of another's situation. But this definition falls short of capturing what it means to identify what is morally salient about a situation. We are closer to understanding how appraisals can be morally significant by employing the concept of ethical perception and by pairing this with the moral motivation to act so as to alleviate need or undeserved suffering. What is missing from de Waal's argument for attributing moral sentiments to chimpanzees is a more precise account of how such emotional states are connected to morality. I suggested in this chapter that what may contribute to de Waal's incomplete explanation of this point is his belief that morality is characterized by levels requiring increasingly more complex intellectual capabilities. On this view, emotions contribute to morality as simple affective states at the lowest level of morality. These moral sentiments are ones that de Waal believes chimpanzees share with human beings. Judgments and cognitions add another layer to morality in such a way that approximates the moral practices and deliberations of adult human beings. But this account of morality ignores the necessary conditions that make emotions morally significant in the first place, and that is by construing these as perceptions of the morally salient features of a situation. Developing ethical perception to read a situation with "insight and clarity" is like developing a skill. It is not a natural capacity but one that requires reflection about direct experience and practice to more closely approximate understanding what is morally relevant about another's situation and how to appropriately respond to these moral particulars. In this sense displaying emotional responsiveness to the morally salient features of a situation is more like the display of virtue. Morally laden emotions cannot be so easily carved off from judgments in the way de Waal seems to suggest.

Still, it might be thought that chimpanzees or other animals are sufficiently like children at an early stage of moral development. Perhaps what they share are simple emotions that motivate caring behavior. The comparison between the affective capabilities of children and animals were discussed in chapter 6. Here I examined the popular idea of *childhood animality* as an explanation for why children and animals are classified together as either morally appraisable or as exempt from ascriptions of moral responsibility, praise, and blame. For example, according to R. Jay Wallace's account of what it means to be a proper target of the reactive attitudes, children and animals are exempt from moral accountability because they fail to have reflective self-control. Wallace may be right that most young children fail to have reflective self-control in the sense that he defines it, but in this chapter I supplied reasons for thinking that this rationality condition is too strong to capture our practical regard for children's normative competence. It seems that even young children can grasp moral concepts and engage in ethical inquiry about these concepts. Children may grasp simple moral reasons that prohibit some actions and they are capable of recognizing simple moral paradigms of kindness, fairness, and so on. To allow for these kinds of moral assessments of children and what they do we need a less rationalistic account of moral responsibility.

In chapter 7 we explored whether or not both children and animals should be held morally responsible because they satisfy the Intentionality Condition (I), a weaker condition about voluntary action suggested by Aristotle. Here I had the opportunity to say more about how morally appropriate emotional states and emotional responsiveness are developed in children. By a closer examination of the moral practices in which children participate it is possible to distinguish the very different ways in which their affective responses to moral particulars are different from an animal's "simple" emotional states. We may be tempted to believe that educating children in ethical perception is like training an animal. After all, the educator/trainer aims to develop the critical capacities of each kind of being. But this is a misunderstanding about what it means for children to acquire the skill to see or perceive what matters ethically in a situation. The mistake made by those who claim that children and animals share morally laden emotional states is to underestimate and underdescribe the moral practices that surround the moral development of children. Recognizing this reveals the limitations of the Intentionality Condition for being morally responsible. If we adopt such a principle we will fail to properly explain how children are morally appraisable and why animals are not.

The general line of argument that I have examined throughout these chapters is one that begins by attributing morally laden emotions to some animals and inferring from this that animals are moral beings. The Moral Kinship Hypothesis is the view that animals and humans share the more fundamental property of being moral. Recall that *moral kinship* as I am using the expression entails that animals are like us with respect to morality, not because they satisfy highly rationalistic conditions for moral agency and not because they are merely morally considerable by being moral patients, but because they perform right or wrong actions for which they can be morally commended or blamed. One reason for initially believing that some animals have this more elevated moral status is that they can be properly credited with morally laden emotional states that are connected to morality in at least one of the ways that we have investigated.

Do some animals have morally laden emotional states? I do not believe that the arguments I have surveyed here establish this conclusion. The general failure characteristic of all these attempts to establish that animals have morally laden emotions is a lack of clarity about what emotions are. I suspect that many writers who credit animals with morally laden emotions are tempted by the commonsense idea that animals are emotional beings. This commonsense attribution seems true to most people, especially those of us who have any dealings with animals. After all, the idea that animals have emotions allows us to predict how animals will behave, it makes possible the training of animals, and it makes sense of the close affinity we have with our pets. However, if we do not specify what emotions are, it is possible to imagine that attributing morally laden emotions to animals is an instance of the same kind of commonsense ascription. The intuitive obviousness of the idea that animals have fear, joy, and anger masks the more philosophically nuanced claim that even fear, joy, and anger in particular contexts may imply something about the moral qualities of the subject who has these emotions. Once we attribute a morally laden emotion to an animal we commit ourselves to a particular way of defining the emotions in that contextual setting. The analysis of emotion state terms and moral concepts that I have undertaken throughout this work reveals more precisely what would be involved in order to justifiably credit animals with morally laden emotions. By engaging in this conceptual analysis it becomes clear that attributing morally laden emotions to animals not only goes beyond our ordinary commonsense ways of talking about animals, but it also goes beyond much of the empirical evidence about animal behavior to which many writers appeal. Of course, we may not notice this if emotional states are left unanalyzed altogether or if they are defined in a way that fails to explain how emotions are actually used in particular narrative settings about our emotional kinship with animals. This is exactly why I begin the philosophical analysis in each chapter with a narrative about animal emotion that fixes the context for the inquiry that follows. The analysis I have provided might require some care in how we ordinarily talk about our emotional and moral kinship with animals. But the real burden of proof falls on those who would use the attribution of emotion to animals to conclude that the Moral Kinship Hypothesis is true.

OTHER PHILOSOPHICAL APPROACHES

Other philosophers have concluded that animals fail to have moral emotions but for different reasons than I have offered here. Richard Joyce argues that in order for any being to have a moral emotion she must be capable of making judgments and appraisals about evaluative language. This means that moral emotions are restricted to those creatures that have the linguistic competence to consider or "semantically assent" to moral language that is used to express normative standards.[6]

Robert C. Roberts sees the difficulty created by using a cognitive-evaluative theory of the emotions to attribute emotions to some animals. Roberts recommends characterizing the emotions of animals as *construals*, or ways of perceptually organizing an animal's concern or interest in certain aspects of the world. But moral emotions take as their objects propositions that are identified and defined by such moral concepts as *culpable, responsible,* or *just.* These, Roberts says, are available only to language users. Because animals fail to have this linguistic competence they do not have moral emotions.[7]

Marc Hauser maintains that animals do not have moral emotions such as guilt, shame, embarrassment, or empathy; although they do, he believes, experience emotions like fear, anger, or surprise. This is so because animals do not have self-awareness or "a sense of self that relies on a richly textured set of beliefs and desires." Another obstacle to attributing these kinds of emotions to animals is that moral emotions involve an evaluation that actions are either right or wrong. But, according to Hauser, research on animal emotion has not conclusively shown that animals make these evaluations that accompany shame, for example, when we associate shame with "violating a norm."[8]

These approaches to our topic have something in common. All entail that the moral emotions constitute a kind of emotional state where a single capacity is necessary in order to have this kind of emotion—either language or self-reflection. I agree that many moral emotions do require linguistic competence, but the general argument that all moral emotions constitute a kind of psychological state that is characterized by a univocal criterion of attribution is a much harder one to make. The limitations of this way of arguing are that it leaves us at the mercy of debates about what counts as a language or self-awareness—notoriously difficult issues to settle. We might also wonder whether or not *all* moral emotions have this particular feature as a necessary condition for their correct attribution.

I believe the topic of animal emotion is more fruitfully explored by examining particular contexts of attribution as I have done here. If we confine our attention to those narrative settings where a particular emotion is attributed to an animal, we can ask whether or not *this* emotion in *this* context of attribution is a morally laden one. And if our answer is yes, we can rely on the narrative context to help us specify how the emotion is conceptually connected to morality. In other words, the methodology here is not general. It does not seek to deny these kinds of emotions to animals by identifying a single criterion of attribution that animals fail to satisfy. Rather, the inquiry proceeds by looking at individual cases where it is claimed that animals are like humans in sharing emotions and then investigating what moral background conditions are necessary to make sense of this particular emotional attribution. These moral background conditions may include judgments or concepts that require linguistic competence or sufficiently complex cognitive states. But I've also described how crucial it is to understand other moral concepts that cluster around the moral emotions such as virtue, the development of moral character, the idea of ethical perception, and the moral practices that surround our moral appraisal of children. My analysis is responsive to the particular details about what it is claimed we share with animals. For this reason my conclusions are less sweeping than those of Joyce, Roberts, or Hauser, since I have argued only that the particular attempts I've examined here fail to establish that some animals have morally laden emotions.

If so, then what should we infer about the Moral Kinship Hypothesis? As we have seen, a popular way of arguing that humans and animals are moral kin is by attributing to animals morally laden emotions. By showing that some standard and initially plausible ways of characterizing our emotional kinship with animals do not entail our moral kinship with animals, we may come to doubt that animals are moral beings like ourselves. This way of reasoning, of course, does not show that the Moral Kinship Hypothesis is false since there may be other ways of trying to establish this conclusion that we have not considered here. Whatever inferences about human uniqueness we may be tempted to draw should be qualified in the same way. For the reasons I've discussed throughout it is probably true that humans are unique with respect to morally laden emotional states and also with respect to morality.

HUMAN UNIQUENESS WITHOUT SUPERIORITY

To even suggest that human beings may be unique is a controversial claim. Because human uniqueness has been historically associated with human superiority, it might seem as if I am supplying an easy rationale for the morally suspect treatment of animals and any human beings characterized as animal-like.

The critic might reason in the following way. Historically the emotions have been characterized as unruly bodily states that are irrational and unreflective. By characterizing the emotions in a pejorative way as passions that we do not choose and cannot control, attributing emotions to animals was a way of marking how animals are different from humans—and a way of marking their inferiority as well. In the present work, instead of assuming that emotions are irrelevant (or even injurious) to morality, many writers correctly identify a place for the emotions in a moral theory like virtue ethics or in our moral appraisals of agents and why they act. By casting suspicion on the claim that some animals have morally laden emotions it might seem that I am recommending that animals are inferior because they do not have the more revered kinds of emotional states that are associated with morality.

Now that I have articulated the worry, let me lay it to rest. Even if it has been sometimes thought that morality *elevates* human beings over other kinds of living things, there is no necessary connection between describing differences between humans and animals and valuing one feature or attribute over another. Human uniqueness does not entail human superiority. And I am not in this work advocating that human beings are somehow better than animals because they may be unique with respect to certain kinds of emotions or morality as a whole. How we characterize the moral emotions is intimately connected to the details of human moral practices. These practices are complex as we have seen by examining the various ways in which emotions are conceptually connected to morality. To say that animals do not have emotions in this sense is just to say that animals may not participate in these kinds of human moral practices. There is no neat and tidy measure for marking this boundary between humans and animals; just a complex collection of concepts, attitudes, and ways of describing morality that more correctly apply to human beings. We should not be tempted to conclude that describing these kinds of differences between humans and animals entails that human beings are superior in these respects.

Still, some might believe that undertaking a project that seeks to identify differences between humans and animals cannot possibly contribute to cultivating a moral concern for animals. Perhaps we are more likely to treat animals disrespectfully, indifferently, or even cruelly if we say they are not moral kin with us or that they do not share with humans certain kinds of emotional states. Mary Midgley wonders about the same idea when she asks, "Can we be concerned at all with anything which is not fundamentally the same as ourselves?"[9] She quotes Spinoza as an example of how some philosophers have answered this question.

> It is plain that the law against the slaughtering of animals is founded rather on vain superstition and womanish pity than on sound reason. The rational quest of what is useful to us further teaches us the necessity of associating ourselves with our fellow-men, but not with beasts, or things, whose nature is dif-

ferent from our own; we have the same rights in respect to them as they have in respect to us. Nay, as everyone's right is defined by his virtue, or power, men have far greater rights over beasts than beasts have over men. Still I do not deny that beasts feel; what I deny is, that we may not consult our own advantage and use them as we please, treating them in the way which best suits us; for their nature is not like ours, and their emotions are naturally different from human emotions.[10]

Spinoza certainly gets off on the wrong foot by referring to "womanish pity" in a disparaging way. But more importantly, consider Spinoza's reasoning that because animals are unlike humans with respect to reason and emotion we may "use them as we please." The particular way that Midgley criticizes Spinoza is instructive. Midgley characterizes Spinoza as an egoist for grounding our moral concerns for others in our likenesses with them. Midgley concedes that while there is much that is "splendid" about Spinoza's ethics, "[w]hat is not splendid, what is downright wrong, is his notion about other people. What would a world be like in which we only cared for others in proportion as they were like ourselves, where we never welcomed or delighted in the fact that they were *different?* Still more, what would a world be like where we only admitted that they had any claim on us in proportion to their likeness?"[11]

Most people will agree with Midgley that grounding our moral concern for others (either humans or animals) in how much alike we are with respect to reason is mistaken. But if so we should surely reject grounding our moral concern for others (either humans or animals) in how much alike we are with respect to emotion. We do not have to follow Spinoza to the conclusion he draws. We can and should concern ourselves with what is owed to animals and how they ought to be treated irrespective of our "advantage" and "what best suits us." The very possibility that humans are unique with respect to morality or with respect to morally laden emotions does not preclude regarding animals as morally considerable and as the sorts of beings that may make moral claims on us. The details of these kinds of arguments have been well documented and discussed thoroughly by other philosophers, so I will not consider them here.[12] Despite the fact that human superiority and a moral disregard for animals have enjoyed a certain amount of historical currency, these views do not follow automatically from specifying how humans are different from animals.

The one idea that I hope I have conveyed to readers throughout this book is that philosophical analysis has a particular role to play in examining our ordinary ways of thinking about animal emotion. The number and variety of stories we tell about both fictional and real animals is testimony to our particular fascination with how human beings are animal-like, and how animals are human-like. The role of philosophical analysis is not necessarily to displace our ordinary ideas about these issues or to show how common sense consistently misleads us. It is to identify first what needs explaining, clarifying, and further justification. In his wonderfully eloquent little book *The Problems of Philosophy*, Bertrand Russell writes, "Philosophy, if it cannot *answer* so many questions as we could wish, has at least the power of *asking* questions which increase the interest of the world, and show the strangeness and wonder lying just below the surface even in the commonest things of daily life."[13] I initially began this inquiry by saying that stories about animal emotion and morality are an occasion for doing philosophical analysis about the meaning and use of the concepts *animal, emotion,* and *morality.* I've examined a number of narrative settings where these themes intersect, but, admittedly, I haven't come close to examining all such stories about these themes. I hope at least to leave the reader with a philosophical interest in the topic. This philosophical interest might inspire us to continue to explore the "strangeness and wonder lying just below the surface" of the stories we tell about animals.

NOTES

1. As quoted in Keith Thomas, *Man and the Natural World: A History of the Modern Sensibility* (New York: Pantheon Books, 1983), pp. 31–32. Thomas cites the author as an early Stuart doctor, Hart, *Diet of the Diseased*, 36 (following Pliny, *Natural History*, xi. 37).

2. Ibid.

3. Ibid., p. 36.

4. Ibid., p. 41.

5. See Colin Allen and Marc Bekoff, *Species of Mind: The Philosophy and Biology of Cognitive Ethology* (Cambridge, MA: MIT Press, 1997), p. 2.

6. See Richard Joyce, *The Evolution of Morality* (Cambridge, MA: MIT Press, 2006), p. 104.

7. Robert C. Roberts, "Propositions and Animal Emotion," *Philosophy* 71 (1996): 154–55.

8. Marc D. Hauser, *Wild Minds: What Animals Really Think* (New York: Henry Holt and Company, 2000), p. 250.

9. Mary Midgley, *Beast and Man: The Roots of Human Nature* (London: Routledge, 1978), p. 351.

10. B. Spinoza, "The Ethics," in *The Chief Works of Benedict de Spinoza: On the Improvement of the Understanding; the Ethics; Correspondence*, pt. 4, prop. 37, no. 1 (New York: Dover Publications, 1955).

11. Ibid., p. 352.

12. The literature on this issue is considerable. For a start, see Tom Regan, *The Case for Animal Rights* (Berkeley: University of California Press, 1983); and Peter Singer, *Animal Liberation* (New York: Avon Books, 1975).

13. Bertrand Russell, *The Problems of Philosophy* (Oxford: Oxford University Press, 1959), p. 16.

ACKNOWLEDGMENTS

For their help and encouragement in writing this book I owe my thanks and appreciation to the following people:

First, to Mark Holden for the innocent but inspirational remark he made to me many years ago, "Maybe you should write about something that interests you." To all my riding friends and instructors who guided me in horsemanship and conversed with me about animals, especially the Edwards family at Willow Hill Farm in Keeseville, New York, and the Landry family at La Crinière in Napierville, Quebec. Thank you also to the students in my philosophy classes at SUNY Plattsburgh who over the span of many years have listened to, commented on, and read about these ideas as they have gradually and painfully emerged. To Tom Moran, Doug Skopp, and the rest of my colleagues at SUNY Plattsburgh who have populated the Institute for Ethics in Public Life. To this group I owe my gratitude for many inspiring and dynamic conversations about ethics. For comments on early drafts of the manuscript, special thanks to Ish Haji and several anonymous reviewers. Thanks also to the expert team of editors and staff at Prometheus Books for moving this project along so effortlessly.

As a role model for how to think I am indebted to Matt for the right kind of skeptical attitude about everything. And, finally, my sincere and heartfelt gratitude goes to Chuck, who deserves most of the credit and none of the blame for this bit of writing. Not only did he read and comment on multiple drafts of each chapter, but also his love, support, and his devotion to getting things right philosophically have sustained me throughout.

BIBLIOGRAPHY

Aiken, William, and Hugh LaFollette, eds. *Whose Child? Children's Rights, Parental Authority, and State Power.* Totowa, NJ: Littlefield, Adams & Co., 1980.

Allen, Colin, and Marc Bekoff. *Species of Mind: The Philosophy and Biology of Cognitive Ethology.* Cambridge, MA: MIT Press, 1997.

Appiah, Kwame Anthony. *Cosmopolitanism: Ethics in a World of Strangers.* In *Issues of Our Times* series, edited by Henry Louis Gates. New York: W. W. Norton & Company, 2006.

Aristotle, ed. *The Complete Works of Aristotle: The Revised Oxford Translation.* In *Bollingen Series Lxxi.2*, edited by Jonathan Barnes. 2 vols. Princeton, NJ: Princeton University Press, 1984.

———. *Nicomachean Ethics.* 2nd ed. Translated by Terence Irwin. Indianapolis: Hackett, 1999.

Arras, John D. "Nice Story, But So What? Narrative and Justification in Ethics." In *Stories and Their Limits: Narrative Approaches to Bioethics*, edited by Hilde Lindemann Nelson, 65–88. New York: Routledge, 1997.

Ascione, Frank R. *Children and Animals: Exploring the Roots of Kindness and Cruelty.* West Lafayette, IN: Purdue University Press, 2005.

Barnett, Samuel. "The Expression of Emotion." In *A Century of Darwin,* edited by S. A. Barnett. New York: Books for Libraries Press, 1958.

Bavidge, Michael. *Mad or Bad?* In *Mind Matters,* edited by Judith Hughes. New York: St. Martin's Press, 1989.

Bekoff, Marc. *Minding Animals: Awareness, Emotions, and Heart.* Oxford: Oxford University Press, 2002.

———. "Mixing Science and Emotion." In *The Smile of a Dolphin: Remarkable Accounts of Animal Emotions,* edited by Marc Bekoff, 21–27. New York: Discovery Books, 2000.

———. "A Nurturing Nature." In *The Smile of a Dolphin: Remarkable Accounts of Animal Emotions,* edited by Marc Bekoff, 40–41. New York: Discovery Books, 2000.

———, ed. *The Smile of a Dolphin: Remarkable Accounts of Animal Emotions.* New York: Discovery Books, 2000.

———. "Wild Justice and Fair Play: Cooperation, Forgiveness, and Morality in Animals." *Biology and Philosophy* 19 (2004): 489–520.

Bekoff, Marc, and Colin Allen. "Cognitive Ethology: Slayers, Skeptics, and Proponents." In *Anthropomorphism, Anecdotes, and Animals,* edited by Robert W. Mitchell, Nicholas S. Thompson, and H. Lyn Miles, 313–34. Albany: State University of New York Press, 1997.

Bekoff, Marc, Colin Allen, and Gordon M. Gurghardt, eds. *The Cognitive Animal: Empirical and Theoretical Perspectives on Animal Cognition.* Cambridge, MA: MIT Press, 2002.

Bekoff, Marc, and Dale Jamieson, eds. *Readings in Animal Cognition.* Cambridge, MA: MIT Press, 1996.

Bennett, W. L, and M. S. Feldman. *Reconstructing Reality in the Courtroom: Justice and Judgment in American Culture.* New Brunswick, NJ: Rutgers University Press, 1981.

Bernhard, J. G. *Primates in the Classroom.* Amherst: University of Massachusetts Press, 1988.

Blake, Nigel, Paul Smeyers, Richard Smith, and Paul Standish, eds. *The Blackwell Guide to the Philosophy of Education.* In vol. 9, *Black-*

well Philosophy Guides, edited by Steven M. Cahn. 13 vols. Oxford, UK: Blackwell Publishing, 2003.

Blum, Lawrence. "Compassion." In *Explaining Emotions*, edited by Amelie Oksenberg Rorty, 507–17. Berkeley: University of California Press, 1980.

Boakes, Robert. *From Darwin to Behaviorism: Psychology and the Minds of Animals*. Cambridge: Cambridge University Press, 1984.

Booth, Wayne C. *The Company We Keep: An Ethics of Fiction*. Berkeley and Los Angeles: University of California Press, 1988.

Burroughs, John. "Real and Sham Natural History." In *The Wild Animal Story*, edited by Ralph Lutts, 129–43. Philadelphia: Temple University Press, 1998.

———. "Science and Sentiment." *Independent*, February 15, 1912.

Byrne, Richard W. "What's the Use of Anecdotes? Distinguishing Psychological Mechanisms in Primate Tactical Deception." In *Anthropomorphism, Anecdotes, and Animals*, edited by Robert W. Mitchell, Nicholas S. Thompson, and H. Lyn Miles, 134–50. Albany: State University of New York Press, 1997.

Caporael, Linnda R., and Cecilia M. Heyes. "Why Anthropomorphize? Folk Psychology and Other Stories." In *Anthropomorphism, Anecdotes, and Animals*, edited by Robert W. Mitchell, Nicholas S. Thompson, and H. Lyn Miles, 59–73. Albany: State University of New York Press, 1997.

Charon, Rita. "Narrative Contributions to Medical Ethics: Recognition, Formulation, Interpretation and Validation in the Practice of the Ethicist." In *A Matter of Principles? Ferment in U.S. Bioethics*, edited by R. Hamel, E. R. DuBose, and L. J. O'Connell, 260–83. Valley Forge, PA: Trinity Press International, 1994.

Coetzee, J. M. *Disgrace*. New York: Penguin, 2005.

Crisp, Roger. "Evolution and Psychological Unity." In *Readings in Animal Cognition*, edited by Marc Bekoff and Dale Jamieson, 309–21. Cambridge, MA: MIT Press, 1996.

Crist, Eileen. *Images of Animals: Anthropomorphism and Animal Mind*. Philadelphia: Temple University Press, 1999.

Dadlez, E. M. *What's Hecuba to Him? Fictional Events and Actual Emotions*. University Park: Pennsylvania State University Press, 1997.

Dagg, Anne Innis. "A Furious Complaint." In *The Smile of a Dolphin: Remarkable Accounts of Animal Emotions,* edited by Marc Bekoff, 104–105. New York: Discovery Books, 2000.

Darwin, Charles. *The Descent of Man; and Selection in Relation to Sex.* Amherst, NY: Prometheus Books, 1998.

Davidson, K. "Scientists Debate Animal Motives." *San Francisco Examiner,* August 28, 1996.

Davidson, Richard J., Klaus R. Scherer, and H. Hill Goldsmith, eds. *Handbook of Affective Sciences.* In *Series in Affective Science,* edited by Richard J. Davidson, Paul Ekman, and Klaus Scherer. Oxford: Oxford University Press, 2003.

Davis, Michael. "Developing and Using Cases to Teach Practical Ethics." *Teaching Philosophy* 20, no. 4 (1997): 353–85.

Davis, N. Ann. "Moral Agency, Individual Responsibility, and Human Psychology." *Public Affairs Quarterly* 12, no. 1 (1998): 51–78.

DeGrazia, David. *Taking Animals Seriously: Mental Life and Moral Status.* Cambridge: Cambridge University Press, 1996.

De Waal, Frans B. M. "Anthropomorphism and Anthropodenial: Consistency in Our Thinking about Humans and Other Animals." *Philosophical Topics* 27, no. 1 (1999): 255–80.

———. *The Ape and the Sushi Master: Cultural Reflections of a Primatologist.* New York: Basic Books, 2001.

———. *Chimpanzee Politics: Power and Sex among Apes.* Baltimore, MD: Johns Hopkins University Press, 1998.

———. "The Chimpanzee's Sense of Social Regularity and Its Relation to the Human Sense of Justice." In *The Sense of Justice: Biological Foundations of Law,* edited by Roger D. Masters and Margaret Gruter, 241–55. Newbury Park, CA: SAGE Publications, 1992.

———. *Good Natured: The Origins of Right and Wrong in Humans and Other Animals.* Cambridge, MA: Harvard University Press, 1996.

———. "Morally Evolved: Primate Social Instincts, Human Morality, and the Rise and Fall of *Veneer Theory.*" In *Primates and Philosophers: How Morality Evolved,* edited by Steven Macedo and Josiah Ober, 3–80. Princeton, NJ: Princeton University Press, 2006.

———. *Peacemaking among Primates.* Cambridge, MA: Harvard University Press, 1989.

De Waal, Frans B. M., and Jessica C. Flack. "'Any Animal Whatever': Darwinian Building Blocks of Morality in Monkeys and Apes." In *Evolutionary Origins of Morality*, edited by Leonard D. Katz, 1–29. Bowling Green, OH: Imprint Academic, 2000.

———. "Being Nice Is Not a Building Block of Morality." In *Evolutionary Origins of Morality*, edited by Leonard D. Katz, 67–77. Bowling Green, OH: Imprint Academic, 2000.

Diller, Ann. "Knowing Better." In *Thinking Children and Education*, edited by Matthew Lipman, 708–18. Dubuque, IA: Kendall/Hunt, 1993.

Dixon, Beth. "Narrative Cases." *Teaching Ethics* 3, no. 1 (2002).

———. "Review Essay on *Good Natured: The Origins of Right and Wrong in Humans and Other Animals*, by Frans De Waal." *Human Ecology Review* 6, no. 1 (1999): 63–68.

Dunlap, Thomas R. "The Realistic Animal Story: Ernest Thompson Seton, Charles Roberts, and Darwinism." In *The Wild Animal Story*, edited by Ralph Lutts. Philadelphia: Temple University Press, 1998.

Dwyer, Susan. "Moral Competence." In *Philosophy and Linguistics*, edited by Kumiko Murasugi and Robert Stainton, 169–90. Boulder, CO: Westview Press, 1999.

———. "Moral Development and Moral Responsibility." *Monist* 86, no. 2 (2003): 182–99.

Ekman, Paul. "Expression and the Nature of Emotion." In *Approaches to Emotion*, edited by K. Scherer and P. Ekman, 319–43. Hillsdale, NJ: Erlbaum, 1984.

Ekstrom, Laura Waddell, ed. *Agency and Responsibility: Essays on the Metaphysics of Freedom.* Boulder, CO: Westview Press, 2001.

Evans, E. P. *The Criminal Prosecution and Capital Punishment of Animals.* London: Faber and Faber, 1987.

Evans, Nicholas. *The Loop.* New York: Dell Publishing, 1998.

Farber, Paul. *The Temptations of Evolutionary Ethics.* Berkeley: University of California Press, 1994.

Feinberg, Joel. *Harm to Self.* 4 vols. Vol. 3, *The Moral Limits of the Criminal Law.* Oxford: Oxford University Press, 1986.

Fischer, John Martin. "Responsiveness and Moral Responsibility." In *Responsibility, Character, and the Emotions*, edited by Ferdinand Schoeman, 81–106. Cambridge: Cambridge University Press, 1987.

Fischer, John Martin, and Mark Ravizza, eds. *Perspectives on Moral Responsibility*. Ithaca, NY: Cornell University Press, 1993.

———. *Responsibility and Control: A Theory of Moral Responsibility*. Edited by Gerald Postema, *Cambridge Studies in Philosophy and Law*. Cambridge: Cambridge University Press, 1998.

Flack, J. C., and F. B. M. de Waal. "Any Animal Whatever: Darwinian Building Blocks of Morality in Monkeys and Apes." *Journal of Consciousness Studies* 7 (2000): 1–29.

Flavell, John H., and Lee Ross, eds. *Social Cognitive Development: Frontiers and Possible Futures*. Cambridge: Cambridge University Press, 1981.

Fouts, Deborah, and Roger Fouts. "Our Emotional Kin." In *The Smile of a Dolphin: Remarkable Accounts of Animal Emotions*, edited by Marc Bekoff, 205–207. New York: Discovery Books, 2000.

Francione, Gary L. "Animals—Property or Persons?" In *Animal Rights: Current Debates and New Directions*, edited by Cass R. Sunstein and Martha C. Nussbaum, 108–42. Oxford: Oxford University Press, 2004.

Frankfurt, Harry. "Freedom of the Will and the Concept of a Person." In *Agency and Responsibility*, edited by Laura Waddell Ekstrom, 77–91. Boulder, CO: Westview Press, 2001.

French, Peter, ed. *The Spectrum of Responsibility*. New York: St. Martin's Press, 1991.

Freud, S. *Totem and Taboo: Some Points of Agreement between the Mental Lives of Savages and Neurotics*. Translated by J. Strachey. New York: Norton, 1950.

Gaita, Raimond. *The Philosopher's Dog: Friendships with Animals*. New York: Random House, 2002.

Garner, Dwight. "Ideas and Trends; Best Sellers That Woof and Meow." *New York Times*, July 15, 2007.

Ghiselin, Michael T. *The Triumph of the Darwinian Method*. Berkeley: University of California Press, 1969.

Goodall, Jane. *The Chimpanzees of Gombe: Patterns of Behavior.* Cambridge, MA: Belknap Press, 1986.

———. *Through a Window.* Boston: Houghton Mifflin, 1990.

Gottlieb, G. "Comparative Psychology and Ethology." In *The First Century of Experimental Psychology,* edited by E. Hearst. Hillsdale, NJ: Erlbaum Publishing, 1979.

Gould, Steven Jay. "A Lover's Quarrel." In *The Smile of a Dolphin: Remarkable Accounts of Animal Emotions,* edited by Marc Bekoff, 13–17. New York: Discovery Books, 2000.

———. "Tales of a Feathered Tail." *Natural History,* November 2000.

Graff, Gerald. *Clueless in Academe: How Schooling Obscures the Life of the Mind.* New Haven, CT: Yale University Press, 2003.

Grier, Katherine C. *Pets in America: A History.* Chapel Hill: University of North Carolina Press, 2006.

Gruen, Lori. "The Morals of Animal Minds." In *The Cognitive Animal,* edited by Marc Bekoff, Colin Allen, and Gordon M. Burghardt, 437–42. Cambridge, MA: MIT Press, 2002.

Haidt, Jonathan. "The Emotional Dog and Its Rational Tail: A Social Intuitionist Approach to Moral Judgment." *Psychological Review* 108, no. 4 (2001): 814–34.

———. "The Moral Emotions." In *Handbook of Affective Sciences,* edited by Richard J. Davidson, Klaus R. Scherer, and H. Hill Goldsmith, 852–70. Oxford: Oxford University Press, 2003.

Haji, Ishtiyaque. *Moral Appraisability: Puzzles, Proposals, and Perplexities.* New York: Oxford University Press, 1998.

Haji, Ishtiyaque, and Sefaan E. Cuypers. "Moral Responsibility, Love, and Authenticity." *Journal of Social Philosophy* 36, no. 1 (2005): 106–26.

Harnden-Warwick, David. "Psychological Realism, Morality, and Chimpanzees." *Zygon* 32, no. 1 (1997): 29–40.

Harrison, Peter. "The Virtues of Animals in Seventeenth-Century Thought." *Journal of the History of Ideas* 59, no. 3 (1998): 463–84.

Hauser, Marc D. *Wild Minds: What Animals Really Think.* New York: Henry Holt and Company, 2000.

Hearne, Vicki. *Adam's Task: Calling Animals by Name.* New York: Vintage Books, 1987.

————. *Animal Happiness.* New York: HarperCollins, 1994.

Higgins, J. "Forensic Psychiatry Symposium: The Origins of the Homicide Act 1957." *Journal of Medical Ethics* 12 (1986): 8–12.

Hornaday, William T. *The American Natural History.* New York: Scribner's Sons, 1927.

Hurley, Patrick J. *Logic.* 4th ed. Belmont: Wadsworth, 1991.

Hursthouse, Rosalind. "Virtue Theory and Abortion." *Philosophy and Public Affairs* 20 (1991): 223–46.

Iamblichus. "Lives of Pythagoras." In *The Pythagorean Sourcebook and Library,* edited by K. S. Guthrie. Grand Rapids, MI: Phanes Press, 1987.

Ingold, Tim, ed. *What Is an Animal?* London: Unwin Hyman, 1988.

Irwin, Terence. "Reason and Responsibility in Aristotle." In *Essays on Aristotle's Ethics,* edited by Amelie Oksenberg Rorty, 117–55. Berkeley: University of California Press, 1980.

Izard, Carroll. *Human Emotions.* New York: Plenum, 1977.

Jaggar, Alison M. "Love and Knowledge: Emotion in Feminist Epistemology." *Inquiry* 32 (1989): 151–76.

Jamieson, Dale, and Marc Bekoff. "Afterword: Ethics and the Study of Animal Cognition." In *Readings in Animal Cognition,* edited by Marc Bekoff and Dale Jamieson, 359–71. Cambridge, MA: MIT Press, 1996.

Joyce, Richard. *The Evolution of Morality.* Cambridge, MA: MIT Press, 2006.

Kael, Pauline. "Current Cinema." *New Yorker,* November 13, 1989.

Kahn, Peter H., Jr., and Stephen R. Kellert, eds. *Children and Nature: Psychological, Sociocultural, and Evolutionary Investigations.* Cambridge, MA: MIT Press, 2002.

Katz, Leonard D., ed. *Evolutionary Origins of Morality: Cross-Disciplinary Perspectives.* Bowling Green, OH: Imprint Academic, 2000.

Kenner, Lionel. "On Blaming." In *The Spectrum of Responsibility,* edited by Peter French, 189–97. New York: St. Martin's Press, 1991.

Kitcher, Philip. "Ethics and Evolution: How to Get Here from There." In *Primates and Philosophers: How Morality Evolved,* edited by Stephen Macedo and Josiah Ober, 120–39. Princeton, NJ: Princeton University Press, 2006.

Knoll, Elizabeth. "Dogs, Darwinism, and English Sensibilities." In *Anthropomorphism, Anecdotes, and Animals,* edited by Robert W. Mitchell, Nicholas S. Thompson, and H. Lyn Miles. Albany: State University of New York Press, 1997.

Kohlberg, Lawrence. *The Philosophy of Moral Development: Essays on Moral Development.* Vol. 1. San Francisco: Harper & Row, 1981.

Korsgaard, Christine M. "Morality and the Distinctiveness of Human Action." In *Primates and Philosophers: How Morality Evolved,* edited by Stephen Macedo and Josiah Ober, 98–119. Princeton, NJ: Princeton University Press, 2006.

Leighton, Stephen, ed. *Philosophy and the Emotions: A Reader.* Toronto, ON: Broadview Press, 2003.

Lipman, Matthew. *Getting Our Thoughts Together: Instructional Manual to Accompany Elfie.* 2nd ed. Montclair, NJ: Institute for the Advancement of Philosophy for Children, 2006.

———. *Lisa.* Montclair, NJ: Institute for the Advancement of Philosophy for Children, 1983.

———, ed. *Thinking Children and Education.* Dubuque, IA: Kendall/ Hunt Publishing, 1993.

Lipman, Matthew, and Ann Margaret Sharp. *Ethical Inquiry: Instructional Manual to Accompany Lisa.* 2nd ed. Lanham, MD: University Press of America, 1985.

Long, William J. "The Modern School of Nature-Study and Its Critics." In *The Wild Animal Story,* edited by Ralph H. Lutts, 144–52. Philadelphia: Temple University Press, 1998.

Lopez, Barry Holstun. *Of Wolves and Men.* New York: Touchstone, 1978.

Lutts, Ralph H., ed. *The Wild Animal Story.* Edited by Clinton R. Sanders and Arnold Arluke, *Animals, Culture, and Society* series. Philadelphia: Temple University Press, 1998.

———. "The Wild Animal Story: Animals and Ideas." In *The Wild Animal Story,* edited by Ralph H. Lutts, 1–21. Philadelphia: Temple University Press, 1998.

———. "Will the Real Wild Animal Please Stand Up! The Nature Fakers." In *The Wild Animal Story,* edited by Ralph H. Lutts, 268–90. Philadelphia: Temple University Press, 1998.

Lyons, W. *Emotion.* New York: Cambridge University Press, 1980.

MacDonald, Robert H. "The Revolt against Instinct: The Animal Stories of Seton and Roberts." In *The Wild Animal Story*, edited by Ralph H. Lutts, 225–36. Philadelphia: Temple University Press, 1998.

Macedo, Stephen, and Josiah Ober, eds. *Primates and Philosophers: How Morality Evolved.* In *University Center for Human Values* series, edited by Steven Macedo. Princeton, NJ: Princeton University Press, 2006.

MacIntyre, Alasdair. *After Virtue: A Study in Moral Theory.* 2nd ed. Notre Dame, IN: University of Notre Dame, 1984.

Mackie, J. L. "The Straight Rule of Responsibility." In *The Spectrum of Responsibility*, edited by Peter French, 123–28. New York: St. Martin's Press, 1991.

Masson, J. M., and S. McCarthy. *When Elephants Weep: The Emotional Lives of Animals.* New York: Delacorte, 1995.

Masson, Jeffrey Moussaieff. *Dogs Never Lie about Love: Reflections on the Emotional World of Dogs.* New York: Three Rivers Press, 1997.

Masters, Roger D., and Margaret Gruter, eds. *The Sense of Justice: Biological Foundations of Law.* Newbury Park, CA: SAGE Publications, 1992.

Matthews, Gareth B. "Animals and the Unity of Psychology." *Philosophy* 53 (1978): 437–54.

———. "Concept Formation and Moral Development." In *Philosophical Perspectives in Developmental Psychology*, edited by James Russell, 175–90. Oxford: Basil Blackwell, 1987.

———. *Dialogues with Children.* Cambridge, MA: Harvard University Press, 1984.

———. *Philosophy and the Young Child.* Cambridge, MA: Harvard University Press, 1980.

McGinn, Colin. "Evolution, Animals, and the Basis of Morality." *Inquiry* 22 (1979).

McGuire, Terry R. "Emotion and Behavior Genetics in Vertebrates and Invertebrates." In *Handbook of Emotions*, edited by Michael Lewis and Jeannete Haviland, 155–66. New York: Guilford Press, 1993.

McKeon, Richard, ed. *The Basic Works of Aristotle.* New York: Random House, 1941.

Midgley, Mary. *Beast and Man: The Roots of Human Nature.* London: Routledge, 1978.

Mighetto, Lisa. *Wild Animals and American Environmental Ethics.* Tucson: University of Arizona Press, 1991.

Mitchell, Robert W. "Anthropomorphic Anecdotalism as Method." In *Anthropomorphism, Anecdotes, and Animals,* edited by Robert W. Mitchell, Nicholas S. Thompson, and H. Lyn Miles, 151–69. Albany: State University of New York Press, 1997.

Mitchell, Robert W., Nicholas S. Thompson, and H. Lyn Miles, eds. *Anthropomorphism, Anecdotes, and Animals.* Albany: State University of New York Press, 1997.

Mivert, St. G. J. "Darwin's Descent of Man." *Quarterly Review,* no. 131 (1871): 47–90.

Morgan, C. Lloyd. *An Introduction to Comparative Psychology.* London: Walter Scott, 1894.

Murasugi, Kumiko, and Robert Stainton, eds. *Philosophy and Linguistics.* Boulder, CO: Westview Press, 1999.

Murphy, Jeffrie G. *Evolution, Morality, and the Meaning of Life.* Totowa, NJ: Rowman and Littlefield, 1982.

Myers, Gene. *Children and Animals: Social Development and Our Connections to Other Species.* In *Lives in Context* series, edited by Mihaly Csikszentmihalyi. Boulder, CO: Westview Press, 1998.

Newman, Aline Alexander. "Do Animals Have Feelings?" *National Geographic World,* June 2001.

Nichols, Shaun. *Sentimental Rules: On the Natural Foundations of Moral Judgment.* Oxford: Oxford University Press, 2004.

Nussbaum, Martha. *Aristotle's De Motu Animalium.* Princeton, NJ: Princeton University Press, 1978.

———. *The Fragility of Goodness: Luck and Ethics in Greek Tragedy and Philosophy.* Cambridge: Cambridge University Press, 1986.

———. *Love's Knowledge: Essays on Philosophy and Literature.* New York: Oxford University Press, 1990.

———. *Poetic Justice: The Literary Imagination and Public Life.* Boston: Beacon Press, 1995.

————. *Upheavals of Thought: The Intelligence of Emotions.* Cambridge: Cambridge University Press, 2001.

Oakley, Justin. *Morality and the Emotions.* London: Routledge, 1992.

Palmeri, Ann. "Childhood's End: Toward the Liberation of Children." In *Whose Child? Children's Rights, Parental Authority, and State Power,* edited by William Aiken and Hugh LaFollette, 105–23. Totowa, NJ: Littlefield, Adams, & Co., 1980.

Paul, Ellen Frankel, Fred D. Miller Jr., and Jeffrey Paul, eds. *Responsibility.* Vol. 16, no. 2, *Social Philosophy & Policy.* New York: Cambridge University Press, 1999.

Piaget, Jean. *The Moral Judgment of the Child.* New York: Free Press, 1965.

Pitcher, George. *The Dogs Who Came to Stay.* New York: Dutton, 1995.

Pluhar, Evelyn B. *Beyond Prejudice: The Moral Significance of Human and Nonhuman Animals.* Durham, NC: Duke University Press, 1995.

Plutchik, Robert. *Emotion: A Psychoevolutionary Synthesis.* New York: Harper and Row, 1980.

Pritchard, Michael S. *On Becoming Responsible.* Lawrence: University Press of Kansas, 1991.

Rachels, James. *Created from Animals: The Moral Implications of Darwinism.* Oxford: Oxford University Press, 1990.

Radner, Daisie, and Michael Radner. *Animal Consciousness.* In *Frontiers of Philosophy* series, edited by Peter H. Hare. Amherst, NY: Prometheus Books, 1996.

Railton, Peter. "Darwinian Building Blocks." In *Evolutionary Origins of Morality,* edited by Leonard D. Katz, 55–60. Bowling Green, OH: Imprint Academic, 2000.

Regan, Tom. *The Case for Animal Rights.* Berkeley: University of California Press, 1983.

Richards, Robert. *Darwin's Ideas on Animal Behavior, Mind, and Morals.* Chicago: University of Chicago Press, 1987.

Roberts, Charles G. D. *The Kindred of the Wild: A Book of Animal Life.* Boston: L. C. Page, 1902.

Roberts, Robert C. "Propositions and Animal Emotion." *Philosophy* 71 (1996): 147–56.

Rollin, Bernard E. "Anecdote, Anthropomorphism, and Animal Behavior." In *Anthropomorphism, Anecdotes, and Animals*, edited by Nicholas S. Thompson, Robert W. Mitchell, and H. Lyn Miles, 125–33. Albany: State University of New York Press, 1997.

Rorty, Amelie Oksenberg. *Essays on Aristotle's Ethics*. Berkeley and Los Angeles: University of California Press, 1980.

Rosenstand, Nina. *The Moral of the Story*. Mountain View, CA: Mayfield, 1994.

Ruse, Michael. *Taking Darwin Seriously*. Amherst, NY: Prometheus Books, 1998.

Russell, Bertrand. *The Problems of Philosophy*. Oxford: Oxford University Press, 1959.

Russell, James, ed. *Philosophical Perspectives in Developmental Psychology*. Oxford, UK: Basil Blackwell, 1987.

Sapontzis, S. F. *Morals, Reason, and Animals*. Philadelphia: Temple University Press, 1987.

Savage-Rumbaugh, Sue, Stuart G. Shanker, and Talbot J. Taylor. *Apes, Language, and the Human Mind*. Oxford: Oxford University Press, 1998.

Schoeman, Ferdinand, ed. *Responsibility, Character, and the Emotions*. Cambridge: Cambridge University Press, 1987.

Seton, Ernest Thompson. *Lives of the Hunted*. New York: Charles Scribner's Sons, 1901.

———. "On His Animal Stories." In *The Wild Animal Story*, edited by Ralph Lutts, 45–47. Philadelphia: Temple University Press, 1998.

———. *Wild Animals I Have Known*. New York: Charles Scribner's Sons, 1911.

Sherman, Nancy. *The Fabric of Character*. Oxford, UK: Clarendon Press, 1989.

———. "The Habituation of Character." In *Aristotle's Ethics: Critical Essays*, edited by Nancy Sherman, 231–60. Lanham, MD: Rowman and Littlefield, 1999.

Shweder, Richard A., Elliot Turiel, and Nancy C. Much. "The Moral Intuitions of the Child." In *Social Cognitive Development*, edited by John H. Flavell and Lee Ross, 288–305. Cambridge: Cambridge University Press, 1981.

Silverman, Paul S. "A Pragmatic Approach to the Inference of Animal Mind." In *Anthropomorphism, Anecdotes, and Animals*, edited by Robert W. Mitchell, Nicholas S. Thompson, and H. Lyn Miles, 170–85. Albany: State University of New York Press, 1997.

Singer, Peter. *Animal Liberation.* New York: Avon Books, 1975.

Smeyers, Paul, and Colin Wringe. "Adults and Children." In *The Blackwell Guide to the Philosophy of Education*, edited by Nigel Blake, Paul Smeyers, Richard Smith, and Paul Standish, 311–25. Oxford, UK: Blackwell Publishing, 2003.

Smith, Adam. *The Theory of Moral Sentiments.* Oxford, UK: Clarendon Press, 1976.

Sober, Elliott. *From a Biological Point of View.* Cambridge: Cambridge University Press, 1994.

———. "Morgan's Canon." In *The Evolution of Mind*, edited by D. Cummins and C. Allen. Oxford: Oxford University Press, 1997.

Sorabji, Richard. *Animal Minds and Human Morals: The Origins of the Western Debate.* Ithaca, NY: Cornell University Press, 1993.

———. *Necessity, Cause, and Blame: Perspectives on Aristotle's Theory.* Ithaca, NY: Cornell University Press, 1980.

Spinoza, B. "The Ethics." In *The Chief Works of Benedict de Spinoza: On the Improvement of the Understanding; the Ethics; Correspondence.* New York: Dover Publications, 1955.

———. *The Ethics and Selected Letters.* Translated by S. Shirley. Edited by S. Feldman. Indianapolis: Hackett, 1982.

Strawson, Galen. *Freedom and Belief.* Oxford, UK: Clarendon Press, 1986.

Strawson, Peter. "Freedom and Resentment." In *Perspectives on Moral Responsibility*, edited by John Martin Fischer and Mark Ravizza, 45–66. Ithaca, NY: Cornell University Press, 1993.

Sunstein, Cass R., and Martha C. Nussbaum, eds. *Animal Rights: Current Debates and New Directions.* Oxford: Oxford University Press, 2004.

Thierry, B. "Building Elements of Morality Are Not Elements of Morality." In *Evolutionary Origins of Morality*, edited by Leonard D. Katz, 60–62. Bowling Green, OH: Imprint Academic, 2000.

Thomas, Elizabeth Marshall. "A Friend in Need." In *The Smile of a*

Dolphin: Remarkable Accounts of Animal Emotions, edited by Marc Bekoff, 184–85. New York: Discovery Books, 2000.

———. *The Hidden Life of Dogs.* New York: Houghton Mifflin, 1993.

Thomas, Keith. *Man and the Natural World: A History of the Modern Sensibility.* New York: Pantheon Books, 1983.

Tobias, Michael. "A Gentle Heart." In *The Smile of a Dolphin: Remarkable Accounts of Animal Emotions,* edited by Marc Bekoff, 171–73. New York: Discovery Books, 2000.

Tomlinson, Tom. "Perplexed about Narrative Ethics." In *Stories and Their Limits: Narrative Approaches to Bioethics,* edited by Hilde Lindemann Nelson, 123–33. New York: Routledge, 1997.

Turner, Susan M., and Gareth B. Matthews, eds. *The Philosopher's Child: Critical Perspectives in the Western Tradition.* Rochester, NY: University of Rochester Press, 1998.

Turski, W. George. *Towards Rationality of the Emotions: An Essay in the Philosophy of Mind.* Athens: Ohio University Press, 1994.

Verbeek, Peter, and Frans B. M. de Waal. "The Primate Relationship with Nature: Biophilia as a General Pattern." In *Children and Nature: Psychological, Sociocultural, and Evolutionary Investigations,* edited by Peter H. Kahn Jr. and Stephen R. Kellert, 1–27. Cambridge, MA: MIT Press, 2002.

Von Kreisler, Kristin. *Beauty in the Beasts: True Stories of Animals Who Choose to Do Good.* New York: Jeremy P. Tarcher/Putnam, 2001.

Wade, Nicholas. "Scientist Finds the Beginnings of Morality in Primate Behavior." *New York Times,* March 20, 2007.

Wallace, R. Jay. *Responsibility and the Moral Sentiments.* Cambridge, MA: Harvard University Press, 1996.

Waller, Bruce N. "What Rationality Adds to Animal Morality." *Biology and Philosophy* 12 (1997): 341–56.

Watson, Gary. "Free Agency." In *Agency and Responsibility,* edited by Laura Waddell Ekstrom, 92–106. Boulder, CO: Westview Press, 2001.

White, E. B. *Charlotte's Web.* New York: HarperCollins, 1952.

Wise, Steven M. *Drawing the Line: Science and the Case for Animal Rights.* Cambridge, MA: Perseus Books, 2002.

———. *Rattling the Cage: Toward Legal Rights for Animals.* Cambridge, MA: Perseus Books, 2000.

Wolf, Susan. "The Reason View." In *Agency and Responsibility*, edited by Laura Waddell Ekstrom, 205–26. Boulder, CO: Westview Press, 2001.

Wolff, R. P. *In Defense of Anarchism.* New York: Harper Torchbooks, 1970.

Zagzebski, Linda Trinkaus. *Virtues of the Mind: An Inquiry into the Nature of Virtue and the Ethical Foundations of Knowledge.* Cambridge: Cambridge University Press, 1996.

INDEX